BUSINESS CORRESPONDENCE

(A Textbook of B.Com.(Hons.), B.A. (V.S.), D.C.L., M.Com., M.B.A. and a reference manual for I.C.W.A. (Inter.), C.S. (Prel.), C.A. and other Professional and Competitive Examinations)

DR. R. K. CHOPRA

M.Com., LL.B., D.C.L. (I.L.I.), D.L.L., L.F.I.I., Ph.D.

Associate Professor, Deptt. of Commerce,
College of Vocational Studies,
University of Delhi
NEW DELHI - 110 017

Himalaya Publishing House

• Mumbai • Delhi • Bangalore • Hyderabad • Chennai
• Ernakulam • Nagpur • Pune • Ahmedabad • Lucknow

© AUTHOR
No part of this publication should be reproduced, stored in a retrieval system, or transmitted in any form or by any means, electronic, mechanical, photocopying, recording and/or otherwise without the prior written permission of the author. Breach of this will be liable for legal action.

First Edition : 2010

Published by : **Mrs. Meena Pandey**
for HIMALAYA PUBLISHING HOUSE,
"Ramdoot", Dr. Bhalerao Marg, Girgaon, Mumbai-400 004.
Phones : 23860170/23863863 Fax : 022-23877178
Email : himpub@vsnl.com
Website : www.himpub.com

Branch Offices

Delhi : "Pooja Apartments", 4-B, Murari Lal Street, Ansari Road, Darya Ganj, New Delhi-110 002
Phones : 23270392, 23278631 Reliance : 30180392 to 396
Fax : 011-23256286 Email : hphdel@vsnl.com

Nagpur : Kundanlal Chandak Industrial Estate, Ghat Road, Nagpur-440 018
Phone : 2721216, Telefax : 0712-2721215

Bangalore : No. 16/I (old 12/1), Ist floor, Next to Hotel Highland, Madhava Nagar, Race Course Road, Bangalore-560 001
Phones : 22281541, 22385461 Fax : 080-2286611

Hyderabad : No. 3-4-184, Linampally, Besides Raghavendra Swamy Matham, Kachiguda, Hyderabad-500027
Phone : 040-655501745, Fax : 040-27560041

Chennai : No. 2, Rama Krishna Street, North Usman Road, T-Nagar, Chennai-600 017
Phone : 28144004, 28144005 Mobile : 09380460419

Pune : No. 527, "Laksha Apartment", First Floor, Mehunpura, Shaniwarpeth, (Near Prabhat Theatre), Pune-411 030
Phone : 020-24496333, 24496333, 24496323

Lucknow : C-43, Sector C, Ali Gunj, Lucknow - 226 024
Phone : 0522-4047594

Ahmedabad : 114, Shail, 1st Floor, Opp. Madhu Sudan House, C.G. Road, Navrang Pura, Ahemdabad-380 009
Mobile : 9327324149

Eranakulam : No. 39/104A, Lakshmi Apartment, Karikkamuri Cross Road Eranakulam, Cochin-622 011, Kerala
Phone : 0484-2378012, 2378016

Typeset at : Elite-Art, N.S, Marg, Daryaganj, New Delhi-110002
Printed at : A to Z Printers, Daryaganj, New Delhi-110002

BUSINESS CORRESPONDENCE

PREFACE

The Genesis:

Mark Twain once said, *"The difference between the right word and the almost right word is the difference between the lightning and the lightning bug."* Everyone would agree with Theo Haimann that *"The success of all managerial functions depends on successful communication–whether oral or written"*. Mark H. McCararck remarked, *"Words you use tell a lot about you"*.

While I was working on my book on **Communication Management** during the last two years, the above words inspired me to write on Business Correspondence as well. Hence the Book.

The Purpose of the Book:

In modern day world, business communication is made up of huge complexities of dimensions, coverage, effectiveness and so on. Professional and result-oriented organisations are always looking for managers who can communicate persuasively and competently.

Researches have revealed that about nine-tenths of a Manager's time is spent in communicating, one way or the other–orally or in writing. That is why, Modern Management Education stresses the importance of Communication–oral as well as written.

A business concern can keep itself in close touch with its customers, dealers, investors, suppliers, Government and other sections of society through various forms of communication–mostly written communication–called business correspondence. The subject **'Business Correspondence'**, therefore, is of great importance in the context of utilitarian usefulness for the Professionals, Managers, Students and Teachers of the subject.

The book prepares students for the accelerated pace of business communication by clearly connecting every aspect, topic and example to the modern work place. It is a very humble attempt to present the voluminous subject in a very simple, brief yet innovative way for complete learning experience of the Reader.

Thematic Structure of the Book:

While the aim of the book is to present comprehensive coverage of real-world concepts in Business letter-writing in an interesting and lively manner, the structure of the book is outlined below:

1. In Business, numerous situations may arise every day, necessitating writing of a (large) number of Business letters. These situations can't be enlisted or enumerated as they may run in hundreds and thousands and even more. Newer situations may arise every day and letters may have to be written according to each individual situation. There can be no exhaustive list of situations warranting business letters. This book is only a modest attempt

to make the reader aware about some of the more common topics (situations) and few examples of pre-written business letters, within certain specified parameters.

2. The topics (situations) have been arranged subjectwise–alphabetically, to allow easy access to the required subject/topic.
3. Apart from alphabetical categories, certain specific categories have also been incorporated in Zed list. All these categories have also been alphabetically arranged.
4. Whereas in most of the books, the authors provide just the body of the letters, this book tries to provide the glimpse of a complete letter containing all the elements of a good business letter.
5. Though the topics and examples of pre-written letters are not at all exhaustive, the book encourages the reader to put his imagination, mental ability and knowledge of English language in practice in writing/drafting of business letters.
6. Chapters on **'Essentials of Effective Business Letter'**, **'Structure of a Business Letter'**, and **'Business Letter Formats'**, prepare the reader in understanding all aspects of Business Correspondence in theoritical detail.
7. **"Quick Tips for Writing Letters"** on different topics/situations have been given with every alphabetical category. These may serve as guidelines for writing business letters on any and every conceivable situations.
8. University Examination Questions at the end of the book (upto the end of year 2009) will help the students in understanding the level of questions asked to help him prepare accordingly.
9. Appendices may be used as supporting material. A large number of appendices for **'Writing Better English'** have been included at the end of the book. These include: *'Business Jargon Simplified', "French and Latin Words used in English', 'English Synonyms and Antonyms', 'Words often mis-spelt or confused', 'Negative words and words with Negative connotations, 'How to organise positive and informative messages', 'Body language', 'Business Correspondence Glossary and Vocabulary* etc., to help the business letter writer in writing result-oriented effective correspondence.
10. While the Bibliography contains all the books, websites and other materials referred to in writing the book, any adaptation, from any source is duly acknowledged at appropriate places. Index at the end of the book, enhances the utility of the book.

While the book is geared specifically for the University and Professional students, it is equally suitable for the Teaching Community and Practicing Managers.

Acknowledgements

Any ideas for the improvement of the book would be appreciated and thankfully acknowledged. I express deep gratitude to Mr. Neeraj Pandey, Director, as also to the team of Mr. Sudhir Joshi, Director, particularly Mr. V.S. Rawat and Mr. Pramod Kumar of the Himalaya Publishing House and Mr.

B.K. Bhatt of M/s Elite-Art, the printers who have helped in the execution of this book with remarkable speed and excellence.

I am also grateful to a large number of subject-teachers, colleagues, friends and students who have directly or indirectly contributed in the preparation of the Book, special thanks are due to my wife, Mrs. C.K. Chopra, Associate Professor in Commerce, Vivekananda College, Delhi University, Mrs. Ankita Bhatia, Assistant Professor in Commerce, Lakshmi Bai College, Delhi University, Mrs. Priyanka Gauri, Assistant Professor (Guest) in Commerce, Shri Ram College of Commerce, Delhi University and Mr. Ashish Chopra for their invaluable support in the preparation of this text.

DR. R.K. CHOPRA
627, Dr. Mukherjee Nagar,
Delhi-110 009

January, 2010

CONTENTS

LIST OF LETTERS

Sl.No.	Topics	Page No.
30.	Letter Replying to Status Enquiry/Credit Verification (Slightly unfavourable reply)	116
31.	Letter Replying to Credit Verification (Unfavourable reply)	117
32.	Letter Granting Credit	118
33.	Letter Refusing Credit	119
34.	Letter Complaining Delay in the Execution of Order	120
35.	Reply to Complaint of Delay in Execution of Order	121
36.	Letter about Supply of Wrong Goods	122
37.	Letter for Goods received in a Damaged Condition	123
38.	Letter Informing Defective Supplies	124
39.	Letter Claiming Replacement of Defective Goods	125
40.	Reply to Letter Claiming Replacement of Defective Goods	126
41.	Letter Conveying Delay in Execution of Orders	127
42.	Letter Refusing order due to lower Prices	128
43.	Letter Refusing Supply unless outstandings are Paid	129
44.	Letter declining direct order to company	130
45.	Letter Offering Substitutes of Brands Ordered	131
46.	Request for Payment	134
47.	Debt Collection Letter : First Reminder	135
48.	Debt Collection Letter : Second Reminder	136
49.	Reply to Collection Letter : Disputing Claim	137
50.	Reply to Collection Letter : Explaining Delay in Payment	138
51.	Letter : Making Part Payment & Explaining for Balance	139
52.	Letter Allowing Extension of Time for Payment	140
53.	Collection letter indicating legal action for non-payment	141
54.	Resignation Letter	147
55.	Termination Letter/Lay-off Letter	148
56.	Letter to Post Master complaining about non-delivery of a Speed Post/ Registered Article	152
57.	Letter to State Electricity Board for change of name and load enhancement	153
58.	Letter to Income Tax Officer for Issue of I.T.C.C.	154
59.	Letter to Railway Authorities Complaining about damage of parcel in transit	155
60.	Letter Applying for Replenishment Licence	156
61.	Request Letter for Octroi-Exemption	158
62.	Letter Requesting Information	165
63.	Letter Sending Information	166
64.	Letter of Invitation	167
65.	Letter Indicating Expression of Interest	168

Sl.No.	Topics	Page No.

Chapter 1

BUSINESS CORRESPONDENCE

CONTENTS

PURPOSE OF A BUSINESS LETTER

A business letter is a formal way of communicating between two or more parties/businesses. Every business, whether big or small, is required to maintain contacts with its suppliers, customers, prospects, government departments and other parties. A businessman is required to exchange information of varied types with different parties, for instance:

- making/soliciting enquiries;
- placing orders for goods/services;
- acknowledging and executive orders;
- applying for/granting credit;
- sending statements of account to debtors;
- requesting for settlement of account;
- complaining on various issues;
- follow-up of various issues;
- promotion of new products/goods/ideas;
- communicating with government departments, such as Sales Tax, Income Tax, Excise, VAT etc.; and
- a lot of similar issues.

There are many different uses of business letters. Business letters can be informational, persuasive, motivational, promotional or goodwill letters[1]. Business letters facilitate business transactions. Business correspondence is rightly regarded as the mental side of commercial activity.

SIGNIFICANCE OF BUSINESS CORRESPONDENCE

The following points underline the significance of Business correspondence :

1. With the expansion of business activities, the number of its suppliers and prospects increase manifold making it difficult to maintain personal contact with all these persons and institutions. The best method of contacting such a large audience is through correspondence. Though there are other means of communication as well — like telephone, fax, e-mail, telegram etc., but written communication is a better form of communication than these other means because :-

(i) It is less expensive than Phone, Fax, e-mail, telegram etc.

(ii) It provides a record of correspondence,

(iii) It leaves durable impression on the receiver's mind.

2. Business correspondence establishes contact between parties separated by long distances, who might never meet each other or might not recognise each other, when they meet. A letter

1. "A good business letter serves as a master key that opens locked doors. It opens the way for your goods or your services. It tells the story of the real character of the firm." *H.N. Casson*

works as a messenger and does all the talking for the business. It has largely extended the opportunities of trade and commerce.

3. Business correspondence provides a written evidence of communication between two businesses. In most cases, the communication over the telephone or telegram is confirmed by means of a letter. The letters with the following opening lines :

"With reference to our telephonic conversation -----"

"We are pleased to confirm our order sent by telegram ----"

"Kindly refer to our e-mail dated -----"

are too common in the business now-a-days.

4. In many cases, business correspondence saves business relations as opposed to public contact. For instance, an argumentative customer insisting on price reduction may invite a discourteous or stiff refusal which might upset him; but a polite refusal in a letter, explaining the reasons for it, might not spoil the relations at all.

The above factors have made business correspondence an indispensable and essential element of business success. It has now become an invariable pre-requisite of most business actions.

ELEMENTS OF A GOOD BUSINESS LETTER

1. The most important element of writing a good business letter is writer's ability to identify and write to the audience. A good writer anticipates the audience :

What is the reader like ?

How will the reader react to the message ?

What is the profile of the reader ?

What the writer knows about the reader's education, belief, culture and attitudes ?

What response (neutral, positive or negative) of the reader can be expected ?

After anticipating the audience's profile, the writer will decide about, the language, (formal or informal), tone and content of the message in the letter. Thus, if the letter is being addressed to the H.R. Department of a company, the writer should avoid using highly technical terms that only engineers would understand. Even if the letter is addressed to an engineering company, chances are that the H.R. personnel may not have an engineering background.

2. The next element is that the writer make sure to present his objectives in a clear and concise manner. The writer should not be vague about his objective. The recipient may not have the patience to sit and guess the meaning of the letter or the time to read a long-winded letter. The letter should just get to the point without going into unnecessary details.

3. Skilled communicators create a positive tone in their messages by using a number of adaptive techniques; such as

(i) highlighting receiver's benefits ;

(ii) cultivating a 'you' attitude;

(iii) avoiding gender, racial, age and disability bias;

(iv) be courteous by using familiar words, and choosing precise words .

4. Another important element of a good business letter is to remain professional. Even if the writer is writing a complaint letter, the tone should be polite and courteous. The writer should simply state the problem, with the relevant facts but be sure to avoid threats and slander.

It must be remembered that a good business letter can open up more channels for the business, get more customers, retain old customers, reduce bad debts and do hundreds of other favourable acts for the business.

WHAT A GOOD BUSINESS LETTER CAN DO ?

According to L. Gartside,[2] a business letter can ;

(i) provide a convenient and inexpensive means of communication ;
(ii) seek or give information ;
(iii) furnish evidence of transactions entered into ; and
(iv) provide a record for future reference ;

Good letter writing is an art, which may be learned by practice and experience. A good letter is a great power. It can do the following to the business :

1. Sell goods and services
2. Retain old customers
3. Bring back lost customers
4. Secure new customers
5. Settle disputes/claims
6. Collect Doubtful Debts.
7. Reduce Bad Debts
8. Creates Goodwill.
9. Strengthen business relations
10. Enhances Image
11. Build Brands
12. Open new markets
13. Creates lasting impression
14. Motivates personnel
15. Widens area of operations.

On the other hand, a bad business letter can undo all above things and becomes a part of the dust-bin.

It is rightly said, "A good letter can pacify an angry customer as much as a bad one can anger a friendly one. It may sell a new product or spoil the sales of an established one, collect debts without hurting the customer feelings or lose both the money and the customer, refuse a request yet with respect or grant the request yet incur ill-will."[3]

2. L. Gartside : Modern Business Correspondence.
3. U.R. Koli & Urmila Rai : Commercial correspondence.

WHO WRITES BUSINESS LETTERS?

Most people who have an occupation or business have to write business letters. Some write many letters every day while others write only a few letters during their entire career. Business people also receive letters on a daily basis. The person who writes the letter is known as the *sender* and the individual person/group who receives the letter is called the *recipient*. Here are some example of senders and recipients.

- Business to Business
- Business to Consumer
- Consumer to Business
- Job applicant to Company
- Employer to Employee
- Staff Member to Staff Member
- Business to Government Department & Vice Versa

WHY WRITE BUSINESS LETTERS?

Business letters may need to be written for many reasons, stated briefly, as :

- to inform
- to persude
- to express thanks
- to request
- to apologise
- to recommend
- to remind
- to order
- to acknowledge
- to reject an offer
- to accept an offer
- to introduce a person or policy
- to follow up
- to collect debts
- to invite or welcome
- to formalise decisions
- to congratulate
- to settle claims
- to make amends
- to announce results
- to make policy statement
- to appoint, promote or terminate
- to argue or plead etc.

WHO, HOW, WHY, WHEN AND WHERE OF BUSINESS CORRESPONDENCE

WHO : (Recipient)

- MR. Ashish Chopra
- Acquaintance (Met Twice before, Interviewed)
- Title : For Manager, Marketing
- Address : 257, Silveroak Apartment, I.P. Estate. N. Delhi-110 002

WHY : (Reason)

- To Make an offer to join as Manager, Marketing Department
- Other Board Members Suggested that he is a fit candidate for this position.
- No other candidate has been found suitable for the job.

HOW : (Specific Details)

- If he decides to join, he will need to revamp the marketing Department.
- Manager level staff are sometimes asked to take on extra duties such as coordinating and hosting social events etc.

WHEN : (Response)

- He will need to join by 1st October, 2009
- He can intimate this by phone or e-mail.

WHERE : (Organisation)

- Give Return address of our company
- Title and Address of Ashish Chopra
- Salutation : Dear Mr. Ashish Chopra
- *First Paragraph* : Introduce the company, remind Ashish where he met before, Provide reason for writing (offer of the Job of Manager, Marketing).
- *Second Paragraph* : Refrence his expression of interest to join as Manager, Marketing. Explain the type of commitment, the position will involve (Fixing & Distribution of Targets, Follow up, Motivation, Achievement of Targets, Rewards, Management Reporting, Public Relation etc).
- *Third Paragraph* : Provide deadline for response & how to contact.
- *Close* : Express thanks.

Chapter 2

ESSENTIALS OF AN EFFECTIVE BUSINESS LETTER

CONTENTS

INTRODUCTION

One of the best ways to test the effectiveness (and appropriateness) of a Business Letter is by putting the sender in the position of recipient of the letter and thinking how the recipient would react on the letter.

Would it irritate or annoy the receiver ?

Would the letter serve the purpose for which it was written ? or

Would it be thrown in the waste-box ?

Some people recommend that the sender should read the letter aloud or have someone else to read it to him. It is said that *"Our ears will catch flaws that our eyes may have missed."*

A Business Letter is considered to be a *"Written piece of conversation"*, or *"a piece of conversation by post"*, therefore, it should he written naturally as the sender would have talked to the receiver, about the subject-matter of the letter, if he had the opportunity to talk to the receiver in person.

Business Letters are different from Personal letters since a business letter is written to achieve a definite purpose and often gives rise to legal consequences. As such, the writer should be more accurate, clear, correct, courteous, precise, brief and reasonable in approach.

ESSENTIALS OR CHARACTERISTICS OF A GOOD BUSINESS LETTER

The effectiveness of a Business Letter can be achieved only if the sender/follows certain *principles of communication*. These *principles* are also called the essential elements or *characteristics* of a good Business Letter. These principles are also called ***"7 C's of written communication"*** which are :

1. Clarity
2. Completeness
3. Conciseness
4. Consideration
5. Coherence
6. Courtsy
7. Correctness[1]

There are discussed in the following paragraphs :

1. Clarity

Clarity as an essential elements of good/effective business correspondence involves two aspects :

1. According to Meenakshi Raman and parkash Singh (Business Communication : Oxford : p. 256), the seven C's of Business Letter Writing are : (i) clear, (ii) consice, (iii) correct, (iv) courteous, (v) conversational, (vi) convincing, and (vii) complete.

(a) Clarity of thought,

(b) Clarity of expression.

A. Clarity of Thought : Clarity of thought is the essence of every business letter. A business letter should not be a piece of literature nor it should be regarded as an essay or unseen passage. The sender of the letter must be clear about the following 3 points :

(i) objective of communication ;

(ii) content of communication ; and

(iii) medium of communication

According to L. Gartside,[2] "He, who would write clearly ought first to think clearly." Clear thinking is a habit which has to be nurtured, However, thorough knowledge of the content (subject matter) of communication proceeds clear thinking. If, for instance, the letter is to place an order for supply of goods, the letter must contain ;

(i) the specifications of the goods required ;

(ii) instructions about the mode of transport ;

(iii) instructions about packing of goods ;

(iv) schedule of delivery ;

(v) place of delivery ;

(vi) mode of remittance ; and

(vii) the *most suitable channel of communication, e.g.,* a written letter sent by Courier or by Post or a Fax or through e-mail or instructions over Telephone followed by a written letter or a Messenger.

The decision about the most suitable channel of communication depends on the following factors ;[3]

(a) Importance of the message,

(b) Amount and speed of feedback required.

(c) Necessity of permanent record ;

(d) Cost of the channel ;

(e) Degree of formality desired.

---

2. Modern Business Communication

3. Mary Ellen Guffey : Business Communication; Process & Product; Thomson : South Western p.107 3rd Ed. 2005.

The following will illustrate the choice of communication channels :

Choosing communication channels.[4]

Channel	*Best use*
Face to Face conversation	• To persuade • To communicate bad news • To share a personal message
Telephone Call	• To gather quick information • When non-verbal cues are unimportant • When meeting for face to face conversation is not possible • To obtain quick response
Voice mail	• To leave important information • To leave routine information • When receiver is allowed to respond to when convenient to him.
Fax	• Effective for communicating with a dispersed audience • When message must cross time zones or national boundaries • When the message is not secret or classified • When a record is significant • When speed is important
e-mail	• When feedback required but not immediately. • Effective for communicating with a large but dispersed audience. • When speed is important. • Is followed by written communication.
Video-conferencing Teleconferencing or Telepresence	• Where group consensus and interaction are important • Where members are geographically dispersed. • To obtain quick decisions. • Huge saving on Travel Time & Cost of executives.
Memo	• When written record is required to clearly explain certain policies • When procedures are explained • When information need to he collected within an organisation.
Letter	• When a written record of correspondence with customers, government departments, suppliers or other organisation is required.
Report or proposal	• When delivering extensive data internally or externally.

4. *Ibid.* (Adapted)

B. Clarity of Expression : Once the writer is clear about what to write, he need to express it in words. Here he should be careful about the words, their meaning and organisation. The following points about clarity of expression may be noted :

(i) Use Simple Words : Simple and short words are more effective than heavy and pompous words. For instance :

Avoid	*Use*
• acquaint	inform, tell
• compensate	pay
• facilitate	help
• demonstrate	show
• visualise	see
• utilize	use
• schedule	begin
• interrogate	question
• terminate	end

(ii) Use single words (avoid long phrases) : A simple word often communicates better than a long phrase. Take for example ; all the following phrases can be avoided / substituted by the use of one single word, that is — 'because'.

- On account of : because
- In consequence of : because
- Due to the fact : because
- Owing to the fact : because
- In view of : because
- In the light of : because
- On the grounds that : because

A large number of other examples (some given below) may be used to simplify expression.

Long Phrases (Avoid)	*Single Word (use)*
• for the purpose of	: for
• to the fullest possible extent	: fully
• will you be kind enough	: Please
• in the event that	: if
• despite the fact that	: although
• prior to	: before
• subsequent to	: after
• at all times	: always
• at a later date	: later
• in the absence of	: without
• to come to a decision	: determine

- to provide further confidence : assure
- to investigate & test officially : review, inspect
- in view of the fact that : because
- the manner in which : how
- until such time as : until

(iii) Avoid Double words : Many a times, we use two words conveying the same meaning, such phrases can he easily avoided and replaced by single meaning words, for example :

Double Words (Avoid)	*Single Words (use)*
return back	: return
actual fact	: fact , factually
mental state of mind	: state of mind
5.00 p.m. in the evening	: 5 p.m.
earlier experience	: experience
previous experience	: experience
end result	: result
absolutely O.K.	: O.K.
viable alternative	: alternative
costs a sum of	: costs
during the year 2009	: During 2009
revert back	: revert
period of one month	: one month
absolutely fine	: fine

(iv) Replace nouns with verbs : Often the use of verbs in place of nouns brings about simplicity and clarity. For example :

Nouns (Avoid)	*Verbs (use)*
making a decision	: decide
coming to a conclusion	: conclude
submit a proposal	: propose
make an announcement	: announce
in continuation of our agreement	: as we agreed
conduct a discussion of	: discuss
create a reduction in	: reduce
engage in the preparation of	: prepare
give consideration to	: consider
make an assumption of	: assume
perform an analysis of	: analyse
take action on	: act

(v) Avoid vague expressions : It is said that concrete expressions create visual images. The business letter writer should try to avoid vague and general statements (unless there is a specific objective in being general). For example :

Vague & General (Avoid)		*Concrete & Specific (use)*
• Goods will be despatched in a week	:	Goods will be despatched on 7th December.
• Order will be executed shortly	:	Goods will be despatched on 7th December
• The product is inexpensive	:	The product costs only Rs. 350 per pc.
• You can own the car at a down payment of 10% and easy EMIs later	:	You can own the car at a down payment of Rs. 35,000 and 36 EMIs of Rs. 7,352 each.
• Your savings can earn a handsome rate of interest	:	Your savings earn 9.50% p.a.

(vi) Avoid Jargon : Jargon refers to the specific, technical words used in a particular trade, profession or area of study. We may have legal jargon, business jargon, technical jargon, IT jargon and so on. Jargon makes it difficult to understand for a common reader. Jargon sometimes consists of garbage words which should be dropped altogether or replaced by simple words.

For example :

Jargon (garbage words)
(That may be dropped altogether)

- as regards
- as soon as possible
- for your information
- for the purpose of
- in due course
- in respect to
- in the case of
- please be advised
- please he informed
- we beg to
- and oblige
- with reference to
- undersigned
- with kindest regards.
- thank you for your attention
- instantly
- per pro
- this is to inform you.

Jargon that needs to be substituted[5]

Jargon (Avoid)		*Substitute word (use)*
• above mentioned	:	above
• accompanied by	:	with
• this is to acknowledge your letter	:	thanks for your letter
• all concerned	:	everyone
• are in agreement	:	agree
• as soon as	:	when

5. Also see section on "Business Jargon simplified" at the end of the Book.

- attached hereto : attached
- enclosed herewith : enclosed
- due to the fact that : because
- it is anticipated : I except
- it is required : must
- it will be necessary : must
- number of occasions : often
- under separate cover : separately

---- and so on.

(vii) Be Positive : Certain negative words create ill-will because they appear to blame or accuse readers[6]. 'Certain loaded words which does not serve any purpose, but may land the writer in trouble are :

- complaint
- defective
- criticism
- failed
- mistake
- relegated
- declined
- rejected
- disagree
- unpleasant
- unwelcome
- damage
- wrong

To avoid angry reaction, the reader should restrict negative words and try to find positive ways to express ideas, for example :

Negative Expression (Avoid)		*Positive Expressions (use)*
• You failed to include your credit card number, so we can't mail your order	:	We will despatch your order as soon as we receive your credit card number.
• You wouldn't be sorry that	:	You will be happy that ....
• The problem can't be solved without the coneant of Top Management	:	The problem can be solved with the consent of Top Management
• You returned a defective laptop, as described in your letter	:	Your letter described the laptop you returned.
• You can't park your vehicle here till December 15th	:	You may park your vehicle here starting December 15th.

.... and so on.

6. Mary Ellen Guffey : op. cit, p. 115

Example : Being Positive[7]

How to deliver Bad News to customers
Here is a checklist for delivering Bad News to customers : **1. Begin Indirectly :** Express appreciation. Show agreement on some point (if possible), review facts and /or show understanding. But don't thank the reader for his request you are going to refuse. **2. Provide reasons :** Justify the Bad news with objective reasons. Avoid blaming the customer. Don't hide behind company policy. Look for receiver's benefits. Be courteous but frank in credit denials. Stay away from Negative words. For instance, "Your complaint about our product...," instead write "We are sorry our product was not upto expectations". **3. State the Bad News :** Give the Bad news objectively or imply it in clear, no-nonsense terms. Although resale or sales promotion is appropriate in order letters, it may offend the reader in claim letters or credit refusals. Don't give the bad news in the opening paragraph itself. If the bad news result in loss to the reader, present relevant facts and details honestly and state the efforts you undertook to minimise his loss. **4. Close pleasantly :** Suggest alternative action, look forward to future business. Refer to gifts, use resale sensitively. Don't repeat the Bad news offer best wishes. **5. Follow up:** A follow up letter or action may help in regaining a lost customer. Show sincerity in approach. Don't give up. Continue with a positive approach.

Here are some more examples of words that generate positive viberations and are considered *'pleasing words'* which can replace negative expressions :

Negative (Avoid)	***Positive (use)***
• complaint department	: customer service department
• complaint department	: customer care department
• down payment	: initial investment
• cheaper	: economical
• headed	: supervised
• pulled up	: motivated
• removed	: reconciled

The following positive words may be frequently used :

- please
- praise
- appreciate
- satisfactory
- thank you
- pleasure
- agree
- courtesy
- welcome
- happy
- cheerful
- admire

7. Mary Ellen Guffey : *op,cit.* p. 111. (Adapted)
8. Ibid. p. 143

2. Completeness

In business correspondence, completeness of facts is of absolute importance. A business letter must be complete in all respects. Incomplete communication irritates the reader and require further communication (both way) to complete the information. This would waste precious time and money. In urgency, the receiver might use his own judgement regarding the missing information, which may result in disputes in future. For instance, in a purchase order for the supply of mobile phones, the communication must clearly include the following details :

- Brand name
- Specific Model No.
- Quantity
- Price
- Colour
- Catalogue Number
- Mode of Packing
- Mode of Transport
- Mode of Payment
- Delivery Schedule
- Trade / cash discounts
- any other relevant information

In the absence of any of these details, the order may not be executed at all or would require further correspondence to fill the gaps of information. The sender / writer should organise the message in such a way that the receiver has no doubts about anything contained in it.

Again, while answering a letter, all the questions raised or queries mentioned should be clearly answered, point by point, leaving some of the question unanswered, creates frustration and irritates the receiver.

3. Conciseness (Brevity)

While a letter should be complete in all respects, it must at the same time, be brief and short. Brevity, however, should not come in the way of clarity, correctness, completeness, or courtesy.

There is no hard and fast rule about the length of a letter. However, following points are worth-noting :

- A letter should be as long or as short as is necessary to tell the story effectively. A ten line letter may seem to be too long while a two-page letter may seem short depending on the contents of the letter.
- Lengthy expressions and unecessary discussions should be avoided.
- Utmost economy of words must be enforced. Lengthy letters without content often go unattended.
- Time is money for all businessmen. A busy manager does not have the time to go through long letters containing irrelevant matter.
- Courtesy words or phrases should not be dropped for the sake of brevity.
- Brevity does not mean use of telegraphic language in business letters.
- The following simple rules will serve the purpose of conciseness (brevity) in a business letter :

  (i) *Include only relevant facts.* Avoid unnecessary details.

  (ii) *Avoid repetition* to avoid monotony and irritation.

(iii) *Avoid lengthy expression* : use one word for many, whenever possible.

(iv) *Organise the message well* by using simple and short sentences.

The 5-step Process for Writing Business Letters
1. List out the topics you want to cover. Put the topics in order of importance
2. List keywords, examples, arguments, facts etc. in each topic.
3. Prepare an outline for relevance of the subject.
4. Delete anything that is not relevant.
5. Sequence the outline into the best order for the receiver

4. Consideration

A Business letter must show consideration for the reader. This can be achieved in the following ways :

(i) Cultivate 'You' attitude : Skilled communicators develop the 'you' attitude. They emphasize second-person pronouns (you, your) instead of first person pronouns (I/we, us, our), whether the objective is to persuade, inform or promote goodwill, the catchiest words the writer can use are **you** and **your.**[9] For example :

'I/we' attitude (Avoid)		*'you' attitude (use)*
• *I* wish to express my sincere thanks for the good words ---,	:	Thank *you* for *your* kind words ----
• We have three different insurance plans in which customers can invest ---	:	*You* have a choice of 3 insurance plans in which *you* can invest.
• *I* have granted you leave from ---	:	*You* have been granted leave from ---
• *I* am asking all employees to submit their views in the attached format ----	:	Since your ideas count, please complete the attached form ----

However, the **'you'** view should not be overused or misused. Readers appreciate genuine interest; they resent obvious attempts at manipulation. "Some sales managers, are guilty of overkill when they include **'you'** dozens of time in a direct mail promotion." In short, avoid using **'you'** for general statements that suggest blame and could cause ill-will." Skilled communicator are able to convey sincerity, warmth and enthusiasm by the words they choose,. "The writer should not be afraid of using phrases such as "I am pleased ...." or "we are delighted ...."

(ii) Be receiver focussed : "The most successful messages are receiver based." Effective communication envision the receiver and focus on benefits to that person. Ben Franklin, on effective writing, observes, "To be good it ought to have a tendency to benefit the reader." According to him, a powerful message can :

(i) show the reader how he can meet his goals ?

(ii) how he can save himself from frustration ?

(iii) how he can benefit from the message ?

9. Mary Ellen Guffy : op. cit. P. 111

Sender of business letter can be receiver focussed by putting himself in receiver's shoes. It is called empathy. "They try, to give something to the receiver, solve the receiver's problems, save the receiver money or just understand the feeling and position of that person." For example :

Sender-focussed (Avoid)		*Receiver-focussed (use)*
• To enable *us* to update our records, we request the enclosed form be returned	:	To ensure that you receiver prompt statements of accounts, please return the enclosed form
• *Our* warranty becomes valid only when the owners register with *us.*	:	*Your* warranty becomes valid as soon as you register with *us.*
• *Our* life policy provides twin benefit of endowment and insurance cover.	:	*You* may get twin benefits of endowment and insurance, with our life policy.

(iii) Avoid Gender-bias : The writer must ensure that his language is sensitive and bias free. He must be cautious about expressions that might be biased in terms of gender, race, age, ethnicity and disability. For example :

Gender-biased (Avoid)	*Bias-free (use)*
• female doctor	: doctor
• woman attorney	: attorney
• waiter / waitress	: server
• author / authoress	: author
• man-kind	: humanity
• man-hour	: working hours
• man-made	: artificial
• office-girls	: office employees
• executives & their wives	: executives & spouses
• workman	: worker
• salesman	: sales representative
• chairman / chairwoman	: chair person
• businessman	: business person

Generally, the writer can avoid gender - biased language by substituting the words man or woman to gender - free words - *person* or *representative*.

Racial or Ethnic Biased (Avoid)		*Bias-free (use)*
• An Indian doctor ---	:	A doctor
• An African engineer was hired	:	An engineer was hired
• Ashutosh, an Indian born American, applied for the job	:	Ashutosh applied for the job

Age-biased (Avoid)		*Bias-free (use)*
• People over 60 get the concession	:	senior citizens get the concession
• Nitin Madan, 30, was appointed	:	Nitin Madan was appointed

Disability-biased (Avoid)	*Bias-free words (use)*
• afflicted with	: has
• suffering from	: has
• crippled by	: has
• disease	: condition
• confined to a wheelchair	: uses a wheelchair

Sensitive communicators avoid gender, racial or ethnic and disability biases and prefer the use of bias-free words, instead.

5. Coherence

Clarity of thought and expression (stated above) must be supported by unity of expression or coherence. Coherence means the following :

- one idea / thought / information should naturally follow another.
- each sentence must show proper sequence.
- writer must show proper respect to logic.
- writer must plan an orderly arrangement of the subject matter and put it in proper words.

Expressions to Build Coherence[10]

To Strengthen	*To Show Time or order*	*To Clarify*	*To Show Cause & Effect*	*To Contradict*	*To Contrast*
Again Also Besides Likewise Moreover Further In Addition to Further more	Before After Earlier Finally Firstly Secondly Next Now Previously Meanwhile	For Instance For example In other words I mean that is thus it means To put it another way	Accordingly Consequently So for the reason therefore, under the circumstances	But Actually However in fact Instead rather though yet still	As opposed to On the otherhand On the contrary by contract at the same time Conversely In contradiction whereas

6. Courtesy

Courtesy and friendliness are inseparable terms . Courtesy demands a considerate and friendly behaviour towards others. "Maintaining a courteous tone involves not just guarding against rudeness but also avoiding words that sound demanding or preachy." The tone of the letter should be polite and its language should not offend the reader.

The following statements should guide the writer :

1. Some people regard bluntness as a sign of strength; which is absolutely wrong. Infact, it is a sign of bad manners and lack of etiquette.

10. Ibid. P. 143.

2. If a person receives a rude letter, he may be tempted to reply in the same manner. It spoils business relations.
3. Courtesy make friends, which, in business are very important.
4. Even when courtesy does not make a friend, it will, atleast not make an enemy.
5. However, there should always he maintained a balance between courtesy and self respect. It never pays to lose self-respect and behave like a subordinate or servile. Frankness coupled with honest statement of facts and polite language is perfectly O.K.

Principles : The following principles can help the writer to promote courtesy :

(A) Answer the letters promptly, preferably on the same day or within 2-3 days at the most. If the letter can't be answered quickly for want of gathering information/ reference/ clarifications from different departments, atleast the letter should be acknowledged promptly indicating the time required to send a complete reply.

(B) Thank Generously for a favour

(C) Apologise sincerely for any errors or omissions

(D) Avoid irritating expressions : Some negative words combined/used with 'you' or 'your' become very irritating. These should be strictly avoided. For example :

Discourteous (Avoid)		***Courteous (use)***
• You must complete the task before Tuesday.	:	Will you please complete the task by Tuesday?
• You are probably ignorant.	:	This may, perhaps, not be in your knowledge.
• We disagree with you.	:	Your opinion may be different than ours.
• Your irresponsible approach.....	:	Your approach may lack responsibility.....

So, even when you are justifiably angry, courteous language is the best way to achieve your objectives. Courteous tone creates goodwill and gives more options to receiver.

7. Correctness

A business letter must mention accurate facts and figures. The sender must not transmit any message unless he is absolutely sure of its correctness. Correctness of the facts and figures may be verified from many sources like ;

- an office file
- old correspondence file
- an office department (Like Sales, Purchase, Production, Accounts) etc.
- a colleague
- office archives
- an encyclopaedia/dictionery/grammar book
- internet search

Figure are liable to be wrongly stated. Therefore it is always advisable to write in Words and figures both, to avoid ambiguity (just as in the case of Cheques, Drafts, Bills of Exchange,

Promissory Notes etc). Amount, Quantity, Rate, Percentage discount, Commissions, Tax rates, Handling charges etc. are to be given in figures, and should be carefully checked.

The following guiding principles may be noted :

- Business letters often have legal consequences. Incorrect facts may land the writer in trouble later.
- Correctness does not mean that writer disclose business secrets.
- Correctness means exactness, accurate and definite as far as possible.
- Distorted/inaccurate facts, misrepresentations or dishonesty when exposed to the receiver offends him and he may not like to deal with the party at fault.
- Correctness implies the following :

  — stating correct facts and figures;

  — sending message at the correct time;

  — sending message in the correct style.
- "Style in Business Correspondence" is discussed in greater detail in the following pages.

EFFECTIVE COMMUNICATION : CRITICAL ELEMENTS

It is said that there are 3 critical elements of all effective communication. These critical elements are the basic requirements of all business correspondence. Ignoring any of them would mean non-effective communication, resulting in wasteful effort and/or inviting trouble. These critical elements are :

1. Think clearly : Thinking comes after knowing. One must know something before one can communicate it. And the better one knows, the more clearly one can communicate it. Consider, for example, the following types of speakers :

(i) Those who speak above your head;

(ii) Those who use big words and jargon;

(iii) Those who speak profoundly and sound scholarly; and

(iv) Those who really know what they are talking about.

It is only the last category of person who can connect right to the heart of the matter. These people (ivth category) can simplify and clarify even the most difficult subject matter. And if they can't do such things, it is a sign of their communication incompetence. Exactly similar is the case of business letter writer. The first critical element of effective communication is clear thinking before writing.

2. Feel Deeply : The business letter writer must not only know the subject matter or the concept, he is communicating, he must also feel deeply about them. However, in business communication, one rarely see the deep-down, straight-out, down-to-earth, truthful communication.[11]

11. As a joke, it is said that, "when a diplomat says 'yes', he means 'Perhaps', when he says, 'Perhaps', he means 'No', but when he says 'No', he is not a diplomat." As quoted in hodu.com

However, when true emotions enter the communication process, the recipients are more inclined towards it. If a communicator gets to feel deeply, the listeners feel deeply. " And if the communicator has lost his passion for what he does, say, or sell, may be it is time he should quit."

Simply speaking, if communicator feels deeply about the concept/subject and acts passionately, their is every reason, that the listner or the reader feels interested and have feelings about the concept/subject matter.

3. Act Consistently : Communicator's knowledge and feeling must be supported by the consistency of his acts. In the words of B.T. Washington, "The world cares very little about the knowledge or feelings of a person, it is what the person does or is able to do, that counts."[12]

If the communicator is :

(i) not doing, what he is talking; or

(ii) not walking his talk; or

(iii) not acting consistently, then

he/she will surely have problems in communicating his/her message. In other words, if the communicator acts consistently with what he thinks and feels, he/she will enjoy greater amount of credibility and the better communicator he/she will be.

It must be clearly understood that **"same rules are not applicable at all times and for all lines of business."**

In a nut shell, communication in any form should not be impersonal, overly formal, long-winded and difficult or tedious to read or understand. A good communication should be effortless to read or understand, it should be clear and concise, short and simple, keeping to the facts and in the interest of the receiver/listener and should bring in the action or reaction, the communicator wants.

12. See also the McGraw Hill handbook of Business letter by Roy W. Poe., A Handbook of Model letters for the Busy Executive By Dianna Booher (amazon. Com), and Business writing Make-overs By Hawley Roddick etc.

Chapter 3

STRUCTURE OF A BUSINESS LETTER

CONTENTS

INTRODUCTION

Business communication involves two types of message — verbal & non-verbal. Verbal messages are conveyed by words chosen by communicator. Non-verbal messages are conveyed by means of a document. If one compares a variety of such documents, (letters and memos) from different organisations, one finds that some look more attractive and professional than others. The attractive and professional looking documents suggest that they were sent by people who are informed, intelligent, careful and successful. One is more likely to take seriously documents that use better stationery and professional formatting techniques.

A set structure of writing business letters has evolved over the centuries out of certain practices, conventions, customs and experience. Although such conventions and practices offer some choices (of letter formatting and punctuation styles), most business letters follow standard formats. To ensure that the non-verbal documents (letters, memos etc.) carry favourable impression of the sender and the company, special attention need to be given to the stationery and formatting of the letters, envelopes, memos, fax cover sheets, e-mail etc.[1]

The appearance of a letter is as important as its contents. A letter bearing an unpleasant appearnace fails to catch the reader's/receiver's attention, even if it contains an attractive proposition.

According to Koli & Rai, "A letter is looked at before it is read, and the first impression which it makes on the reader's eye is often an important factor which influences the reader's opinion of the sender of the letter." A letter often works as a representative or salesman of the sender organisation.

PHYSICAL APPEARANCE OF A BUSINESS LETTER

Stationery

Most organisations use high-quality stationery for business documents (letters, memos etc). This is generally printed on BOND paper or other high quality paper which can withstand filing, erasing, is durable and also looks graceful. Some basic guidelines for use of stationery are given below :

A. Paper :

- Use A4 or 8.5 inch × 11 inch paper or letterhead.
- Use 2.5 cms. or 1 Inch margins on all four sides.
- Use 12 point font (may vary as per requirements)
- Use simple font (Times New Roman or Ariel)
- Lay out the letter so that it fills the paper appropriately.
- Single space within paragraphs.
- Double space between paragraphs.
- Double space between last sentence and closing (sincerely, faithfully etc.).
- Leave 3-4 spaces for signature of sender.

1. Adapted
2. Commercial Correspondence

- Cc (meaning "copies to") comes after the typed name.
- encl. (meaning "enclosure") comes next to cc, (if necessary).
- Fold horizontally (in three) before placing in the envelope.

B. Colour

Most business letters are written on white paper with black print. Scientists now claim that black ink on white paper gives a strong glare and is hard on eyes. Hence the use of coloured paper offers two distinct advantages :

(i) *Colour coding:* Colour coding makes papers (letters etc.) stand out and they are easy to trace at any time. If an organisation sends its letters always on a particular colour paper, the colour becomes the symbol of the organisation. Such letters become colour coded in other offices.

(ii) *Psychological effect:* Colours also have psychological effect. Adopting a single colour or colour combination in logos, trademarks, advertisements, letters etc. helps to project an image of the organisation. The following points should be kept in mind while selecting colours for stationery :

(a) Light colours are easy on eyes. They should be preferred over dark colours like Red, deep yellow or dark blue/green etc. which should be avoided.

(b) Light colours allow reproduction of documents on copying machines similar to white paper.

Choice of colour also reflect the moods and attitude of the writer, which is illustrated below :

Colour	:	***Reflecting Moods & Attitudes***
Yellow	:	Cheerfulness, vigour
Orange	:	High rank, status
Brown	:	Strength, usefulness
Pink	:	Faminity, gracefulness, healthiness
Grey	:	Confidence, wisdom
Blue	:	Sincerity, Harmony
Green	:	Life, freshness, coolness, natural
Red	:	Excitement, Danger

C. Envelope

Envelopes must also be impressive. Envelope should match with the document paper. The receiver sees the envelope before the letter is opened or read. It is said that the envelope determines the fate of the letter.

D. Letterhead

Outgoing letters must be typed on a letterhead of the organisation. Modern latterhead contain the following information (neatly printed or embossed) :

(i) Full name of the firm or The Individual

(ii) Complete Address

  (a) Address of registered Office; and

  (b) Address of the Branch, in case of a limited company.

(iii) Pin Code
(iv) Telephone Numbers (including ISD/STD codes)
(v) Fax Number (including ISD/STD codes)
(vi) E-mail address
(vii) Website address
(viii) Refrence no. and Date of the letter with blank spaces.

Letterhead of different organisations are found to incorporate the above information on the letterhead in any of the following ways :

- on the right hand top portion;
- on the left hand top portion;
- on the middle of the Top portion; or
- with name at the Top portion and other information at the middle of the bottom portion.

Some organisations also print their logo or trademark or tradename, symbols or slogans or some appropriate pictures as a watermark in the middle of the letterhead.

E. Continuation Sheets

Most Business letters are a one-page document. However, when a letter requires more than one page, an additional sheet of the same paper size, colour and paper quality should be used as continuation sheet. The continuation sheet should necessarily be a blank sheet (not a printed letterhead). Continuation sheets are used for second and subsequent pages of the letter. The continuation sheet should not spoil the impression created by the impressive letterhead.

The continuation sheet/s must indicate the following clearly on the top of the sheets :

- The name of the receiver
- Page Number
- Letter no, and date

Continuation sheets must be properly attached/ affixed/ stapled to the main/first page of the letter/letterhead.

PARTS OF A BUSINESS LETTER

The term "business letter" makes many people nervous. Generally, people with English as a second language think that their writing is not advanced enough for business writing. However, this may not be the case. An effective Business letter uses short, simple sentences and common-use vocabularly. The easier a letter is to read, the better it is.

To be effective, a business letter must be written in a proper form and style. Professional-looking business letters are arranged in a conventional sequence with standard parts. These standard parts are discussed in the following paragraphs.

1. Letter head

This is the printed part of the Business Letter, displaying the organisation's name, address, telephone and fax numbers, e-mail, website etc. The letterhead may also include the logo, trademark or advertising message etc. (Already discussed above).

2. Dateline

Dateline is placed below the line of the letterhead (Printed Portion). Date may be given in either of the following way :

- 23rd January, 2010, 7th October, 2009 (English style)
- January 23, 2010 October 7, 2009 (American style)
- 23 January 2010, 7 October, 2009 (European style)

The European style (also called as the Military style) does not allow use of *comma, rd* and *th* in the dateline.

In India, English style is generally followed. However, sometimes, the following style, though illogical and irrational are also used :

- 23-01-2010, 07-10-2009 (Indian style)
- 23/1/2010, 7/10/2009 (Indian style)

Both the above styles should certainly he given up in Business correspondence.

3. Refrence Number

The word Refrence Number (Ref.....) is printed with blank space below the printed heading on the letter head. The number of the letter is written in the blank space. The reference is very useful :

(i) for future reference;

(ii) in large firms, where large volumes of letters are handled;

(iii) for the receiver to quote in his reply; and

(iv) in locating an old or previous correspondence.

4. Inside Address

The inside address shows the name and address of the recipient. This information helps prevent confusion. In the inside address, include the appropriate title of respect of the recipient; and copy the name of the company exactly as the company writes it. When the name of the individual is known to the sender, he should address them properly; Mrs., Ms., Mr., Dr. and so on. While writing to a firm, Messrs. or M/s should be used. In the case of a company, the letter should he addressed to some executive of the company such as H.R. Manager, Administrative Manager or the Secretary.

In Business letter, the Inside Address should be given after the date line and Reference Number, on the left hand side of a letter paper. The Inside Address should be the same as given on the envelope. It may be given in three lines, but in case of a foreign addressee, the name of his country should be given in the fourth line. One line blank space should be given before and after the inside address.

5. Salutation

The salutation[3] directly addresses the recipient of the letter and is followed by a comma. Salutation is a way of greeting to the addressee and is similar to a hello or handshake in face-to-face conversation. The following guidelines may be observed for writing salutations :

- The oldest form of salutation is *'Sir'*. However, this is mostly used in official correspondence and not in business correspondence.
- *'Sir'* is also used when an applicant writes an application to a firm.
- The commonest forms of salutations used in Business correspondence are 'Dear Sir' or 'Dear Madam'.
- If the firm is being addressed, or a letter is addressed to two or more person, 'Dear Sirs' or 'Gentlemen' should be used.
- If the recipient is familiar, the writer may use his/her name, like: 'Dear Mr. Saxena', 'Dear Mrs. Suman', and so on.
- The writer must make sure that he/she spells the recipient's name correctly.
- The writer should also confirm the gender and proper title of the recipient. Use *'Ms'* for women and *'Mr.'* for men. Use 'Mrs', if it is 100% sure that the woman is married.
- The commonly used salutations are given below :
  - Dear Sir
  - Dear Sirs
  - Dear Madam
  - Gentlemen
  - Dear Mr. Chopra
  - Dear Ms. Prinyanka
  - Dear Mrs. Hans
  - Dear Valued Customer
  - Dear Ramesh Lamba

6. Subject Line

It is also called as the caption line. It is customary to use subject line to enable the recipient to quickly identify the subject of the correspondence. It may be placed in-between the inside address and the salutation or in-between the salutation and the body (opening paragraph) of the letter. In big organisations, subject line facilitate the work of filing. The subject or caption line is

---

3. Sometimes, an *Attention line* precedes *Salutation*. An attention line directs the letter directly to the specific individual, executive or department. Attention line may be typed in all caps or in bold upper-and-lowercase letters. Some writers donot use Attention line because they feel that letters addressed to Individuals at companies may be regarded as private letters. They fear that if the individual has moved on, the letter may not even be opened.

usually made distinct by placing the words, *sub.*, or *Ref.* or *Re.* before it. sometimes, the subject line is given in bold font or is heavily underlined. Subject live not only helps the receiver to connect to the previous correspondence but also helps in passing the letter quickly to the concerned person/department for necessary action. Some examples of the use of subject line are given below:

Subject : complaint against defective goods.

Reference : Your order no. 113/09 dated 28th Sep. 2009

Sub. : Your application for REP. licence

Ref. : Your enquiry of 10th September,2009.

Good subject lines are, specific, concise and appropriate for writer's purposes and the response writer expect from the reader. Remember that :

- When there is a good news, put it in the subject line.
- When the information is neutral, summarise it concisely in the subject line.
- When the information is negative, and if the negative is sender's error, use a negative subject line.
- If the information is negative and the reader may not reed the message or needs the information to act, use a negative subject line.
- When the letter contains a request that the reader can easily grant, put either the subject of the request or a direct request in the subject line.
- When the sender needs to persuade a reader who is reluctant, he should use a common ground, or a reader benefit or a direct subject line that makes the issue clear.[4]

A subject line is a title of the document. It aids in filing and retrieving the document, tells readers why they need to read the document, and provides a framework in which to set what you're about to say. A survey of business people in Southwest U.S.A. found that 68% of them considered a subject line in a letter to be important, very important or essential; only 32% considered subject lines to be somewhat important or unimportant.[5]

7. Body of the letter

The body of the letter is its most important part. It is generally divided into three or more paragraphs, each having its own function, as follows:

The first paragraph is known as introduction paragraph.

The second paragraph (or middle paragraphs) constitute the main body and contain the text of the letter.

The third (or last) paragraph is known as the concluding paragraph.

4. Adapted from : Business communication, Building Critical Skills by Kitty O. Locker & Stephen Kyo, P. 149
5. *Ibid* p. 168.

If the letter contains more than three paragraphs, they are usually numbered for ease of reference and reply.

The First Paragraph. The first or opening paragraph links up the correspondence and establishes repport with the reader/receiver. In most business letter, it is common to use a friendly greeting in the first sentence of the letter. Some examples are given below:

- Thank you for your letter dated ....
- We are happy to announce the launch of ....
- We are glad to offer you a ....
- It was a pleasure meeting you in connection with ....
- It gives me great pleasure to ....
- I came across an ad for your company in today's Hindustan Times regarding ....
- We are pleased to receive your letter no...........dated ....
- We appreciate the suggestions contained in your letter dated ....

Following opening lines should be strictly avoided, since they are no longer in use[6]

- I beg to apply for the post of ....
- I/we beg to acknowledge ....
- We beg your esteemed attention ....
- Your esteemed favour of ....
- We regret to inform you ....
- We are sorry to ....

After the short opening sentence, the main point of the letter may be stated in one or two sentences in the first paragraph itself such as :

- I am writing to enquire about ....
- We would like to place an order ....
- We would like to make an exclusive offer ....
- I am interested in the job opening ....
- We would like to ....

Second Paragraph : The second paragraph should deal with the main text of the letter (the subject matter) *i.e.,* the subject proper. If necessary, the point made in the second or main paragraph is elaborated or further developed upon, a third or even fourth paragraph may be used. Proper paragraphs should be made to deal with the whole matter systematically. It may be noted that any negative message or news should be disclosed only in the second (or third) paragraph.

6. These opening lines relates to the period of British Rule in India and are regarded as hackneyed phrases.

If the subject matter may be discussed in one paragraph only, one should not write an extra paragraph to make the letter look longer. If the letter includes any sensitive material such as rejecting an offer or informing an employee of lay off or retrenchment, it is advised to include such information in the second paragraph rather than opening with it. Some examples of expressing negative news follows :

- We regret to inform ....
- After careful consideration of the subject ....
- It is with great sadness that we ....
- We are unable to ....
- It is unlikely that ....

Third (Final) Paragraph : The final or concluding paragraph should be written in good spirit and should present the writer's point of view with force but politely. This paragraph should include requests, reminders, enclosures, assertions, actions, warnings, intentions, expectations, information about next step, and such other information, as may be required under the circumstances. If necessary, writer may give his contact information in this paragraph. The following are some common phrases used while closing a business letter:

- We look forward to ....
- Please respond at your ealiest convenience ....
- For further details please contact ....
- If you require more information ....
- I may also remind you that ....
- Thank you for considering ....
- I appreciate any feedback you may provide ....
- Please feel free to contact me by phone or e-mail.

The following stereolyped phrases may however *be strictly avoided* as they have lost all charm and convey almost nothing:

- Thanking you in anticipation,
- Hoping for an early reply,
- Awaiting an early response,
- Apologising for our mistake.

Opening Lines & Closing lines in Business Correspondence

Opening lines : We need an opening line in a business letter :

(i) to make reference to previous correspondence; or
(ii) to indicate why the letter is being written; or
(iii) to tell how you found the recipients name and address.

Examples of opening lines : Here are some examples of good opening lines in a business letter :

- With reference to your letter of 10th September, I ....
- With reference to your advertisement in ...., I ....
- I am writing to enquire about ....
- Having received your address from ...., I ....
- I/we recently wrote you about ....
- Thank you for your letter of 15th October, I ....
- Thank you for your letter regarding ....
- In reply to your letter of 2nd October, ...
- I received your address from .... and would like ....

Opening lines may be drafted according to the requirements of each particular case.

Closing lines : We need a closing line in a business letter;

(i) to seek a reply of the letter; or
(ii) to repeat a thankyou or an apology; or
(iii) to make a reference to a future event; or
(iv) to remind something *e.g.*, an offer of help etc.

Examples of Closing Lines : Some examples of good closing lines in a business letter are given below :

- I look forward to your reply.
- Looking forward to hearing from you.
- I look forward to seeing you.
- If you require any further information, feel free to contact me.
- Looking forward to a continuing business relationship in the future.
- Once again, please accept our congratulations.
- Once again, I apologise for any inconvenience.
- I would appreciate your immediate attention to this matter.
- Assuring you of our best services at all times.
- Assuring you of our best attention.
- Kindly expedite the matter at the earliest.
- Awaiting an early response.
- Hoping that needful will be done.

Just like opening lines, closing lines may be drafted according to the requirements of each particular case.

8. Complimentary Close (or Subscription)

It is a form of saying good-bye. It comes just below the body of the letter. It has to match in tone with the salutation. The more informal is the salutation, the more informal will be the complimentary close, and *vice versa*. The most common forms of complimentary close used in business correspondence are :

- Yours sincerely,
- Sincerely yours,
- Sincerely,
- Yours faithfully,
- Yours truly,
- Yours respectfully,

If the writer does not use a comma or colon in the salutation, then a comma or colon may not be used after the closing phrase.

Some writers also use the following phrases just before the complimentary close :

- Thank you,
- Best wishes,
- Best of luck,
- All the best
- Warm regards,

However, the following phrases in complimentary close **should be strictly avoided** in business correspondence :

- Yours affectionately,
- Yours very truly
- Yours very sincerely,
- Yours obediently,
- Yours fly,
- Yrs fly,
- Coordially yours, etc.,

The writer may design his own complimentary close, but he should be careful not to use florid or wordy phrases. Remember that only the first letter is capitalised, and the close is always followed by a comma.

"Your faithfully" versus "Yours sincerely"
When to use ? There are no hard and fast rules for using the words, 'yours faithfully', or 'yours sincerely' in a business letter; yet the following guidelines may be of help to a business letter writer : A. *When the name of the recipient is not known* Dear Sir .... Yours faithfully Dear Madam .... Yours faithfully Dear Sir/Madam .... Yours faithfully, B. *Addressing two or more persons or whole of a department/section/unit of a company* : Dear Sirs .... Yours faithfully. C. *When the Recipient's, name is known* : Dear Mr. Mongia .... Yours Sincerely. Dear Mrs. Suman .... Yours Sincerely. Dear Miss Seema .... Yours Sincerely. Dear Mrs. Jasvinder ----------- Yours sincerely. Now a days, even 'yours' word is being dropped and in case of acquaintances, only 'sincerely' word is used in business correspondence e.g., Dear Mrs. Sarvjeet ----------- Sincerely. D. *When the recipient is a colleague or good friend or old business friend, both 'yours faithfully' as well as "yours sincerely' may be dropped : such as -* Dear Yogesh .... Best wishes Dear Suman .... Regards Dear Ashish .... Best Regards.

9. Signature

Usually, the name of the writer is typed four lines below the complimentary close and signatures are handwritten in-between. As in most cases, the signatures are illegible, it is customary to type the name of the siganatory below his siganture. Signature serves the following purposes :

- The signature is an authentic proof as to by whom the letter is written.
- The status of the signatory has a great bearing on the importance of the letter.
- The signature must be accompanied with (a) the name of the Firm/Co. for whom the letter is being written, and (b) the designation of the person signing the letter.
- Every business letter must be signed. An unsigned letter even on a corporate letterhead is nothing more than a piece of paper.

The formats regarding signatures are as follows :

(i) Where the individual signs in his own rights	.... (Medhansh Bhatia)
(ii) Where an individual signs in his capacity in the organisation :	.... (Medhansh Bhatia Marketing Manager)
(iii) Where an individual signs as a representative of a firm :	For CATALYST corporation .... (Medhansh Bhatia) Partner
(iv) Where an individual signs as a representative of a company	For CATALYST INDIA LTD .... (Medhansh Bhatia) Managing Director
(v) Where an individual signs as an attorney holder	For M.L. Bhatia .... (Medhansh Bhatia) Attorney Holder
(vi) Where an individual signs with the authority of another individual.	Per Pro M.L. Bhatia .... (Medhansh Bhatia)

In legal sense, the signatures have great significance, because it is the mark of the sender who is identified and held responsible for whatever is written in the letter.

10. End Notations

In business correspondence, it is common to find, below the signature block, several abbreviations or phrases that have important functions :

(a) Initials : Initial in all capital letters are those of the writer of the letter. Similarly, as a rule, the initials in all small letters (lower case letters) after the colon are those of the typist.

(b) Enclosures : This word is always written in the left side of the letter below the signature block. It is marked either as 'Encl.' or 'Enc.' Any documents, invoices, bills, statements, cheques, certificates, photocopies of earlier correspondence, resume, price lists, quotations, write ups, minutes of meetings, agenda, summary of accounts, etc.. etc.. that are sent along with the letter are mentioned against the enclosures in their proper sequence. If more than one documents are enclosed, they should he numbered and attached/stapled to the letter in the same sequence. If the enclosure is lost, the recipient will know. The despatcher must carefully see that the enclosures mentioned are actully enclosed with the letter.

(c) Copies to : If the writer wants to send copies of the letter to different individuals, he/she should indicate the fact among the end notations. If the writer was sending a copy of the letter to the superior/boss of the receiver or to the customer care centre or to his lawyer for further action, he may refer it thus :

cc : to The Director Marketing
cc : to The Customer Care Executive
cc : to Mr. Parveen Hans, Advocate

(d) Post Script : If after the completion and signing of the letter, the writer wants to convey some more information, or an after-thought (new idea) is required to be conveyed to the receiver, the writer may put P.S. (Post Script) and write below that. The writer should invariably sign below the matter written in the Post Script. A signed post script becomes a part of the main letter.

As far a possible, Post Script should be avoided as it gives the impression that the writer lacks stability and coherance.

However, in some cases, post scripts may be used effectively and gain attention of the reader, such as :

- In announcing the launch of a Product.
- In mentioning the last date of receipt of Tenders/offers/proposals,
- In highlighting an exclusive offer.
- In making a declaration.
- In reminding of an important date/event.
- In announcing a reduction sale.

If such a declaration/invitation/announcement/reminder is typed or printed in a letter or a circular, it need not be signed or initialled. Such a Post Script catches the eye of the recipient and also creates an impression in his mind. A post script in such a sitution, is justified as being more effective than the letter in itself. It may be noted that in any and every case, no salutation or complimentary close is required before or after a Post Script.

WRITING TIPS

The following guiding principles for writing of effective business letters may be noted :

- Double check gender and spelling of names.
- Use a conversational tone.
- Use active voice (wherever possible)
- Use polite words (would in place of will)
- Ask direct questions.
- Be positive always .
- Never give negative news in the opening paragraph.
- Always refer to yourself as 'I'.
- Don't use 'we' unless you represent a department, a committee or a group.
- Avoid Vagueness
- Don't forget to include the date (day-month-year is conventional).

PROOF READING A BUSINESS LETTER

'Proofread' means to read a text carefully to check it for errors and contents as well as general tone of the letter. A business letter writer should always proofread a business letter before sending it. The following checklist will help in proofreading a business letter :

Checklist for Proofreading
• Have you read the letter after it is typed ?
• Have you allowed some time to pass after writing the leter before proofreading it ?
• Are you requests, requirements, offers, concerns, declarations clear ?
• Are there any long sentences that need to be broken into parts.
• Do all questions contain a question mark ?
• Is your tone polite ?
• Is your style positive ?
• Did you spell the recipient's name correctly ?
• Did you include the date (Day, month, year) ?
• Are there any passive sentences that may be changed to active ones.
• Have you spell-checked confusing words ?
• Have you used a standard business letter format ?
• Have you mentioned (clearly) and attached all enclosures to the letter.
• Have you signed it ?

Quick Tips for Proofreading Business Letters

- Donot try to proof a document by reading it on your computer screen. Read from a printed copy.
- Proofread after you have composed the first draft of the message.
- Take out the print-out in double space. This makes it much easier to read because the added white space helps your eyes rest between all the text.
- Allow time to proofread. When you are rushed, you can't do a good of proofreading.
- Reading your message aloud is a great technique for finding errors in construction.
- The final look should be for capitalisation, spelling of names, and number used in sentences. Double-check all the names because it is often easy to mis-spell a person's name.
- Remember every single piece of written correspondence you send out is a representation of your company. The errors you missed will be quite obvious to the reader and whether you like it or not, they will judge you.
- Proofread for the finishing touch.[7]

7. ***Source :*** Business Communication : Meenakshi Raman and Prakash Singh : Oxford, p. 240-249.

STYLE IN BUSINESS CORRESPONDENCE

Writing Business correspondence differs in certain important ways than writing Reports. The following points of advice may help in adding style to your business correspondence.

1. State the Main Purpose or Subject Matter First : Let the reader know from the very first sentence what the letter is about. The first concern of a receiver of a letter is to know (i) What the letter is about; (ii) What is its subject matter; and (iii) Why he/she should spend time to read it.

For instance, if one is writing to apply for a job; the letter should start like;

"I am writing to apply for the post of ....".

Similarly, a letter acknowledging receipt of an order may start like this

"We thank you for your order dated ...." or

"We acknowledge having received your order.................".

However, negative or bad news should not be broken in the first sentence. They may be included in the second or third sentence.

2. If responding to a letter, its reference and date be identified in the First Sentence or Paragraph : A busy recipient, who writes many letter might not remember the contents of every letter. It is therefore, that the subject and date of the letter responded be mentioned first.

3. Keep it short : As far as possible, business letters should not exceed one page, except in exceptional circumstances. It must be remembered that business letters are read differently than articles, reports or books. Generally, they are read rapidly.

The Paragraphs of business letters should be kept short, some only one sentence long. As a generally accepted norm, a paragraph of a business letter should be between three to six lines long. Big, thick, dense and long paragraphs containing over 10 lines, which require concentration may not be read properly — or not read at all.

In business letters, paragraphs that are made up of only a single sentence are very common and perfectly acceptable. Rather, they add style to the letter.

4. Compartmentalise the Contents : The contents of the letter should be compartmentalised. Each different segment of the discussion or each different topic of the subject matter should be placed in a separate paragraph of its own. For instance, in a fire insurance claim letter, the following compartmentalisation may be adopted :

- A description of outbreak of fire with relevant facts and action taken.
- An estimate of loss assessed by claimant.
- Requesting the Insurance Co. to send surveyors and complete formalities.
- A request for early settlement of claim.

Each paragraph must be complete in its contents purpose and function. If a paragraph does more than one thing, it should better he split into two paragraphs. Similarly, if two paragraphs perform the same function, they should be clubbed into one.

8. "Be positive, even if your blood group is B negative". Dr. R.K. Chopra.

5. Provide Topic Indicators : Every paragraph should, if and when possible, provide topic indicators at the begining of individual paragraphs . For instance, in the above letter (claim for fire) the words like 'Fire' 'Policy', 'Claim', 'Settlement' etc. may give recipient a clear sense of the content and purpose of each paragraph.

6. Position important information stratigically : Important information in a business letter should be placed strategically *i.e.*, in high visibility points. The following guiding principles may be followed :

(i) Information in first and last lines of a letter to be read and remembered better.
(ii) Information provided in the middle paragraphs or middle of long paragraphs is easily overlooked or forgotton.
(iii) For saying difficult things, a good strategy is to de-emphasise them by placing them in the areas of less emphasise.
(iv) Negative or detrimental information, should be placed in less-highly visible areas of the business letter.
(v) Just don't emphasise weak or negative points unnecessarily.

7. Convey bad news in a Positive Way : Bad news or negative information should not be conveyed in direct or straight forward manner. Be tactful and adopt positive approach, as far as possible, to avoid/reduce the chance of spoiling/ending business relations with the recipient. To convey bad news in a positive way, avoid the use of the following words, as much as possible :

Deny	Restrict	Can't	Fail
Refuse	Forbid	Impossible	Prohibit
Out of question	Unable	Against	Rejected

8. Adopt "You attitude" : The letter should not be self-centered, foccusing only the concerns of the business letter writer. It should address the concerns of the recipient by making the recipient the focus of the letter. This recipient-oriented style is often called the 'you attitude' in business correspondence, which adds a style to the letter.

9. Use simple, plain, common-sense language : Writer of a business letter must keep in mind the following guidelines :

- Avoid Business Jargon
- Avoid Inflated, legal-sounding phrases
- Avoid puffed, information sounding language.
- Present yourself as a plain-talking, down-to-earth person.
- Use common-sense in writing.
- Be honest.
- Avoid Slang.

10. Give the 'Business letter', an 'action ending' : Never leave the Business letter with open ending. Whenever appropriate, a business letter must be given an 'action ending,' requesting or setting a schedule (an expected date or period) for action desired or contemplated. Avoid the following :

(i) Non-committal statements
(ii) Unspecified action

(iii) Ineffective conclusions
(iv) Non-viable promises/commitments
(v) Vague or ambiguous language.,

at the end of a business letter.

Following the above guidelines will add a style to the business letters, in line with the making of effective communication.

HOW TO USE NUMBERS IN BUSINESS LETTERS

Numbers Versus Words : Follow the following rules

- Donot start sentences with numerals-write the number out or better still, rephrase the sentence so that the numeral does not begin the sentence.
- Make a firm decision on how to handle 0 and 1 when they refer to key, exact values.
- For decimal values less than 1, add a 0 before the decimal point; for example .05 should be 0.05.
- Use numerals for important, exact values.
- Use words when values are below 10, say five, seven, nine etc. but use numerals when values are above 10.
- Use numerals for important, exact values even when those values are below 10.
- Use words for numerical values that are unimportant, such as in the sentence.
  "There are six data types in the C programming language".
- When you use fractions, avoid the symbols that may be available in the character set used by your software or typewriter. Write the fraction like this : 3-1/4. Be sure to put the hyphen between the whole number and the fraction.
- Stay consistent with either decimals or fractions in these situations.
- Donot make numerical values look more exact than they are. For example, do not add '.00' to a Rs. amount if the amount is rounded or estimated.
- For large amounts you can write like Rs. 65,000, but not Rupees sixty five thousand.[9]

DO'S AND DONT'S IN BUSINESS CORRESPONDENCE

Business correspondence is a skill which may be acquired by constant practice, training and observation. In addition to the command on language, the writing process and drafting skills in writing business letters, the following points should also be kept in mind as Do's and Dont's in correspondence.[10]

'Do's

(1) Your letterhead must be attractive and give the full name, complete address and other details accurately.

(2) Where there are a number of addresses, make it clear where the correspondent is supposed to reply to you. Suppose the registered office of a company is in Delhi, its factory at

9. Adapted from Business Communication : Meenakshi Raman and Prakash Singh, Oxford. p. 198.
10. Adapted from Business communication by Pradhan N.S. & Pradhan Homai, Himalaya Publishing House, p. 121, 122 & Google Search.

Greater Noida and its godown at Noida, the letterhead should make it clear where the recipient is expected to reply. This is done by printing on the letterhead in bold letter. "Please reply here" (indicating the address).

(3) Whatever form your secretary uses in typing letters, see to it that every letter looks beautiful and pleasing. Corrections, omissions, gestures, uneven spacing etc., spoil the beauty of a letter. Where computers are used, most of these problems are taken care of. However, spelling mistakes might still occur, through some computers do have 'spell check' facility.

(4) The envelope must be typed with care. If this is to be done on the computer, adhesive labels are printed and then stuck on the envelopes.

(5) When using window envelopes, see to it that the inside address coincides with the window; otherwise letter is likely to be miscarried or delayed.

After the inside address on the letter is aligned with the window, it is a common practice to staple the envelope, so that the address continues to be seen in the window.

(6) Be courteous, and positive always.

(7) Ensure the 'you attitude'.

(8) Check before signing.

(9) Check enclosures.

(10) Check dates. Every writer of business letter must be date conscious. The errors in documents are often those of dates. In fact, every person must look at the date every time a paper, latter or document comes into his hands.

(11) Your letter should be to the point, precise and clear. Clarity in correspondence comes through clear thinking. In practice, we find that only a very few persons are able to think clearly and, therefore, write clearly.

(12) Give clear instructions. The writer has to indicate whether the letter will go under certificate of posting, recorded delivery, registered A.D., insured post, by hand delivery, by a special messenger. etc.

(13) Reply promptly.

Don'ts

(1) Do not delay a reply but do not also be in a hurry. You may wait till you have all the relevant facts before you.

(2) Do not be confused

(3) Never be rude. You can be firm, yet polite.

(4) Do not be unfair/unreasonable.

(5) Do not make a personal attack or personal criticism.

(6) Do not miss any relevant points when replying to letters.

(7) Don not write to a wrong person or wrong authority.

(8) Do not use jargon, unless the technicalities of the subject matter require such use.

(9) Don't violate any 'do' mentioned above.

(10) Don't be negative.[11]

11. "Be positive, even if your blood group is B negative" : Dr. R.K. Chopra.

GENERAL RULES FOR ALL BUSINESS CORRESPONDENCE

1. Address it to a particular person by name

Send your letter to the person who should receive it. If you do not have a contact name, call the firm. A purchase order may be sent to Sales Manager, sales promotion letter to the Purchase Manager, collection letter to the Account Manager and so on.

2. Letters should be kept to one page only

Your letter should not be more than one page in length. If it is more than one page, you are probably giving the reader too much information. keep your letter focussed, brief and to the point. Letter exceeding one page in length usually don't get read.

3. Remember the aesthetics

Print on high quality paper. Your letter should be free of spelling and grammatical mistakes Proofread! Have someone review your letter to get feedback regarding style and content.

4. Construct a letter that is unique and specific to the individual

This will make you stand out from the others. Moreover, it creates interest and also gets quick response.

5. Keep a copy of the letter and response for your records

This allows your to avoid confusion later. Sometimes, such records need to be quoted in future correspondence or prove useful in legal matters.

Letter-Writing Categories[12]			
Acceptances	Compliments	Fundraising	Referrals
Acknowledgements	Avoid Spaces	Get-Well	Refusals
Advice	Confirmations	Gifts	Reprimands
Announcements	Congratulations	Goodwill	Requests
Apologies	Cover Letters	Government	Reservations
Applications	Credit	Holidays	Resignations
Appointments	Delegation	Inform/Notify	Responses
Appreciation	Disagreements	Inquiries	Sales
Approvals	Discipline	Introductions Interview	Social Events
Authorizations	Dismissals	Invitations	Suggestions
Business Memorandums	Encouragement	Job Offers	Sympathy
Cancellations	Endorsements	Legal forms	Terminations
Circulars	Promotions	Orders	Thank You
Claims	Errors	Persuasion	Transmittals
Collections	Proposal letters	Recommendations	Aooid spaces
Complaints	Farewells	References	Welcome etc.
Contracts	Follow-Up		
Complaints-Response Letters			

12. Adapted from : http://www.write express.com.

Chapter **4**

BUSINESS LETTER FORMATS

CONTENTS

INTODUCTION

There are certain standards for formatting a business letter, though certain variations are acceptable in American and British styles. In India, business correspondence is written in British English language, accent, grammar and style. So, while writing a business letter, one of the common formats should be selected. The common formats[1] include the following :

1. Block Format
2. Semi-Block Format
3. Alternative-Block Format (Modified Block Format)
4. Simplified Letter.

1. Block Format

Block Format is the most common format used in business today. With this format, nothing is centered. The sender's address, the recipient's address, the date and all new paragraphs begin at the left margin. The Block format is the simplest format, as all of the writing is flush against the left margin. (See Fig. 1)

The numerals given in the figure 1 (Block format letter) denote the following :

1. *Address* : (Not needed if the letter is typed on Printed Letterhead of the organisation). The address represent the return address of the letter so that the recipient can easily know where to send a reply to. One line spacing is desired between the address and the date.

2. *Date* : Date when the letter was written is to be written here in the format (Day, month and year) e.g., 25th September, 2009. Skip one line space between the date and the inside address. (Some people skip 2-3 lines)

3. *Inside Address* : The address of the receiver alongwith the name of the recipient, their title and company name. If sender is not sure who the letter should be addressed to, he may leave it blank but must put in a title *i.e.*, "The Marketing Manager". Again, skip one line spacing between the date and the salutation.

4. *Salutation* : Dear Mr./Mrs./Ms. Last Name (Sirname); or Dear Manager (H.R.); or 'To whom it may concern; if the recipients' name is unknown. Note that there is a colon after the salutation.[2] Again skip a line between the salutation and the subject line or body.

5. *Subject Line* : This is an optional line. Subject line makes it easier for the recipient to find out what the letter is about. Skip one line spacing between the subject line and the body of the letter.

---

1. Some authors on the subject enumerate the following as the common business letter formats :
   (i) Indented form
   (ii) Hanging Indent form
   (iii) Block form
   (iv) Semi-Block form
2. *Sources* : Letter writing guide.com
   Io.com
   Hodu.com

6. ***Body of the Letter*** **:** The Body is the most important part of the letter. The body is where content of the letter is written. The Body may be divided into two, three or more paragraphs depending on the information to be conveyed. The paragraphs should be single spaced with a skipped line between each paragraph. Skip a line between the last (final) paragraph of the body and the complimentary close.

7. ***Complimentary Close*** **:** This marks the end of the body of the letter. It usually ends with Thanking you, Thank you, Yours Sincerely, Yours Faithfully and so on. It may be noted that (i) There is a comma after the end of the closing; (ii) only the first letter of the closing is capitalised; and (iii) skip 3-4 line spacing between the closing and the Printed name of the sender, so that the sender may put his signature below the closing line.

8. ***Signature*** **:** Sender's signatures will go under this section. It is also called as 'Signature Block'. The sender should use only blue or blank[3] ink only for putting his signatures here. Signatures should be hand written, always.[4]

9. ***Printed Name*** **:** The printed version of sender's name, and in most cases in business correspondence, the title or position of the sender is also typed/printed alongwith name, on the line underneath it. Skip a line between the printed name/title/position and the enclosures.

10. ***Enclosures*** **:** If certain documents/papers/forms etc. are to be sent to the receiver alongwith the letter, the letter will include the word "Enclosure"/"Enclosures". It is always advisable to write the detail of the documents in enclosures than writing merely the numbers (2,3 and so on) or writing a/a (as above mentioned). The number mentioned should not count the letter itself.

11. ***Reference Initials*** **:** If someone other than the sender had typed the letter, the initials of the typist should be given here. The letter dictator's initials should be given in capital letters and the initials of the typist should be given in lower case alphabets.

The Serial Nos. 1 to 11 above is followed in all business letter formats mentioned above and are given in figures 1 to 4 in the following pages :

2. Modified Block Format Letter

In modified Block format letters, the sender's address, date,[5] the close, signature, and printed name of the sender alongwith his title or position are all indented to the right side of the page. Care should be taken to indent the heading and closing in a straight line. However, variation may be made in such a manner that the letter looks presentable.

3. Semi-Block Format Letter

It is also called as the 'Indented' format of Business letters. In the Semi-Block Format, the sender's address, date[6], the closing signature and printed name and title/position of the sender are all indicated to the right side of the page. (The indent should be so spaced that the heading and closing are lined up or variations may be done to make the letter presentable). *In addition, the first line of each paragraph of the body of the letter is also indented.*

---

3. Red & Green should be strictly avoided for signatures.
4. However in Computer Generated letters, signatures may not be required.
5. The date can actually be given on either the left or the right side of the letter.
6. The date can actually be given on either the left or the right side of the letter.

Sender Company Name Line 1 **1**
Address Line 2

Date (Day, Month, Year) **2**

Mr./Mrs./Ms./ Full name of recipient. **3**
Title/Position of Recipient
Receiver Company Name
Address Line 1
Address Line 2

Dear Mr./Mrs./Ms. Last Name: **4**

Subject: Title of Subject **5**

Body Paragraph 1 ....

....

....

Body Paragraph 2 ....

....

....

Body Paragraph 3..

....

.... **6**

Closing (Sincerely) **7**

Signature **8**

Sender's Name (Printed) **9**
Sender's Title

Enclosures (3) **10**
Typist Initials. **11**

Fig. 1. Block format letter

7. Also see related websites : Latter writing guide. Com, about. Com, 4hb.com, is. Com (formats), write express. Com, grossmont. Com., writing business letter. com, wikipaedia, org., Justanswer. Com, writing help. com etc.

Sender Company Name Line 1 **1**
Address Line 2

Date (Day, Month, Year) **2**

Mr./Mrs./Ms. Full name of recipient. **3**
Title/Position of Recipient
Receiver Company Name
Address Line 1
Address Line 2

Dear Mr./Mrs./Ms. Last Name: **4**

Subject: Title of Subject **5**

Body Paragraph 1 ....

....

....

Body Paragraph 2 ....

....

....

Body Paragraph 3..

....

.... **6**

Closing (Sincerely) **7**

Signature **8**

Sender's Name (Printed) **9**
Sender's Title

Enclosures (3) **10**
Typist Initials. **11**

Fig. 2. Modified Block format letter

8. *Ibid.*

Sender Compay Name Line 1 **1**
Address Line 2

Date (Day, Month, Year) **2**

Mr./Mrs./Ms./Full name of recipient. **3**
Title/Position of Recipient
Receiver Company Name
Address Line 1
Address Line 2

Dear Mr./Mrs./Ms. Last Name: **4**

Subject: Title of Subject **5**

Body Paragraph 1 ....
....
....

Body Paragraph 2 ....
....
....

Body Paragraph 3..
....
.... **6**

Closing (Sincerely), **7**

Signature **8**

Sender's Name (Printed) **9**
Sender's Title

Enclosures (3) **10**
Typist Initials. **11**

Fig. 3. Semi-Block format letter [9]
(Also called indented form)

9. Ibid.,

Sender Company Name Line 1 **1**

Address Line 2

Date (Day, Month, Year) **2**

Title/Position of Recipient **3**
Receiver Company Name
Address Line 1
Address Line 2

Subject: Title of Subject **4**

Body Paragraph 1 ....

....

....

Body Paragraph 2 ....

....

....

Body Paragraph 3..

....

.... **5**

Closing (Sincerely), **6**

Signature **7**

Sender's Name (Printed) **8**
Sender's Title

Enclosures (3) **9**
Typist Initials. **10**

Fig. 4. Simplified format letter
(Also called Modified Semi-Block format)

The only difference between the Semi-Block Format letter and Modified Block Format letter is the indentations of the first line of each paragraph of the Body of the letter.

4. Simplified Format Letter : When the sender does not know the title (Position) of the person he is writing to or when he is writing to a Company, Government Agency or Organisation, it eliminates the courtesy salutations (Mr., Mrs., Ms.,) and the complimentary close. The focus of the letter is on the body and what is to be said. Such a letter is called simplified letter.[10]

Some professionals believe that neither the salutation nor the complimentary close are read, and therefore neither should be included. This has produced the 'Simplified letter style." *A very good use of the simplified letter style is when the sender can't identify the name or gender of the person to whom the letter is written. Instead of using a generic "Dear Sir or Madam", salutation, skip the salutation entirely and just identify the subject.*[11]

A Simplified Letter Format takes the same elements as of Block letter with one exception, the greeting or salutation is eliminated. This is a helpful format when sender does not know the recipient's gender is male or female, or Mrs. or Miss.[12]

Figure 4 illustrates a simplified letter format.

DIFFERENCE BETWEEN DIFFERENT LETTER FORMATS[13]

S.No.	*Format type*	*Nature of Difference*	*Indentation*
1.	Block type	All Text is aligned to the *LEFT* Margin	Paragraphs are not indented
2.	Semi-block type	All Text is aligned to the *LEFT* margin	Paragraph are indented
3.	Modified block type	Writer's Address, Date & closing are aligned to *RIGHT* Margin. Rest All text is aligned to the *LEFT* Margin.	Paragraphs are not indented
4.	Simplified Type	Writer's Address, Date & Closing are aligned to *RIGHT* Margin. Rest all text is aligned to the *LEFT* Margin	Paragraphs are indented.

GUIDELINES FOR BUSINESS LETTER FORMAT

- The format of business letters has slowly changed with the culture of business getting less anless formal.
- Variation and customisations are common in Business letter formats. (Not all elements are needed in every type of letter such as job application cover letters, Thank you letters etc.,
- Try to keep the letters to one page only.
- Use letterhead only for the first page., use only blank sheet of paper for continuation pages.

10. Adapted from letter formats KIN 302
11. Adapted from http://www.mc. maricopa.edu/format/2html
12. About.com (Adapted)
13. Simplified type is also called Modified Semi-Block Format (see Business Letter — Wikipedia)

- Sender may enjoy some freedom/variations in how many blank lines to space between blocks and in the margin sizes in order to fit the letter to one single page.
- Not all letters need every element in the format.
- If one element is avoided, donot leave blank lines where the element would have been.
- A business letter may, however, be not resticted to one page; the letter should be as long as it needs to be. Care for the line spacing.
- The continuation sheets (if any) should be of same paper quality, weight and texture as the letterhead stationery.

BUSINESS LETTERS — SPACING CHECKLIST

Margins : Top	1.5″
: Bottom	1.25″
: Side Right	1.25″
: Side Left	1.75″
Address/Dateline spacing	3
Salutation spacing	1
Paragraph spacing	1
Closing line spacing	1
Signature spacing	3-4
Printed name spacing	1
Enclosure Notation	1
End Notations — cc.	1
— Initials	1
Total spacing	13-14

E-MAIL

E-mail is an internet service provided by internet service providers. E-mail lets a person send a message to a person without making a direct contact or knowing where that person is located.[14] To understand what e-mail is and how it works, the following quick points may be observed :

- Subscriber to e-mail services are called users.
- An e-mail user can access messages on his/her system from anywhere—home, office, airport, hotel or anyplace he/she happen to be.
- An e-mail is a method of instant messaging.
- Alongwith an e-mail message, attachments in the form of drafts, document, files, folders, photograph, diagrams, or any such thing can be sent instantly.

14. Business communication : Meenakshi Raman and Prakash Singh : Oxford, p. 380

- Part of the e-mail information included in a message is the address of both the sender and the receiver, which include their unique identification codes, called e-mail id's.
- To obtain an e-mail id, a user has to register at the site of any of the internet service providers.[15]
- Each e-mail system uses a protocol that describes the structure of the message, generally with a header of *To, From, Subject*, followed by *cc, bcc* and *attachments*, followed by the body of the message.

In a study sponsored by Oracle Corp. and conducted by KRC Research, it was observed.

"That 56% of professionals said they could not live without e-mail and 44% said they use e-mail almost twice as much as they use the telephone."[16]

Almost all organisations are rapidly embracing the use of e-mail for communication. E-mail has replaced the telephone as the most frequently used business communication tool around the world.

E-Mail formats are still evolving :

Most E-Mail programmes appear like the following

To	: ________________
From	: ________________
Subject	: ________________
Cc	: ________________
Bcc	: ________________
Attachments	
(Space for Message)	

- *'To'* indicates the name (e-mail id) of the person the message goes to
- *'From'* indicates the name (e-mail id) of the person sending the message
- *Subject* indicates the subject line.
- *cc* denotes computer copies; the recipient will see that these people are also getting the message.
- *Bcc* denotes blind computer copies, the recipient does not see the names of these people.
- *Attachments* : Most e-mail programmes allow the sender to attach documents from other programmes. Thus the sender can attach the documents with formatting, drafts, MS word or Power point slides, or the design for a brouchure cover etc.,

15. Such as Yahoo, Sify, In, Indiatimes, gmail & a host of others.
16. Quoted by Meenakshi Raman etc. op. cit P382

- *Date and Time* : are automatically supplied by the computer. Some programmes also allow sender to write a message now and programme the future time at which the sender wants it to be sent.

Some aspects of E-mail formats are still evolving, for instance :

- Some people treat e-mail messages as informal letters.
- Some treat them as Memos.
- Some writers put a salutation in the Message Box.
- Date & Time are automatic, yet people put them in the Box, some don't.
- Some writers use a Signature Block in an e-mail.
- Some writers repeat subject line in the Box.

E-mail 'Netiquette' Rules[17]

Adherence to the following tips can make an e-mail writer a good "Netizen".

1. Never send angry messages by e-mail. If the sender has a conflict with someone, he should work it out face-to-face, not via e-mail.
2. Use full caps only to emphasise a single word or two. Putting the whole message in caps is considered as shouting.[18]
3. Send only those messages that people need. Avoid unnecessary or irrelevant messages.
4. Send copies to your superior, or boss or CEO of the company only if they have asked you to do so.
5. Messages should be short. Any details, drafts, documents, statements should be sent as attachments. (Not as part of the message).
6. While responding to an e-mail, include only the part of original message that is essential so that the reader understands your posting. The rest may be deleted. If the quoted material is long, sender should put response first and then the original material.
7. When composing a message in a word processor to use it subsequently in e-mail, use it in short line lengths so that awkward line breaks in messages may be avoided.
8. Sending attachments make most sense while sending :
   - A long test document
   - A text document with extreme formatting
   - A non-text file like
     — Power-point slides,
     — html file,
     — spread sheet etc.,
9. A computer virus[19] is a script that harms the computer or erases the stored data. One can't get a virus through e-mail, but viruses can affect attachments/files that are attached to e-mail messages or that the receiver downloads.

17. Also see Kitty O. Locker & Stephen Kyo : op. cit. p. 267.
18. It is considered rude to the recipient if the message is in all caps.
19. Kitty O. Locker & Stephen, Kyo : op. cit. p. 268 (Adapted).

10. To stay virus-free :
    - Install an Anti-virus[20] software on the computer and keep it up-to-date.
    - Give attachments (that are sent with e-mail message), your name. Virus titles are not that specific.
    - When in doubt about an attachment, don't open it.
    - Forward e-mail messages when you are sure of the source and contents.

Formatting Business E-mail

When using an e-mail in business, most of the guidelines for standard formatting in business letters apply. Following are a few differences :

- Choose a subject line that is simple and straight forward.
- Refrain from using key words that might cause an e-mail to go into another's trash Box.
- Repeat the subject line in the body of the e-mail, below the salutation (as in the letter)
- Use the 'cc' address line to copy to more than one person with your correspondence.
- Sender may request for a receipt of important letters.
- Instead of a siganture, sender may type his name and below it include his/her e-mail address, business name and address, phone/fax number, website, etc., if appropriate.
- Many people often print out e-mails, so sender's e-mail address and the subject line would be lost if he/she had not included them in the body of the e-mail.
- Internal e-mails may be formatted more like a memo than a formal letter.

Computer Ethics

The Ten Commandments of Computer Ethics are :[21]

1. Thou shalt not use a computer to harm other people.
2. Thou shalt not interfere with other people's computer work.
3. Thou shalt not snoop around in other people's computer files.
4. Thou shalt not use a computer to steal.
5. Thou shalt not use a computer to bear false witness.
6. Thou shalt not copy or use proprietory software for which thou hast not paid.
7. Thou shalt not use other people's computer resoures without authorisation or proper compensation.
8. Thou shalt not appropriate other people's intellectual output.
9. Thou shalt think about the social consequences of the program thou art writing or the system thou art designing.
10. Thou shalt always use a computer in ways that insure consideration and respect for thine follow humans.

20. There are many anti-virus softwares available like Norton, Mcaffe, AVG, firewall etc.
21. As quoted in Business Communication : Meenakshi Raman and Prakash Singh : Oxford, p.536

Quick Tips for writing E-mail[22]

- Be concise and to the point.
- Answer all questions and pre-empt further questions.
- Use proper spelling, grammar and punctuation, where needed.
- Make it personal.
- Use templates for frequently used responses.
- Answer swifly.
- Do not attach unnecessary files.
- Do not overuse the high priority option.
- Never write in capital letters.
- Read the e-mail before you send.
- Do not overuse reply to all.
- Be careful with formatting and HTML.
- Do not forward claim letters without requesting delivery and read receipts.
- Do not ask to recall a message or attach a message without prior permission.
- Never use e-mail to discuss confidential issues.
- Use meaningful subject avoiding urgent or important.
- Use active voice instead of passive.
- Do not ever forward any junkmail to offence or obscene remarks.
- Do not reply to span.
- Know the Cyber Laws of the land.

E-mail Etiquelte

Because E-mail is fairly immediate and generally less formal than other forms of written communication, one may be tempted to relax the tone, organisation and content of the message. However, the following guidelines work for e-mail messages :

- *Watch your tone :* Because of the conversational aspect of E-mail and the fact that the writer is sitting in privacy, he/she may be tempted to be too casual. Writer's formality will depend on his/her relationship with the receiver.
- *Be concise :* Long, repetitive and meaningless messages are just as ineffective on E-mail as they are in print.
- Send a message only if you have something *important to say.* Frivolous & trivial e-mails can be daunting to the receiver.
- If you receive a message that was not meant for you, *forward it* to the correct name and address. Also, alert the sender of the message for sending it to the wrong address.
- *Be polite :* 'Flaming is an E-mail term meaning to insult, provoke or comment too much about something which is irrelevant or tasteless.[23]

---

22. *Source* : Meenakshi Raman & Prakash Singh : Business Communication; Oxford, p. 580-581 (Adapted).
23. Effective Business Communication : Herta A. Murphy, Herbert W. Hidlebrandt, Jane P. Thomas : McGraw Hill : 7th ed. p. 123-124.

How to use E-mails in Business effectively?

The ever increasing use of e-mail in business communication has also presented certain dangers of its use in business; e.g.,

(i) e-mails can travel long distances (intentionally or unintentionally);
(ii) a dissatisfied customer/client may forward the e-mail to a competitor or adversary;
(iii) even erased e-mails can remain on the disk-drives and may be restored in future to be used against the business;
(iv) some users use e-mail casually, without visualing its negative impact on receiver ;
(v) several e-mail receivers have genuine, complaints of an 'information overdose' or 'information dumping'

It is in the interest of organisations to make e-mails more efficient and less burdensome for users (receivers).

It is claimed (and rightly so) that the benefits of e-mail far outweigh its disadvantages. The following guidelines may be used for effectively using e-mails in

(i) business to customers (B2C)
(ii) business to business (B2B) situations.

Business to customer's (B2C) E-mails

Every organisation sends hundreds of e-mails to customers for situations like :

— acknowledging an order (order confirmation)
— communicating shipping date,
— requesting customer to modify order,
— requesting customer to make advance payments.
— declining an order,
— informing delayed shipping,
— confirming despatch of goods,
— acknowledgeging receipts of payments etc.,
— announcement letters,
— sales letters,

An ill-drafted e-mail may make customers' life miserable; e.g.,

— when aggressive sales letters are repeatedly sent,
— when e-mail does not contain the name and contact number or e-mail id. of the sender,
— when e-mails contain irrelevant information,
— when e-mail confirming dispatch of goods does not specify the date of dispatch.
— when the expected date of delivery is not mentioned.
— when e-mail does not mention the name and designation of the sender.
— when e-mail does not even mention the name of the organisation.
— when a brief e-mail omits necessary and relevant information.

— when an e-mail communicating delay in dispatch fails to convey the expected date of dispatch.

— when the e-mail communicating change of office location does not provide the new office address, etc.[24]

Such e-mails can endanger goodwill, create annoyance and frustration in the mind of customers and all hard work done to acquire a customer/order goes down the drain. When a customer does not get specific information, they get annoyed and angry. There can be no excuse for :

— refusing to respond a customer's phone, fax, e-mail, letter,

— refusing to respond to a customer's genuine requests,

— downplaying customer's requests for timing of dispatch, delivery, discounts, concessions, scheduling of payments etc.,

"Every e-mail is an opportunity to build a relationship with customers. E-mail is one of the most inexpensive tactics for improving customer service. Do that, and your relationship with a customer will be long and fruitful."[25]

Litmus Test for B2C e-mail[26]

(i) sender should pretend he/she is talking to the recipient face to face;

(ii) choose words very carefully so as not to offend;

(iii) sender should organise his/her thoughts, compose carefully and be concerned with correct grammar and punctuation.

(iv) essentials (7c's) of writing business letters should also be religiously followed in e-mail.

Business to Business (B2B) e-mails :

Developing effective B2B e-mails is quite different than developing effective B2C e-mails. It is a common fact that business executives always suffer from scarcity of time and hence want to know the message as quickly as possible. They scan instead of reading the e-mail messages. They appreciate just benefits and facts and not jargon and fluff.

Meenakshi Raman and Prakash Singh[27] list down 20 rules for writing effective business e-mail messages. These are summarised below :

1. Be accurate
2. Care about correctness
3. Be brief
4. Be clear
5. Be genuine
6. Speak recipient's language
7. Put yourself in receiver's shoes.

---

24. What is true about business letters is equally true about business e-mails as well. the 7C's must be followed in e-mail also.
25. Business Communication : Meenakshi Raman and Prakash Singh : Oxford : Ed. 2006, p. 283
26. Adapted
27. Business Communication , op. cit. p. 384-385

8. Watch out for a 'knowledge gap'.
9. Take your time.
10. Remember your e-mail is likely to be passed around.
11. Mimic your verbal presentation.
12. Check you signature block
13. Carefully choose when you actually send the e-mail.
14. Prepare your subject line carefully.
15. Use graphics wisely.
16. Make sure links within your e-mail display and work properly.
17. Be wary about sending attachments
18. Double check before hitting the 'send' button.
19. Be complete
20. Stand out from the rest.

E-mail Abbreviations

With the evergrowing use of internet and online trading, business communication is undergoing enormous transformation by the development and use of e-mail language. There are a large number of e-mail abbreviations commonly used in online messaging. A brief yet indicative list of such abbreviations which are used in e-mails, is given below[28] for quick reference of the reader :

E-mails Acronyms & Abbreviations

GR8	: Great
URGR8	: You are great
YRW	: You are wrong
CIO	: Check it out
GTG	: Got to go
WDYS	: Why did you say ?
AYSOS	: Are you stupid or something ?
CID	: Consider it done.
W4Y	: Waiting for you
2L8	: Too late
atw	: at the weekend
cm	: Call me
idk	: I donot know
dur	: Do you remember ?

28. Also see life's little E-mail Book : Business India I.T. Ltd., and postmaster@axcess.net.in

f2f	: face to face
gal	: get a life.
gmta	: great minds think alike
tnx	: thanks
T2UL	: Talk to you later
4e	: forever
imi	: I mean it
imo	: in my opinion
jam	: just a minute
j4f	: just for fun
KC	: keep cool
nc	: no comment
now	: no way out
o44	: only for you
ptmm	: please tell me more
asap	: as soon as possible[29]
BBL	: Be back later
BFN	: Bye for Now
BRB	: Be right back
BTW	: By the way
FYI	: For your information
<g>	: grin
<G>	: Big grin
HSIK	: How should I Know
IAE	: In any event
IMO	: In my opinion
IOW	: In other words
LOL	: Laughing out loud
NBD	: No big deal
ROFL	: Rolling on floor laughing
TIA	: Thanks in Advance

29. *see also* : Business Communication : Meenakshi Raman and Prakash Singh ; Oxford 579-580

TIC	: Tongue in Cheek
TTFN	: Tata for Now
TTYL	: Talk to you later
WYSIWYG	: What you see is what you get[30]
KAO	: Kind attention of
FAQ	: Frequently asked questions
IMHO	: In my humble opinion
ROFL	: Roll on the floor laughing
BTW	: By the way
AFW	: Away from Keyboard
IMB	: I'am back
BBFN	: Bye Bye for now
BBL	: Will be back later
BFN	: Bye for now
Bg	: Big grin
BO	: Brain Overbad
BRB	: I'll be right back
CMIIW	: Correct me if I am wrong
CU	: see you
CUL8R	: see you later
FIIOOH	: Forget it, I'm out of here
FITB	: Fill in the Blank
G2G	: Got to go
IMO	: In my opinion
LOL	: I'm laughing out loud[31]
RUOK	: Are you O.K.?
TA4n	: That's all for now
All Caps	: Shouting
* Asterisks	: Word/phrase emphasis

30. Effective Business Communication : Herta A. Murphy, Herbert W, Hilderbrandt, Jane p. Thomas; McGraw Hill 7th ed. p. 125
31. Source : Homai Pradhan etc. (Himalaya) p. 20-21

Emoticons

:→)*	Pleasure, humour etc.
%-(8-0	Shocked, amazed
:-] :-]	sarcastic[32]
>->	a devilish remark
>:-<	You are mad and angry
:-D	Laugh
:-(-	a frown
: *	a kiss
: –*	my lips are sealed
% -)	confused
-@	a scream[33]
:-(	Sadness
:-|	Indifferent
:-)	winking
:-C	crying
:-D	Laughing
:-\	undecided
:-P	Tongue hanging out
:-0	Surprised
:- @	Screaming
:- X	Big Lass
::-)	wearing glasses
8-)	wearing sunglasses
:-C	Really sad
:-&	Tongue Tied
X !	A Typical woman
Y !	A Typical man

32. Also see : Meenakshi Raman etc. op. cit. p. 580
33. Homai Pradhan (Himalya) op.cit, p. 20

Chapter 5

WRITING BUSINESS LETTERS

CONTENTS

The letters given on the following pages are arranged in alphabatical headings pertaining to diverse business situations.

> "The difference between the right word and the almost right word is the difference between the lightning & a lightning bug" — **Mark Twain**

In Business, numerous situations may arise every day, necessitating writing of a (large) number of business letters. These situations can't be enlisted or enumerated as they may run in hundreds and thousands[1] and even more. Newer situations may arise every day and letters may have to be written according to each individual situation. There can be no exhaustive list of situations warranting business letters. This book is only a modest attempt to make the reader aware about some of the more common topics (situations) and few examples of pre-written business letters, within the following parameters :

1. The Topics (situation) have been arranged subjectwise-alphabetically. For example ; under Alphabet A, the subjectwise classification goes as under :

- Acceptance letters
- Acknowledgement letters
- Advice letters
- Announcement letters
- Apology letters
- Appreciation letters
- Approval letters
- Authorisation letters

and similarly with other alphabets.

2. Apart from the above common categories, certain specific categories have also been incorporated; such as

- Banking letters
- Company letters
- Circular letters
- Government letters
- Insurance letters
- Letters to the Editor
- Public Relations letters

All these categories have also been alphabetically arranged.

3. Whereas in most of the books, the authors just provide the body of the letter (ignoring the top and bottom parts of the letters), this book tries to provide the glimpse of a complete letter containing all the elements of a good business letter.

4. The book does not provide letters on all the topics mentioned in Alphabetical sections. It is because the author is of the opinion that the reader has a reasonably fair level of understanding

---

1. There are books like "3001 Business & Sales Letters" by Mel Luthy Ph.D., Editor-in-chief : Write express.com $ 19.99 and "4001 Business, Sales & Personal Letters" by Write Express (Manufacturer) $ 34.99 covering 560 Topics and Over 4000 prewritten letters. Even these are not exhaustive lists.

of English language and a few examples of letters in every alphabetical section will guide him/her in writing/drafting of letters according to each specific situation.

5. The author accepts that the lists of topics and sample letters are not exhaustive. These are only indicative and the reader has to put his imagination, mental ability and knowledge of English language to test in writing/drafting every business letter.

6. **Sources & References :** While the bibliography contains a comprehensive list of the books, websites and other materials referred to, while writing this part of the book, the author is particularly inspired by the good work done by the following :

- Effective business communication : Herta H. Murphy, Herbert W. Hildebrandt, Jane P. Thomas : McGraw Hill, 7th Ed.
- Business Communication : Meenakshi Raman & Prakash Singh : Oxford University Press : Ed., 2006
- Business Communication : Building Critical Skills : Kitty O'locker, Stephen Kyo Kaczmarek : McGraw Hill, 2nd Ed.
- Business Communication : K.K. Sinha : Galgotia Publishing Co. Ed. 2006.
- Basic Business Communication : Lesikar and Flatlay : McGraw Hill; 9th Ed. 2002.
- Contemporary Business Communication : Scot Ober : Biztantra, 5th ed.
- Communication in organisations : Dalmer Fisher : Jaico Books. Ed. 2007
- E-Mail, SMS and Online chat. Better Writing. www. ask Oxford. com/better writing/view= UK>.
- Essentials of Business Communication : Rajendra Pal, J.S, Korlahalli : Sultan Chand & Sons, Ed. 2008.
- Business Communication : Homai Pradhan & N.S. Pradhan : Himalaya Publishing House ed. 2009.
- "3001 Business & Sales letters" By Mel Luthy Ph.D. Editor-in-Chief, write express.com.
- http : //www.letter writing guide.com
- http : //www.writing business letters.com
- http : // www.about.com.

Any adaptations out of these and a host of other sources is duly acknowledged at appropriate places.

7. **Disclaimer :** The names, addresses, Telephone & Fax Number, e-mail id's given in the sample letters or elsewhere in the book are pure imagination and unintentional and are given just to complete the sample letters etc,. Any resemblence to any individual, firm or company etc., is purely incidental and sans recourse to the author.

In the following pages, sample letters are provided on different business headings to give the reader a fair and clear idea as to how business letters are generally written in different situations.

A

Given below are some suggested topics under Alphabet 'A'.

Acceptance Letters

- Accept a request to serve in an honorary position.
- Accept a formal invitation to attend a social event.
- Accept a request to give a Media interview.
- Accept an invitation to business appointment.
- Accept an invitation to attend/participate in a seminar.
- Accept a suggestion (and express appreciation)
- Decline to accept an offer.
- Thank someone for accepting your recommendation.

Acknowledgement Letters

- Acknowledge an order[1]
- Acknowledge the receipt of a report/document or letter
- Acknowledge the receipt of an overdue payments.[2]
- Acknowledge the receipt of an article for exchange, refund or credit.
- Acknowledge the receipt of a suggestion for an employee.
- Acknowledge an employee's achievements

Announcement letters (Business Announcement letters)[3]

- Announce a change of Company's name
- Announce a change of Business Address
- Announce a business anniversary
- Announce a Company savings Plan
- Announce a holiday work schedule
- Announce the opening of a new branch, store or office
- Announce a new business location.
- Announcing a business Merger
- Announcing the acquistion of a business
- Announcing the issue of equity shares by the company.
- Announce a new partner (of a firm)
- Announce a routine business meeting
- Announce a special meeting (or extra ordinary meeting)

1, 2. will also be found in order letters under Alphabet 'O'

3. For a very detailed list of suggested topics see: http: //www.writeexpress.com, http: //www.letterwritingguide.com, http: //writingbusinessletter.com, http: // www.about.com etc. Also see "3001 Business & sales letters," "4001 Business, sales and personal letters" by Mel Luthy & a host of other sources.

- Announce the closing of an office or store to employees.
- Announce bonus for employees.
- Announce health insurance scheme for employees.
- Announce a work schedule for employees during holidays.
- Announce a new product or service
- Announce a price decrease
- Announce a price increase
- Announce a sales contest
- Announce a Special Sale/ Discount Scheme/ Complimentary gift or coupon scheme.

Apology Letters[4]

- Announcing the launch of a new product or service
- Apologise for a defective or demaged product.
- Apologise for late payment
- Apologise for shipping delay
- Apologise for missing an oppointment/event
- Appologise for offensive behaviour
- Appologise for inadequate or poor service
- Apologise for providing incorrect information
- Apologise for sending a collection letter by mistake.
- Apologise for cancelling an appointment.

Appreciation letters :

- Express appreciation to a customer for prompt payment.
- Appreciate a customer for purchasing product or services.
- Appreciate an employee on his achievement.
- Appreciate a retiring employee for his/her service.

Approval letters

- Approve a proposal
- Approve a loan
- Approve an extended term of credit
- Approve payments already made.
- Approve a promotion or a raise of pay.
- Approve a credit.

Authorisation letter

- Authorise a report or study or research.
- Authorise legal representation.

4.Ibid

- Authorise medical treatment.
- Authorise someone to take action.
- Authorise special project.
- Authorise someone to do special tasks.

QUICK TIPS FOR WRITING ACCEPTANCE LETTERS

- Even if an offer has been accepted verbally, it is good to write an acceptance letter, making it formal.
- Thank the individual, business or organisation etc. at the beginning of the letter.
- Clearly identify what is being accepted.
- The tone of the letter should always be positive.
- Express that you are obliged.
- Restate the terms of the offer, e.g., the position, the assignment, the terms & conditions, the compensation, the duration of the offer, the standing date, the benefits, the responsibilities etc., as you understand them.
- Proofread the letter carefully for correctness, since the acceptance letter may become a part of permanent records of the organisation making the offer. Errors , may leave bad impressions.
- Close the letter by appreciating the offeror once again.

QUICK TIPS FOR WRITING ACKNOWLEDGEMENT LETTERS

- Promptly send the acknowledgement letter, preferably within 2-3 days of receipt of order, report, letter, documents etc.
- If for any reason, the acknowledgement letter is delayed, express sincere, brief and polite apology for the delay.
- Be courteous in your response when the matter relates to return, exchange, refund or credit for goods returned etc.
- Appreciate the employee when acknowledging his achievements.
- Be sincere, honest and positive.
- Acknowledgement letter should be sent to a specific individual, not to an organisation or company in general.

QUICK TIPS FOR WRITING ANNOUNCEMENT LETTERS

- The announcement letter should be concise, yet to the point, clear and straightforward so that the receiver gets to it quickly and easily.
- If the announcement to be made is positive in nature, it should demonstrate desire to create/maintain business relationship.
- An announcement letter should simultaneously build goodwill, create confidence, boost morale and appreciate loyalty of clients/employees/recipients.
- An announcement letter must provide complete and clear information (e.g., for change of business address : The complete new address, new telephone, fax number, date from when change will be applicable etc.

- Incomplete information in Announcement letter will invite further correspondence resulting in loss of time and money.
- If the announcement is regarding bad news, the language should reflect honesty, consideration, a direct and no-nonsense approach.
- While announcing bad news, if the sender has valid and cogent reasons, these may be briefly stated with consideration and respect.

QUICK TIPS FOR WRITING (BUSINESS) APOLOGY LETTERS

- The apology should be expressed in the opening paragraph of the letter.
- Use polite sentences while apologising ; e.g.,

  — we sincerely apologise for the delay in despatch of your order.......

  — we apologise for the incovenience caused to you due to the late payment ....

  — we regret the inconvenience caused to you due to ....
- If there are reasons for what happened/went wrong, state them briefly in the second paragraph of the letter. This may help in pacifying the receiver to some extent.
- If the situation can be rectified or problem solved, mention the options clearly in the letter.
- Also mention if your action can mitigate the losses suffered by the receiver of the letter.
- A well-worded apology letter may not only save business relationship, it may even strengthen it.
- An Apology letter (honestly written) alongwith an offer of compensation to the suffering party can do wonders in strengthening business relationship.

QUICK TIPS FOR WRITING APPRECIATION LETTERS

- Appreciation letters should be promptly written (perferably within 2 to 4 days of the happening of the event.
- Appreciation letters should preferably be handwritten to create and enhance goodwill, confidence, loyalty and make someone feel special.
- The writer should carefully choose words of admiration, gratitude or recognition, appropriate to the specific situation.
- The subject-matter of appreciation should be clearly stated.
- Be honest and sincere in appreciation.
- Use words simply, clearly and concisely. Avoid using phraseology, Lengthy paragraphs or Jargon in language.
- Appreciation letter should close with 'warm regards' or 'best wishes' or other encouraging/ motivational remarks.

QUICK TIPS FOR WRITING APPROVAL LETTERS

- Approval letters should begin with what is that (the subject-matter) which is being approved.
- If necessary, the reasons for approval may be stated.

- Approval letters should also indicate what further steps are required/expected of the receiver.
- Also mention the schedule (Date, Time, Place etc.) When the approval (e.g., Promotion, Vacation, Transfer etc.) would be applicable.
- State the formalities required (e.g., subsequent to approval of a loan, account, credit etc.) to be complied with by the receiver of the letter.
- The closing paragraph should include appreciation, best wishes, regards, offer of help, motivational or encouraging lines.

QUICK TIPS FOR WRITING AUTHORISATION LETTERS

- As the name suggest, Authorisation letters delagate authority, grants approval, fixes responsibility or permits to do something to someone.
- Authorisation letter should be very carefully written to indicate :
  - The precise parameters of authority.
  - The extent of responsibility coupled with authority.
  - The instructions on how to execute authority.
  - The exact outline/structure/timeframe/schedule for execution of authority.
- Authorisation letter must clearly and in reasonable detail, answer the WHY, WHO, WHEN, BY WHOM, & HOW of the delegation process.
- Authorisation letter must sound business like and not individualistic in approach.
- Authorisation letter must be complete in all respects so as to avoid unnecessary correspondence in future.

A few example letters on some of the topics mentioned in Alphabet 'A' above are given below for quick reference.

LETTER ACKNOWLEDGING RECEIPT

Big Bull Business Co.

F 19, Ambience Towers,
Udyog Vihar,
Gurgaon (Haryana)
Tel. : 09125-3547921

Dated : 25th August, 2009

Sub. : Acknowledgement of Receipt

M/s Apex Trading Co.
262, Khari Baoli,
Delhi 110006

Dear Sir,

We acknowledge having received a cheque no. PXY 0937409 drawn on State Bank of India, Parliament Street Branch, dated 19th August, 2009 for Rs. 1,50,000 (Rs. One Lac Fifty Thousand only) towards partial payment of the debit balance of your account with us.

Please note that a formal receipt of payment will be issued only after clearance of the cheque.

Assuring your of our best cooperation at all times.

Thanking you,

Yours Sincerely,

(Avinash Sood)
Accounts Manager

LETTER INFORMING BUSINESS CLOSURE

Right & Left Finance Co.

327, New Friends Colony,
(New Business District)
Ahmedabad (Gujarat)
Tel. : 75914861, 75864861
e-mail : rlfco@yahoo.com

Dated : 10th September, 2009

Sub : Letter of Business Closure

To all valued Dealers/Suppliers etc.,

We regret to inform you that in the wake of worldwide economic slowdown, our company, which had suffered huge downturn, has decided to close down business w.e.f. 30th Sept. 2009.

Our company, now onwards, will not be placing any new orders for the purchase/supply of any of the traded goods. During the next 20 days, we are targetting out payables and trying to pay any outstanding dues to our valued creditors.

Kindly confirm, if you have any outstanding balance receivable from us so that we can arrange to clear it before the said date.

We would like to thank you for your association with us and the cooperation extended by you during all these years. Kindly feel free to ask for any information or queries before 30th September, 2009.

Yours Sincerely,

Kapil Saxena,
Operations Manager

LETTER ANNOUNCING FRESH ARRIVAL OF STOCK

Aprajit Enterprises
36, Chaurangee Lane
Kolkata
Tel.: 39486566 , 39489898

Dated 20th October, 2009

M/s Kailash Trading Co.
B-54, East of Kailash
New Delhi.

Sub.: Fresh arrival of stock

Dear Sir,

Our new shipment of electronic toys from Shenghai (China) has been unloaded, custom cleared, delivered and is now ready for your review.

We would like you to send your representative/purchase Manager to visit our showroom/godown within a period of one week so that he may view, select, and buy if he likes by placing orders before we run out of stock.

We may assure you that the fresh shipment contains refreshingly new and stunning variety of electronic toys at very reasonable prices.

We look forward to see you soon.

Yours Sincerely,

(Somu Ganguly)
Marketing Manager

PRICE CHANGE NOTICE

Apex Electronics Pvt. Ltd.

135, Ansal Bhawan
Nehru Place,
New Delhi
Tel : 011-29258586

April 7th, 2010

Mr. Ashok Pruthi
M/s A.P. Electronics
Shakti Nagar,
Delhi-110007

Sub. : Intimation of Forthcoming Price change

Dear Sir,

You had been our valued dealer for the sale of our assembled Air-conditioners, Desert Coolers, Heaters and other electrical appliances.

The summer season bumper sale of these electricals is expected to start very shortly, and as you know, the prices of all inputs like steel, motors, coils, switches, compressors, packing materials etc. have skyrocked, we are finding it necessary to raise the price of our products. However, we are trying to limit the price rise to bare minimum so as to remain in competition. A revised price list is enclosed.

We hope you will continue to cooperate with us. You may also register your orders as early as possible to remain unaffected by any further price rises.

We look forward to you for better business relations.

Yours Sincerely,

(Vineet Saxena)
Director (Sales)

Encl. : Price list

LETTER ANNOUNCING DISCOUNT SCHEME

Krantikari Suppliers

317, Esplanade Road
Kolkata (India)
Ph. 68325672 , 65386572

Dated : 19th September, 2009.

To All Valued Dealers

Sub. : Announcement of New Discount Scheme

Dear Sir,

It is with great pleasure that we announce the launch of festival scheme before the onset of the forth-coming festive season. The salient features of the scheme are :

- Period of scheme : 1st Oct. 2009 to 15th Oct. 2009
- Available on : All stocks (including fresh arrivals)
- Scheme offers : 20% flat Discount on Sales upto Rs. 50,000/=
  : 25% Flat Discount on orders beyond Rs. 50,000/= and upto Rs. 2lacs.
  : 30% Flat Discount on orders beyond Rs. 2 Lacs (No upper limit)
- Cash Discount : 2% upfront on Discounted value (for payment on Delivery)
- Credit Terms : Full payment within 15 days.

We hope you will take full advantage of the scheme before we go out of stock.

Sincerely,

(Poorva Banerjee)
Marketing Manager

LETTER ANNOUNCING CHANGE OF ADDRESS

Akhil Advertisers (Pvt.) Ltd.

B-57, Manish Market
Fountain Circle
Mumbai (India)
Tel.: 022-77593241, 77594739
e-mail : akhil@indiatimes.com

Dated : 25th September, 2009

To

All our valued Suppliers/Dealers/Customers

Sub. : Intimation regarding change of address

Dear Sir,

Please be informed that effective 1st October, 2009, Akhil Advertisers (Pvt.) Ltd. will be shifting to its new, well furnished, fully air-conditined and more spacious office at the following address :

Akhil Advertisers (Pvt.) Ltd.
Level III, Raheja Towers,
Vile-Parle Road, (west)
Mumbai (India)

Please also note, our new Phone numbers which are 022-65923333, 65923434.

We are sure, we would be able to serve you much better from the company's new office which is better located and has better infrastructure.

Looking forward to see you there.

Sincerely,

(Rajesh Patil)
P.R.O.

LETTER ANNOUNCING PRICE REDUCTION

Nav Bharat Trading Co.

(Generators & Invertors Suppliers)
31-F, Kamla Market, Ajmeri Gate,
New Delhi 110001
Ph. 011-65057878, 65059696
e-mail : ntc@g-mail.com

Dated : 15th September, 2009

To

All our valued Dealers/Customers,

Sub : Announcement of Price Reduction

Dear Sir,

We have the pleasure to inform you that for a very limited period of time, we are reducing prices on certain items in our catalogue. You may review our enclosed catalogue containing reduced prices circled in red ink that are temporarily reduced.

Please note that

- The reduction is selective and for a period of 10 days from today or till stock lasts, whichever is earlier.
- The reduction ranges from 10% to 40% as indicated.
- Full payment in advance should accompany any order containing price reduced items.

We would urge you to place your order immediately so as to have confirmed suppliers.

I wish to thank you in advance for your order.

Sincerely,

(Mayank Sinha)
Marketing Manager

LETTER INTIMATING CHANGE OF BUSINESS NAME

Complex Systems Ltd.

B-37, South Extension (East)
New Delhi
Tel. : 011-69254567, 69256789.
e-mail : csl@yahoo.com

Dated : 15th September 2009

M/s Business India Corporation
B-527/1 Kesar Ganj Road
Ludhiana (Punjab)

Sub. : Announcement of change of business name

Dear Sir,

As our new letterhead indicates, we have recently changed the name of our business from :

> **Radhika Enterprises Ltd.**] Old Name
> To
> **Complex Systems Ltd.**] New Name,

with the prior approval of the Board of Directors and the General Body of Shareholders.

Please note that there has been no change in management and the company (with its new name) will be providing the same products and fine services on which it has built its reputation in the industry and the market.

We would appreciate if you would bring this announcement to the notice of your accounts department and direct them accordingly.

Thank you for being one of our valued customers. We appreciate your co-operation in this matter.

Sincerely

(Pramod Mehta)
P.R.O.

LETTER OF APPRECIATION (FOR A JOB WELL DONE)

Micro Networks (India) Ltd.

(Network Solutions For Business)
11th Floor, Omax Towers
Bhikaji Cama Place,
New Delhi

Dated : 10th December 2009.

Dear Mr, Ankur Gauri,

Your enthusiasm and ability to motivate your co-workers in implementing the overseas project no. XX437 has resulted in significant increase in company's productivity and profitability.

The company appreciates your efforts and the assistance you offer to your co-workers. Your extra efforts in devoting long hours and dedicated approach in meeting the deadline make you 'reliable and dependable' in the eyes of management.

Please accept my sincere gratitude for your superior work in the Service Department.

(John Mac)
Chief Manager

LETTER OF RECOGNITION

Info System Ltd.
(Leadership Through Innovation)
32, Raheja Chambers, 9th Level,
Backbay Reclamation
Mumbai
Tel. : 022-64321122, 64324455

Dated : 30th Sept. 2009

Professor Inder Mohan
Deptt. of Computer Studies
University of Delhi
North Campus
Delhi 110007

Dear Prof. Inder Mohan,

On behalf of Info System Ltd. and Indian Society for Computers, we would like to recognise your assistance and contribution in the successfully held Annual Conference of the Indian Society for Computers at Delhi on 12th September, 2009.

We gratefully appreciate that you so generously contributed your time in assembling and organising the Penal discussion on *"Providing Network Solutions in the next decade"*. We recognise that the penal's contribution was a major event of the conference and was widely reported in concerned media for the insights and innovative problem solving approach. We are, at our level, prominently bringing out the summary of the proceedings in our quartely publication to be released in October, 2009.

We hope that you enjoyed your time at the conference. As a sponsor of the event, we look forward to your participation in next year's event as well.

Sincerely,

(Prateek Sinha)
Managing Director

B

Given below are some suggested topies under Alphabet 'B'.

Banking Letters (Correspondence)

- Letters to a Bank Manager for opening of a Current A/c.
- Letters to a Bank requesting to stop payment of a cheque.
- Reply of Bank to stop payment of cheque.
- Request letter to Bank for overdraft facility.
- Bank withdrawing overdraft facility
- Complaint for wrongful dishonour of a cheque
- Reply from the Bank
- Request letter for grant of loan against House Property.
- Letter to a Bank requesting for issue of a credit card.
- Letter to a Bank requesting for issue of a debit card.
- Bank's refusal to grant loan on inadequate security.
- Bank Manager's letter to H.O. for sanctioning of loan.
- Letter to a Bank requesting to open an L/C (Letter of credit).
- Letter to a Bank for issue of foreign exchange
- Bank's letter for recovery of loan and penal action.
- Letter of complaint to Customer Care Center of the Bank.
- Letter of complaint to Banking Ombudsman against Bank's inaction/inability/refusal to redress a complaint.
- Letter of Branch Manager to H.O. suggesting ways and means to increase the business of the branch.
- Letter of Branch Manager concerning staff's promotions, transfers, retirement etc. to H.O.
- Letter to H.O. relating general administration of the branch.

QUICK TIPS FOR WRITING LETTERS TO BANK

- Every letter written to a Bank (and Vice Versa) must indicate sender's A/c No. with the Bank, type of Account, Name of the Bank and address of the Bank's Branch, under Reference line.
- Subject line in a Banking letter must clearly mention the subject matter of the letter; e.g.,

  — request for issue of credit card;

  — request for grant of overdraft facility ;

  — request for issue of credit card;

  — complaint for wrongful dishonour of a cheque etc.
- The letter should provide complete information about the sender firm/company/organisation and the relevant details as required under different situations.

- The documents submitted (say Letters, Statement of Account, Report, Final Accounts, Balance Sheets, other documents etc.) should be detailed in the Body of the letter and also mentioned in the enclosures.
- Banking letters should be carefully written as they become legal documents in case of future disputes.
- Any complaint should be duly supported by facts and relevant documents as enclosures to substantiate the complaint.
- The language of the letter should be simple, clear, single meaning and straight forward. Long-winded words or flowery language (with intention to impress) should be strictly avoided.
- Banking letters should be properly preserved for future reference and record.

Abbreviations used in Banking Correspondence

Banks in their daily routine use certain terms and phrases in abbreviated form. The customer should clearly understand these terms etc. so as to properly deal with the Bank. These abbreviations are generally used in the Statement of Account (Pass Book) and are listed below :

Ch. or chq.	— Cheque
Chrgs	— Charges
T/Rd or T/fr	— Transfer
Com.	— Commission
Div.	— Dividend
Int.	— Interest
Clg.	— Clearing
Remitt.	— Remittance
D.D. or D/D	— Demand draft
P.O.	— Pay order
T.T.	— Telegraphic Transfer
M.T.	— Mail Transfer
L.C. or L/c	— Letter of Credit
Dr.	— Debit
Cr.	— Credit
Revsd	— Reversed
Bal.	— Balance
Op	— Opening
Cl.	— Closing
S/A	— Savings Account

C/A	— Current Account
F.D. or R/D	— Recurring Deposit
A/C	— Account
R.D. or R/D	— Recurring Deposit
P/L	— Personal loan
H.O.	— Head Office
R.O.	— Regional Office
C.C.	— Cash Credit
O/D	— Overdraft

Terms and Phrases used while dealing with cheques

While doing correspondence with the customer, especially on Bouncing (dishonour) of the claque, the Bank uses one or more of the following phrases :

- Refer to Drawer.
- Effects not cleared, please present again.
- Cheque is crossed, please present through clearing.
- Not arranged for.
- Exceeds arrangements.
- Drawer's signature differs.
- Amount in words & figures differ.
- No advice.
- Payment stopped by Drawer.
- Endorsement is irregular
- Endorsement — requires payees' signature.
- Ante-dated cheque
- Post-dated cheque
- Irregular discharge by Bank.
- Mutilated cheque.
- Cheque not signed by Drawer.
- Cheque crossed to two Banks.
- Cheque not drawn on us.
- Account closed.
- Account holder expired.
- Full cover not received.

- Joint holder signature required.
- Garnishee order received from court.
- Drawer declared insolvent.
- Outstation cheque.
- Cutting/correction on the cheque requires drawer signature, etc. etc.,

A few example letters on some of the topics mentioned in Alphabet 'B' (Banking letters) above are given below for quick reference.

LETTER TO OPEN A CURRENT ACCOUNT WITH A BANK

Vipul Shah Trading Co. (P) Ltd.

132, Apollo Street, Fort, Mumbai 400022
Tel. : 022-75693231, 75632981
http. : //www.vipulshah. com

Dated : 15th September 2010

The Manager
State Bank of India
Fort Branch
Mumbai-400022

Sub. : Request for Opening a Current Account

Dear Sir,

Kindly refer to the telephonic conversation between your goodself and the undersigned for opening of a Current Account in our company's name with your esteemed Bank. I am enclosing the following documents alongwith the relevant forms duly filled in for the purpose :

1. The current Account opening forms.
2. A copy of the certificate of incorporation of the Company.
3. Certified copy of the minutes of the Board of Director's Meeting containing the proposal to open a Current Account in your Bank.
4. Copy of Memorandum of Association of the Company.
5. Copy of Articles of Association of the Company.
6. Letter of Introduction by Mr. Ashish Chopra, an account holder of your Bank.
7. A draft for Rs. 1,00,000 (Rs. One lac) favouring State Bank of India as initial deposit for account opening.
8. Authority letter on company's letterhead that any of the directors can operate the Bank Account.

You are requested to open a Current Account in the name of our company and issue us

(i) a cheque Book containing 100 cheques;
(ii) a pass Book;
(iii) a pay-in-slip book

to operate the account.

We look forward to a long term fruitful cooperation with your Bank.

Sincerely,

(Surinder Singh)
Director,

Encl.: 8 (as above)

BANK LETTER : REQUEST TO STOP PAYMENT OF A CHEQUE

Alpha Numeric Enterprises (P) Ltd.

(Management Solutions for Tough Challenges)
Vivekananda Road (East)
Matunga, Mumbai-400082
Tel. : 022-44965201, 44952901
http. : //www.alphanumeric.co.in

Dated : 2nd November, 2009

The Chief Manager
State Bank of India
Western Naka,
Borivali (West)
Mumbai-400091

Sub. : Request for Stop Payment

Dear Sir,

You are requested to stop payment of the following cheque, issued by us, but lost in transit by the courier company through which it was sent to the payee :

Cheque No.	:	09367451
Dated	:	27th October, 2009
Amount	:	Rs. 45,500/-
Favouring	:	M/s Perfect Travels (P) Ltd.
Status	:	Crossed Account Payee

Kindly issue the necessary instructions to your staff to record 'Stop Payment' of the cheque.

Sincerely,

(P.K. Srivastava)
Director

BANK LETTER : REPLY OF BANK TO STOP PAYMENT REQUEST

State Bank of India

Western Naka,
Borivali (West)
Mumbai-400091
Tel. : 022-32754291
http. : //customercare@sbi.com

Dated : 4th November, 2009

The Director,
M/s Alpha Numeric Enterprises (P) Ltd.
Vivekananda Road (East)
Matunga, Mumbai-400082

Sub. : Your Request to Stop Payment

Dear Sir,

We are in receipt of your letter dated 2nd November, 2009 asking us to stop payment of your cheque no. 09367451 dated 27th October, 2009 favouring M/s Perfect Travels (P) Ltd. for Rs. 45,500/-.

We have issued the necessary instructions and also recorded the details in your account to stop payment of the cheque. We confirm that till date the cheque has not been presented in clearing.

As a matter of caution, we wish to draw your attention to the following rule (Rule no. 17 of our Current Account Rules); which reads as under :

> "The Bank will register customer's request regarding stop payment of cheques lost, stolen, misplaced, etc. but cannot guarantee him against loss that may arise in such cases in the event of a cheque being paid through oversight, inadvertence, or if other cheque(s) are returned unpaid on account of payment of such a cheque".

Assuring you of our best services at all times.

Sincerely,

(Ganesh Dass Tomar)
Chief Manager

BANK LETTER : REQUEST FOR OVERDRAFT FACILITY

Hi-fly Communications (P) Ltd.

624, Dr. Mukherjee Nagar
Delhi-110009
Tel. : 011-27652459-60
http. : //hifly@yahoo.com

Dated : 29th Sept. 2009

The Chief Manager
Axis Bank Ltd.
Mall Road, Kingsway Camp
Delhi-110009

Sub. : Request for Overdraft facilities

Dear Sir,

We are having Current A/c no. 4765 with your esteemed Bank for the last 6 years. We are grateful for the cooperation and services provided by your Bank during all these years.

As our business is expanding, we need additional working capital to cope with the stock requirements and also for expansion of our marketing needs. We, therefore request you to sanction overdraft facilities with a limit of Rs. 15 lacs.

As required by you, we are enclosing the following documents for the purpose mentioned above :

1. Our Balance Sheets and Profit & Loss Accounts for last 3 years.
2. Projected Balance Sheets and Profit & Loss Accounts for next 3 years.
3. Copies of I.Tax Returns for last 3 years.
4. A cash flow statement for next 3 years.
5. Stock statement with details of Stock held at different godowns, their value etc. as on 31st March 2009.
6. Copies of Franchise agreements with companies.
7. A list of directors, their names and addresses & holding in company's stocks.
8. An application form duly filled in (On Bank's format).

We would be ready to hypothecate our stocks in favour of the Bank for the purpose mentioned above. Alternatively, two of our Directors can provide personal guarantees for the overdraft facility.

We would like you to expedite our request as early as possible so that we may derive full benefit of the forthcoming festival season.

Looking forward to hear from you,

Sincerely

(Bindeshwari Prasad)
Manager

Encl. : 8 (as above)

BANK'S LETTER : WITHDRAWING OVERDRAFT FACILITY

State Bank of India

Kohinoor Mills Compound
Andheri(West)
Mumbai-400019
Tel. : 022-62914646
e-mail : customercare@sbi.com

Dated : 29th October, 2009

The Manager
M/s Freestyle Sports Goods Co.
Jhaveri Bazar, Taraporewala Road
Mumbai-400026

Sub. : Overdraft facility in your A/c.

Dear Sir,

An overdraft limit of Rs. 10 lacs was provided to you by the Bank on your request deted 10th August 2009. We have observed from our records that you have not even once utilised this facility. In the circumstances, the Bank has decided to withdraw the facility from your current a/c w.e.f. 1st November 2009.

The Bank has been forced to take this decision, since this facility granted to you ties up Bank's funds unremuneratively.

May we assure you that the Bank would be pleased to grant you this facility in future, if you so require.

Sincerely,

(G.C. Patil)
Chief Manager

COMPLAINT TO THE BANK FOR WRONGFUL DISHONOUR OF A CHEQUE

Amit Chhabra

Rangoli Garments
Guru Nanak Street, Chaura Bazar
Ludhiana (Punjab)

Dated : 10th October 2009

The Manager
State Bank of Patiala
Chaura Bazar Branch
Ludhiana

Re : Our C/A with your Bank (No. 42359)

Sub. : Wrongful dishonour of our cheque

Dear Sir,

I have just been informed by one of my suppliers M/s India Garments, Ludhiana that my cheque no. 09253410 for Rs. 17,5000/- issued in their favour on 1st October 2009 has been dishonoured by you, giving in your returing memo dated 8th October 2009, "Effects not cleared" as the reason.

According to the passbook updated till 7th October, 2009, there was a clear balance of Rs. 31,729.63 in my account which makes it difficult for us to understand why the cheque for Rs. 17,500/- was returned, negatively affecting my business reputation with my suppliers.

Will you please write back promptly, stating the reasons for the dishonour of the cheque which has caused us a great concern.

Sincerely,

(Proprietor)

BANK'S LETTER : DISHONOUR OF A CHEQUE

State Bank of India

Branch : Chaura Bazar
Ludhiana (Punjab)
Tel. : 0161-3592627

Dated : 12th October, 2009

Mr. Amit Chhabra
Proprietor
Rangoli Garments, Guru Nanak Street,
Chaura Bazar, Ludhiana

Sub. : Dishonour of your cheque

Re : Your C/A No. 42359

Dear Mr. Chhabra

We thank you for your letter dated 10th October, 2009. Complaining about the returning of your cheque no. 09253410 for Rs. 17500/- on 8th October, 2009.

Please note that your balance as on 7th October, 2009 was Rs. 31,729.63 but since you are enjoying a loan of Rs. 5 lacs from the bank, the EMI for which is debited on 8th of every month. After debiting the EMI on 8th October, of Rs. 23,675.00, the balance left with your account was only Rs. 8,054.63. You might have forgotton this fact and also the need to make prior arrangement for overdraft facility in your account.

While, the Bank is always under an obligation and takes every care in its dealings to avoid any incovenience to its customers, in this particular case, we could hardly be blamed for any act of omission or negligence.

We are forwarding an account statement reported till today.

Assuring you of our best services, at all times.

Sincerely,

(Chief Manager)

Encl. : Statement of Your A/c.

REQUESTING A BANK FOR A LOAN AGAINST HOUSE PROPERTY

M.G. Raghvan
Proprietor
'Cheap & Best' Stores
24, 7th Level, Express Towers,
Nariman Point (West)
Mumbai 400021
Tel. : 022-39754244, 39755254
e-mail : cheapnbeststores@gamil.com

Dated : 20th October, 2009

The Chief Manager,
HDFC Bank Ltd.
Branch: Nariman Point (West)
Mumbai-400021

Sub. : Request for loan against House Property

Re : Our C/A No. 0432759 with your Branch

Dear Sir,

We are in an expansion mode. During the last 12 months, we have opened 7 stores in different locations of Mumbai. Our brand has gained recognition and recall value in the minds of Mumbaikars.

We now plan to expand further by opening 5 more stores during this year at different locations of prominence. Those will be franchise outlets, we would require capital for investing in stocks to the time of Rs. One crore.

Though we are able to raise around Rs. 50 lacs from internal accruals, family and friends, we need to fill The gap of Rs. 50 lacs urgently required by us. We, therefore, approach your goodself with a request for granting us a loan of Rs. 50 lacs for a period of 5 years against security of House Property.

I, possess, in my own name, a house, built on 200 square metres plot in the H anuman Street at Ambalal Doshi Marg, Matunga, Mumbai. It has a clear title, free from encumbrances and is currently valued at around Rs. 1.20 crores. A valuer's certificate to the effect is enclosed. I have all the documents, required for the loan, ready with me, the photocopies of which are being enclosed with the loan application from, for your kind consideration. I would request you to process the loan application as early as possible.

Sincerely,

(Proprietor)

Encl. : 8 (As above)

BANK'S REFUSAL TO GRANT LOAN ON INADEQUATE SECURITY

HDFC Bank Ltd.

Branch : Nariman Point (West)
Mumbai : 400021
Tel. : 022-47350221-25

Dated : 23rd October, 2009

Mr. M.G. Raghvan
Proprietor
'Cheap & Best' Stores
24, 7th Level, Express Towers,
Nariman Point (West)
Mumbai 400021

Re : Your C/A No. 0432759 with our Bank
Sub. : Your request for loan against House Property

Dear Mr. Raghvan,

We thank you for your letter dated 20th October 2009 for offering us an apportunity to provide you loan against House Property owned by you.

In this regard, we wish to point out that due to global economic slowdown, the market prices of real estate has taken a severe beating. In some areas, the prices have crashed by 30 to 50 per cent of their peak values, around 12 months ago.

We have observed that the valuer's certificate, submitted by you is more than a year old, is of dated 10th August 2008, when the prices were at an all time high. According to our Bank's valuers, the value of the property mentioned is not over Rs. 70 lacs, currently.

Our Bank provide loans against House Property according to the norms laid down by Reserve Bank of India which allows loan of upto 60% of the value of House property, which amount does not meet your requirement of Rs. 50 lacs.

Under these circumstances, we are unable to accede to your request. You may either reduce the amount of loan or provide additional security of value not less than Rs. 25 lacs to provide you a loan of Rs. 50 lacs.

You may choose the option suited to you and inform us accordingly so that we may expedite the process for grant of loan.

Sincerely,

(Chief Manager)

BANK MANAGER'S LETTER TO H.O. FOR SANCTIONING OF A LOAN

Canara Bank

Regd. Office
36, Lighthouse Hill,
Mangalore (Karnataka)
Parliament Street Branch,
New Delhi 110001
Tel. : 011-35092734-36

Dated : 30th September, 2009

The Chief Manager
Loans Department
Regional Office,
Nehru Place,
New Delhi-110017

Re : Request for Term loan of Rs. 50 lacs of M/s. Balaji Telecom, our C/A holder.

Dear Sir,

I am forwarding a loan application with necessary documents submitted by M/s Balaji Telecom, of C/A No. 043927 with our Branch, along with our comments for your consideration. The details are given in brief, below :

1.	Name of Borrower	:	M/s Balaji Telecom
2.	Address of Borrower	:	367, Ansal Chambers, Bhikaji Cama Place, New Delhi
3.	Telephone No.	:	011-47529250-51
4.	e-mail	:	balajitelecom@in.com
5.	Legal Status of Firm	:	Proprietorship
6.	Name of Proprietor	:	Mr. Nishant Mongia
7.	Nature of Loan Required	:	Term Loan
8.	Amount of Loan Required	:	Rs. 50 lacs
9.	Nature of Security Offered	:	Hypothecation of Stocks
10.	Value of Security Offered	:	Rs. 80 lacs
11.	Margin Required	:	30%
12.	Interest	:	12.75% p.a.
13.	Purpose of Loan	:	Expansion of Business by Taking Distribution right of NOKIA mobile phones for New Delhi Area.
14.	Term of loan required	:	5 years (With reconsideration after every 12 months)
15.	Process fee chargeable	:	2% of sanctioned amount of loan
16.	Pre-payment charges	:	0.5% of prepaid amount
17.	Payment Terms	:	Monthly EMI chargeable by debiting the account with our Branch.
18.	Terms & Conditions	:	As specified by loan Department

Our Comments:

1. M/s Balaji Telecom is an old and valuable customer of our bank. They are engaged in the retail trading of Mobile phones, Sim cards, Top-up cards, Phone accessories etc. of Top Brands in India. According to the Balance Sheets submitted by them, their business is growing @ 50% compound every year. Their net profits are at 3.5% of turnover, which is very satisfactory according to industry standards.
2. M/s Balaji Telecom is offering us hypothecation of Stocks Worth Rs. 80 lacs which provides us a margin of 40% against 30% required by the Bank.
3. M/s Balaji Telecom have a very good reputation in the Market.
4. A Statement of A/c of M/s Balaji Telecom reveals that they are a financially sound party and will be easily able to pay the monthly EMI.
5. The telecom business is growing by 35% every year. It is also the Government Policy to help accelerate growth of Telecom business. The new 3G spectrum regime will provie further boost to Telecom Trade.
6. The Proprietor, himself, is a person of high reupte with excellent managerial capabilities. In our opinion, he would be able to handle the proposed expansion of the business.

Based on the facts, I, confidently recommend M/s Balaji Telecom for a Term Loan of Rs. 50 lacs on terms and conditions decided by the Loans Department of the Bank.

The request for loan may be given a favourable consideration.

Sincerely

(Senior Manager)
Parliament Street Branch

Encl. : 1. Loan Application form duly filled in
2. Other Documents (7)

C

Given below are some suggested topics under Alphabet 'C'.

Cancellation letters

- Cancelling a membership
- Cancelling a subscription
- Cancelling a rent agreement
- Cancelling a service contract
- Cancelling an order
- Cancelling (or postponing) an appointment
- Request to cancel a lost credit card
- Cancellation of an Insurance Policy.

QUICK TIPS FOR WRITING CANCELLATION LETTERS

- Cancellation letter must clearly state the reference no. and subject line to make it clear to the receiver.
- If possible, the reason for cancellation (of membership, subscription, rent agreement, order etc.) be given in the body of the letter.
- The language of the letter should be polite yet firm. The tone of the letter should be positive even if it conveys bad news.
- The letter should contain complete details of the subject matter to avoid future arguments, correspondence or litigation.
- Wherever possible, the options, if any offered to the receiver to rectify or undo the damage done, should be elaborately mentioned in the letter.
- A cancellation letter should be so worded that it does not end business relations, rather ways & means for continuation of business relations be explored.
- A cancellation letter should end with a positive approach for future dealings with the suffering party. Aggressive tone is strictly forbidden for such letters.

Circular letters

- Obtaining a new agency.
- Opening of a new branch.
- Change of Business address.
- Announcing clearance Sale/Price reduction sales.
- Announcing the opening of a new agency.
- Announcing the appointment of a distributor.
- Announcing a discount scheme.

- Sales promotion letters.
- Introducing a new partner in a firm.
- Retirement of a partner in a firm.
- Intimating death of a partner.
- Announcing opening of a new showroom.
- Intimating launch of a new product.
- Appointment as sole selling agent.
- Termination of an agency.
- Closing of a branch or showroom.
- Announcing the change in the constitution of business.

The list of situations demanding circular letters seem to be endless. The above list is neither representative nor exhaustive. It only provides a glimpse of an idea about the variety of circular letters that may be written in business.

QUICK TIPS FOR WRITING CIRCULAR LETTERS

- Circular letters, in many respects, are similar to 'Announcement letters'. Circular letters should also be clear and straight forward and must carry the message to the receiver, easily and quickly.
- It circular letters are positive in nature (e.g.) opening of a new branch, launch of a new product, introduction of a new employee, admission of a new partner etc.), it must simultaneously create goodwill, awarenewss, loyalty and confidence among staff/customers/recipients.
- Circular letters of a negative nature (e.g., termination of agency, intimating retirement/death of a partner, closure of a showroom, termination of a contract etc.) should express grief, sorrow, pain or dissatisfaction over a given situation.
- A circular letter must provide complete and clear information (e.g., for change of business name : the exact and complete new name, the new address and telephone numbers, the new website address, new e-mail ID etc.) to the recipient.
- Incomplete information in circular letters will invite further correspondence resulting in loss of time and money.
- If the circular is regarding unfavourable news, the language should reflect honesty, consideration, a direct and no-nonsense approach. Any valid reasons for the unfavourable news may also be briefly stated with consideration and respect.
- Circulars regarding sales promotion subjects, must properly highlight the promotional activities like discounts/offers/free samples etc. repeatedly in subject line, body of the letter and in post script, wherever possible.
- A circular announcing the admission of a partner should mention the reasons for such admission, e.g., expansion of business, additional investment, better and more efficient

management as well as mention the experience and special knowledge of the partner, as also the change, if any, in the name of the firm. It should also solicit the customers continued patronage.

- Similarly, a circular announcing a change in the constitution of the firm should discuss the following:
  — development of business requiring additional capital,
  — requirement of broad based management,
  — the changed name of the business (firm),
  — the changes in authorities and responsibilities of different partners,
  — request the customers to continue extending their coöperation to the firm.
- A circular letter must contain all relevant details according to the business situation. However, no irrelevant details should be included.

Claim letters

- Letter seeking a warranty claim
- Insurance claim letter
- Claim for reimbursement of expenses incurred
- Claim for damage to property.
- Claim for defective product or service.
- Letter requesting quick settlement of claim.
- Reference of claim to arbitration etc.
- Denying a claim (Rejecting a claim).

QUICK TIPS FOR WRITING CLAIM LETTERS

- The following details, as are applicable, must be highlighted in a claim letter :
  — Policy no. and date in case of insurance claim.
  — Order no./contract no. in case of claim under defective product/service.
  — Intention to make a claim specifying the type of claim (under subject line)
- The letter must describe the circumstances under which the claim arose. All relevant facts must be stated clearly.
- The letter should indicate the following:
  — The extent of damage
  — The amount of claim (in Rupees)
- The date (time) by which action from the recipient is expected.
- Any enclosures such as claim form, damage report, repair estimates, warranty card, copies of invoice, delivery receipt etc. should be mentioned in the letter and properly attached to the letter. (These are called supporting documents).
- Tone of the letter should be courteous, polite yet firm. The language should be simple, clear and straightforward.

- Sender should also give his/company's contact no. so that the other party may easily reach him for further information.
- The claim letter may end with anticipatory thanks to the other party.
- The claim denying letter should be:
  — polite and respectful
  — indicate reasons for rejection of claim
  — state alternate options, if any, available to the claimant.
  — positive even if conveying bad news
  — show sincerity and concern for other party's loss
  — offer of help in whatever ways possible.
  — Indicate a date for making an appeal, information about to whom appeal is to be made and how the appeal may be filed.

Complaint letters

- Complaint letter regarding a defective/faulty product or service.
- Complaint letter regarding delayed shipping or faulty/damaged delivery.
- Complaint regarding poor quality of goods/equipment supplied.
- Complaint regarding an error in the Bills/Invoices.
- Complaint regarding an employee about bad service or offensive behaviour.
- Complaint about sexual harrassment.
- Complaint about gender discrimation.
- Follow up letter on a complaint from a customer.
- Letter accepting a complaint and offering adjustment/compensation/discount in payment etc.
- Letter rejecting a false complaint.
- Reply to a complaint letter.
- Letter about supply of wrong goods.
- Letter claiming replacement of defected goods.
- Reply to letter claiming replacement of defected goods.

QUICK TIPS FOR WRITING COMPLAINT LETTERS

- A a general rule, a complaint letter should be written, **"only for the purpose of getting the wrong righted, and not to pick-up a quarrel with the seller"**
- A compliant letter should be written only when it is utmost essential; i.e., when the complaints are causing considerable financial loss.
- A complaint should not be made only for the sake of making a complaint.
- Complaint should not be made on guess work, flimsy grounds, negligible matters, or assumptions as these will cause irritation and affect the future relationship between the buyer and the seller.

- While writing a complaint letter, the following points should be carefully considered[1] :
  - — That there is a solid and real complaint existing on the date of writing,
  - — That a complaint letter should he written as far as possible, avoiding the word **'complaint'**,
  - — That a complaint letter should be written in a convincing, tactful, polite and forceful manner.
  - — Every effort should be made to see the complaint letter does not affect mutual relationship or interest of the buyer and the seller.
  - — The complaint should appeal to the seller's sense of honesty and transparency in dealings.
  - — The complaint letter should invariably make a claim for compensation, refund, replacement or discount, as the case may be.
- A complaint letter should be honest, straight forward, clear and concise.
- A complaint letter should provide complete detail about the basis of the claim, the damage or loss suffered, the financial aspect and the quantum of loss.
- A complaint letter should avoid the following:
  - — Aggressive tone
  - — Accusing language
  - — Disrespectful attitude
  - — Irrelevant details
  - — Threats that may not be followed through
- The complaint letter should enclose the following :
  - — photocopies of orders/invoices/receipts and other documents
  - — photographs of damaged articles/equipments/supplies
  - — documentary evidence of delayed receipts etc.
- No originals of the abvoe documents be sent alongwith complaint letter, under any circumstances.
- A copy of the complaint letter must be retained for future reference.
- Complaint letter should be direct, tactful, professional and respectful to gain maximum milage of the situation. The complaint should accomplish the objective without damaging business relationships.
- The letter must include sender's contact information(e.g., name, address, phone, e-mail etc.) so that the respondent may reach him for discussion, settlement or resolution of complaint.
- If the first letter of complaint does not elicit favourable response, second or third letters may be sent in firmer yet respectful tone to the same person or his superior or to the President or CEO of the company.

---

1. Also see : Business communication : R.C. Bhatia; Ane Books India.

- A reply to a complaint letter should also be tactful, respectful, honest and straight forward.
- A reply to a complaint letter should follow *'The customer is right'* approach. Therefore
  (i) ***When the customer is right,*** admit the fault at once with a sincere regret/apology for the mistake and set the things right by making good customer's loss.
  (ii) ***When the customer is at fault,*** is unfair or unreasonable, don't react violently. Make him look at your point of view. Accommodate him, if possible. If not, tell him politely, why he cannot be accommodated. Donot end business relations but try for its continuance.
  (iii) ***When the carrier or some other party is at fault:*** Express thanks to customers for pointing out the delay or damage. Show sympathy for inconvenience caused to customer and tell him what actions you have taken. The Carrier, Post Office or Bank whoever is at fault should be sent a claim letter with a copy to the customer. Try to be helpful.
- Don't take shelter behind such words as :
  "It is the policy of our company, not to entertain ...."
  "Our firm's policy is not to ...."
  This will irritate the customer. Politely, but briefly explain to the customer the reason for not accepting his claim.
- Convince the customer that you are helpful. Tell him you are prepared to do all that you can. This will earn you the customers goodwill and expect continuance of business relations.

Compliment letters

- Compliment an employee for his contribution/achievement.
- Compliment a sales staff on overachieving targets.
- Compliment a supplier of a product or service for quality.
- Compliment an employee of another firm/company for his work performance.
- Compliment and motivate a sales force.
- Compliment same one for his/her achievements.

Tips for Writing Compliment Letters

- Please see "Quick Tips for Writing Appreciation Letters".

Confirmation Letters

- Letter confirming an oral agreement.
- Confirming an authorisation given to someone.
- Acknowledging the receipt of a letter/document/report or order.
- Confirming a decision/resolution/contract etc.
- Confirming a transfer/promotion/demotion/termination/lay-off of an employee/s.
- Confirming an appointment of an employee.

- Confirming an order already made.
- Confirming receipt of a bid/order/application/proposal etc.
- Confirming a telephonic order.
- Confirming the loss of a credit card.
- Confirming the request of stop payment of a cheque.
- Confirming an error in accounts and allowing adjustments.
- Confirming the despatch/sending of an order.
- Confirming to speak at or attend a seminar, meeting or conference.
- Confirming travel arrangements (request for).
- Confirming reservation of travel arrangements.
- Confirming a windfall gain to the business.
- Confirming a setback to the business.
- Confirming the release of prospectus/annual accounts/contracts of the company.

Congratulation Letters

- Congratulating an employee/colleague/associate on
  — getting a new job.
  — his/her achievement.
  — winning an award.
  — promotion/advancement.
  — his/her excellent work performance.
  — his/her retirement.
- Congratulating a business friends on
  — winning a new contract.
  — opening of a new showroom.
  — opening of a new store/office.
  — winning a state/national award.
  — receiving an honour.
- Congratulating a senior/boss on his/her
  — accepting an important assignment.
  — going on deputation.
  — joining a higher position in the company.

QUICK TIPS FOR WRITING CONGRATULATION LETTERS

- Congratulation letters should be written quickly and as soon as possible after the announcement/event/acceptance/joining etc. Gap of 2-4 days like in the case of confirmation letters or appreciation letters is not desired in congratulation letters.
- The reason for writing the congratulation letter should be highlighted in the opening paragraph of the letter.

- A congratulatory letter may shower praise or appreciation on the incumbant for his achievement/accomplishment etc.
  — brief and concise (no lengthy details)
  — to the point (discuss only fortunate event)
  — positive always (or don't write it at all)
  — avoid irrelevant details/negative comments or past unfavourable/sad events/news
  — use honest and sincere tone and language
- A congratulatory letter should not smell of sarcasm/exaggeration/mocking of the recipient.

Credit letters

- Approve a credit account to a client/customer.
- Cancel or withdraw a customer's credit account.
- Intimate a customer of bouncing of his cheque.
- Intimate a creditor that you have stopped payment on his account.
- Warn a customer about credit suspension and/or penal action.
- Provide a credit reference.
- Respond to a credit enquiry (Status Enquiry).
- Approve a credit/loan request.
- Decline a credit/loan request.
- Request/apply for a credit account.
- Intimate a customer about receipt of a
  — mutilated cheque
  — unsigned cheque
  — crossed cheque without endorsement
  — cheque with difference in words & figures
  — post dated cheque
  — stale cheque etc.
  and request for a new cheque.
- Request for rescheduling of payment due.
- Accepting request for rescheduling of payment.
- Transmit a payment etc.
- Making part payment and explaining for balance.
- Explaining delay in payment.
- Granting extension of time.
- Letter requesting for credit information.
- Letter supplying trade reterences for credit verification.

QUICK TIPS FOR WRITING CREDIT LETTERS

- A letter containing request for grant of credit should :
  - — State the source of information about the product or service to be purchased.
  - — Place the order (Exact quantity, description, packing etc.)
  - — Indicate the desired terms of credit.
  - — Old customer may also ask for credit facility,
  - — Furnish credit references with whom you are dealing.
  - — Promise to supply additional information, if required.
- A *positive letter* accepting/granting request for credit should;
  - — mention the grant of credit in the opening paragraph. (right in the beginning)
  - — mention that the credit references have been obtained (It is optional)
  - — Explain the terms and conditions of credit in clear terms.
  - — Give details of the time and mode of despatch of order.
- A *negative letter* refusing/declining request for credit should be carefully worded; to contain :
  - — Thank the applicant for the credit request.
  - — Briefly describe the reasons for refusing the credit.
  - — State the credit policy of the company, clearly.
  - — Positive efforts to retain the customer by asking him to make cash payment for the present transaction
  - — Assure/suggest to consider his request for credit in future transactions.[2]
  - — Offer cash discount/other incentives, where possible.
- As a rule, in all credit letters, whether conveying positive or negative news, the tone should be courteous and polite.
- Most credit letters are like collection letters, hence same guidelines should be followed.
- If the credit letter is to decline cr deny a request or application for credit, the letter should have a professional touch by
  - — keeping the door open to future dealings
  - — maintaining business relations rather than its discontinuance
  - — initiating further discussion with the debtor to facilitate recovery of the loan/overdue payment.
- The credit recovery letter though polite should be firm and suggest clearly the penal action in the absence of immediate response to the letter.
- Empty threats, which may not be followed through, should be strictly avoided.
- Credit letters should contain complete information (e.g., the invoice, date, amount, credit policy of the company, the period of delay, options available etc.) but at the same time be brief, straight forward and business like.

---

2. See also Communication Skills : Dr. Nageshwar Rao & Dr. Rajender P. Das; Himalaya Publishing House 2nd Ed. 2009, p. 423.

- A credit letter must also assure the recipient of the sender's fullest co-operation in settlement/resolution etc. of the conflict.
- A credit (or Status) enquiry letter should be based on
  - (i) sound credit policy
  - (ii) careful selection of credit customers, and
  - (iii) prompt collection of overdue credit.
- Before allowing credit, the credit department must get the following information (called 4C's) about the customer :
  - (a) ***Character:***[3] indicating honesty, reputation, reliability, trustworthiness;
  - (b) ***Capacity:*** including business acumen, judgement, experience and financial resources;
  - (c) ***Capital:*** including tangible assets, market value, reserves, debt-equity ratio, asset-liability ratio.
  - (d) ***Condition:*** of customer's business in particular and of the type of business on the whole, which certainly affects customer's business.

Since it is not possible to include letters concerning hundreds of situations demanding circular, credit letters etc. in a small volume of this book, a few sample letters are given in the following pages to illustrate these concepts.

3. Adapted from Essentials of Business Communication : Rajendra Pal and J.S. Korlahalli : Sultan Chand & Sons. Ed. 2008.

CIRCULAR LETTER ANNOUNCING OPENING OF A NEW BRANCH

Light & Sound Store

217, Ferguson College Road,
Shivaji Nagar, Pune-411004
Tel. : 022-3569407, 3566407
http.: //www.lightandsound.com

Dated : 10th September, 2009

Dear ....

OUR AIM IS TO CONQUER INDIA
&
WE HAVE COME TO YOUR CITY

Light & Sound Store has, within a short span of 3 years of being established, become a household name for everyone young and old, male and female, and almost everyone who is interested in Music and T.V., Audio and Video, Films and Entertainment alike.

Already, we have opened 175 stores in all Metro and large Towns throughout the length and breadth of the country. We are now expanding to smaller towns and planning to open 250 stores by the end of the current year.

Our stores have the widest collection of Bollywood & Hollywood Movies, Video Albums, Sound Tracks, Movie and Songs, DVDs and VCD, audio CDs and Cassettes and almost anything concerning Light and Sound.

You would be delighted to know that, we have now opened, on 1st September 2009, a franchise store in your city, at the address given below :

LIGHT & SOUND STORE
A-2, Sabharwal Market
Railway Road,
SONEPAT (Haryana)
Ph.: 2526789

The store is owned and managed by Mr. Surinder Kapoor who will be very helpful with his staff to assist you in your purchase of movies, videos, DVDs or anything of your choice.

As a gesture to welcome you at our above store, we are offering you an inaugural discount of 25% on all your purchases till 30th Sept. 2009.

Happy Shopping.

Sincerely,
for Light & Sound Store

Promotions Manager

CIRCULAR LETTER ANNOUNCING CLEARANCE SALE

WOODSTOCK Apparels

(Creators of Designer Wears)
B-56, South Extension Part I
New Delhi
Tel. : 011-29653029, 29657654
http : //www.woodstockindia.com

Dated : 27th September, 2009

Dear Valued Customer,

Sub. : Announcement of Annual Clearance Sale

As you are aware, we fill our godowns with all new varieties of fresh stocks on the eve of festival season like Diwali, Christmas & New year etc. Before that, we tend to clear our stocks to make way for new arrivals. And this is an annual feature at WOODSTOCK Apparels.
This year also, we are planning a Grand Clearance Sale of our stocks before the arrival of the festival season, as per the following schedule :

Subject	:	**Grand Clearance Sale**
Venue	:	Our South Extension Showroom
Dates	:	1st October to 7th October, 2009 (or Till Stock Lasts, whichever is earlier)
Timings	:	10 A.M. To 7 P.M. (No Lunch hours Closure)
Offering	:	25% To 75% Discount
Covering	:	All items of stock

In addition to the fabulous discount mentioned above, there shall be a DAILY LUCKY DRAW for an ALL EXPENSE PAID holiday to an Exotic Indian Destination for Two.

We welcome you to take advantage of this most lucrative, once in a year, offer.

Hoping to see you there, with your family and friends.

Sincerely,

(S.S. Bedi)
Manager

CIRCULAR LETTER ANNOUNCING THE OBTAINING OF A NEW AGENCY

Perfect Electronics & Travel Services

631, Main Road,
Dr. Mukherjee Nagar,
Delhi-110009
Tel. : 011-27603456, 27607890
e-mail : naveen631@indiatimes.com

Dated : 20th November, 2009

Dear Valued Customer,

We thank you very much for patronising our business since last six years of our establishment. We have always tried to serve you with the excellent quality product in Electronics at most competitive prices. we also endeavour to provide the most satisfactory after sales services to our customers.

Following the same tradition, we now announce with pride and pleasure that NOKIA has appointed us their **'Preferred Dealers'** for the sale and service of World's No.1 Nokia Mobile Phone Handsets and Accessories.

Our showroom has been fully renovated and air-conditioned. The ambience and display of Nokia products is International class keeping in mind the NOKIA standards of quality, fashion and style. You will find all new launches of Nokia mobile phones available at the showroom. A dedicated service counter has also been set up to meet the requirements of the customers.

We are also providing Sim Cards, New connections, Charger coupons, validity coupons of all Telecom companies.

As always, our dedicated staff will be always ready to give you our best and prompt attention. You can also avail of the exchange facility at our showroom.

We look forward to your visit to our newly renovated showroom and experience the pleasure of shopping.

We solicit your patronage and co-operation as in the past.

Sincerely,

(Naveen Sabharwal)
Proprietor

CIRCULAR ANNOUNCING THE CHANGE IN THE CONSTITUTION OF BUSINESS

(Formation of a company)

Professional Publishers

3675, Murari Lal Lane
Ansari Road, Darya Ganj,
New Delhi-110002
Tel. : 011-39654242, 39655252
http: //www.professional-publishers.com

Dated : 15th September, 2009

Sub. : Intimation regarding change in the constitution of business

Dear Valued Dealer,

Your excellent co-operation and valuable support expressed through your patronage of our business during past several years has provided us with necessary stimulus to think big. In the process, we had charted out a plan to increase our capital and capacity four-fold to the present level.

This has necessitated to change the constitution of our firm to that of a limited liability company. From now onwards, our firm will be known as

> Professional Publishers (P) Ltd.
> Regd. Office : 3675, Murari Lal Lane
> Ansari Road, Darya Ganj,
> New Delhi-110002

Our telephone numbers shall remain the same. However, our partners shall now be called as Directors of the newly established company.

You may, however continue to do business with us like ever before. We even assure of still wider varieties of our publication, on a larger scale and at most competitive prices.

Your satisfaction will always remain our main motto.

Looking forward to your continued co-operation and patronage.

Sincerely,
For Professional Publishers (P) Ltd.

Managing Director.

LETTER REQUESTING FOR CREDIT INFORMATION

Neelgagan Stationery Products Co.

(Stationery Manufactures & Suppliers)
237, Khurshid Market,
Sadar Bazar, Delhi 110007
Tel. : 011-27452930, 27453940
e-mail : neelgagan@indiatimes.com

Dated : 1st December, 2009

The Accounts Manager,
M/s Apex Stationery Mart,
26, Nai Sarak,
Delhi-110006

Sub. : Request for Credit Information

Dear Sir,

We have received the name of your firm for credit reference from M/s Jain Bros., Stationery Suppliers, Bazar Sita Ram, Delhi 110006. They have indicated to be dealing with your firm for the last 6 years.

Please provide us with any appropriate information about your credit relationship with M/s Jain Bros. Kindly indicate the average volume of Trade and the credit limit provided to them by you during last 2 years. Any special comments about the credit history will be welcome.

May we assure that the information you share with us will be strictly held in confidence and will be used for credit purposes only.

For your convenience, we are enclosing a self addressed stamped envelope.

Your response shall be highly appreciated.

Sincerely,

(R.K. Sabharwal)
General Manager

LETTER SUPPLYING TRADE REFERENCES FOR CREDIT VERIFICATION

Nirmal Boutique

M-75, Greater Kailash, Part I
New Delhi
Ph. 011-65044848, 65044646
e-mail : nirmalboutique@sify.com

Dated : 3rd October, 2009

The Accounts Manager,
M/s Adam-N-Eve Garments (P) Ltd.
31 F, Gaffar Market,
Karol Bagh, New Delhi-110055

Sub. : Your letter dated 29th Sept. 2009 asking for Trade references.

Dear Sir,

Thank you very much for extending courtesy to open our account in your books. Being in trade, you must have the knowledge that we are distributors for some of the best known brands in the readymade garments industry like Provogue, Cotton County, Charlie Outlaw and Silverline. Our distribution network covers entire Delhi and New Delhi areas and our turnover is sufficiently large to justify credit purchases.

However, as desired by you, we are supplying three references with whom we have been dealing for the past 5 years :

- Indus Trading Co.
  F 29, Lajpat Nagar Part II, New Delhi-110019
  Ph. 011-66925262
- Raghunath Trading Co.
  E 149, Kamla Nagar, Delhi 110007
  Ph. 011-65057733
- Best Wears
  N-72, Model Town Part II, Delhi 110009
  Ph. 011-27459096

Should you require any further information, please feel free to phone or write to us, since we wish to include the variety of stock in our showroom before the onset of festival season.

May we request you to complete the formalities quickly and despatch the stock as promply as possible.

Sincerely,

(Nirmal Bhasin)
Proprietor

LETTER DECLINING REQUEST FOR CREDIT FACILITY

India Business Solutions (P) Ltd.

(Transforming Business Through Networking)
32F, Fountain Circle, 3rd Lane
Mumbai
Tel. : 022-64092373
e-mail : ibs@yahoo.com

Dated : 10th October, 2009.

The Purchase Manager
M/s Unique Data Systems
3-4, D-Mall, 7th Level,
Netaji Subhash Place, New Delhi

Sub. : Your request for credit facilities.

Dear Sir,

Thank you for your letter dated 3rd October, 2009 requesting for the grant of credit facilities to the tune of Rs. 5 lacs. with our company.

At the outset, we may inform you that the credit facilities, as a matter of corporate policy, are offered only to those customers, who have been trading with us for over 6 months.

Secondly, the credit limits are awarded on the basis of average business done by a client during the last quarter. This is further reviewed from time to time.

Thirdly, credit facilities are awarded only to the clients who have a clean track records of payment without default or late payment in the last quarter.

So far, no exception to this corporate policy has been made.

We hope you would understand our policy and continue to patronise us with your valued orders in accordance with our payment terms.

We look forward to being of service to you.

Sincerely,

(Naveen Kohli)
Manager : Accounts

LETTER ASKING FOR ADVANCE PAYMENT OR CREDIT REFERNCES

Adam-n-Eve Garments (P) Ltd.

31 F, Gaffar Market,
Karol Bagh, New Delhi-110055
Tel. : 011-32695684, 32695685

Dated : 29th September, 2009

The Proprietor
M/s Nirmal Boutique
M-75, Greater Kailash Part I,
New Delhi-110047

Sub : Your Purchase order dated 23rd September, 2009

Dear Sir,

We thank you very much for your order no. 135 dated 23rd September 2009 for supply of readymade garments worth Rs. 75,000.00 approximately. We appreciate your interest in our products which are of excellent quality with an assurance of very high level of customer satisfaction.

However, we have noticed that you have neither sent any advance draft nor mentioned any mode of payment with your order.

You, we hope, must be aware of the usual practice in wholesale garment trade that first orders are always paid in advance or on cash-on-delivery basis. We, therefore, would like you to send us a demand draft/payment order for the full amount of the purchase order to enable us to despatch the goods promptly and to avail of cash discount.

In case you wish to avail credit facilities (without the benefit of cash discount), please give us the names of atleast two wholesale dealers of the garment trade with whom you have dealings for more than last 2 years. Since this is our company's policy of credit verification, it is carried out as a normal routine before supplying goods on credit to a new customer.

Looking forward to continued business relations with your esteemed firm.

Sincerely,

(Prakash Chander)
Accounts Manager

LETTER REPLYING TO STATUS ENQUIRY/CREDIT VERIFICATION
(Favourable reply)

Best Wears

N-72, Model Town Part II,
Delhi 110009
Ph. 011-27459096
Dated : 22nd October, 2009

M/s Adam-n-Eve Garments (P) Ltd.
31F, Gaffar Market
Karol Bagh
New Delhi-110015

Sub. : Credit Verification

Dear Sir,

M/s Nirmal Boutique, about whom you have sought credit information vide your letter dated 16th October, 2009, have been in business with us for the last 5 years. Their record of payment and other dealings during this period has been entirely satisfactory. The trade circle treats them as a financially sound party. Even as a businessman, the proprietor is held in high esteem among Co-traders.

Their business with us on an average have been Rs. 2.50 Lacs per month during the last two years. During peak season it goes up to Rs. 7 lacs and above. We do not hesitate to allow them credit of upto Rs. 5 lacs.

We would like to add that our experience and confidence in the firm has never been misplaced.

May we expect that you will keep this information confidential and not divulge it for any other purpose. Further the information shall have no legal consequences, whatsoever.

Sincerely,

(Madan Mohan)
Proprietor

LETTER REPLYING TO STATUS ENQUIRY/CREDIT VERIFICATION
(Slightly unfavourable Reply)

Indus Trading Co.

F-29, Lajpat Nagar Part II,
New Delhi-110037
Ph. 011-66925262

Dated : 21st October, 2009

M/s Adam-n-Eve Garments (P) Ltd.
31F, Gaffar Market
Karol Bagh,
New Delhi-110055

Sub. : Credit Verification

Dear Sir,

M/s Nirmal Bontique, about whom you have sought credit information vide your letter dated 16th October, 2009, have been in business with us for barely past two years. Through, we can vouch safe a credit limit of upto. Rs. 1 lac with the firm, our own experience in the last 6 months is that the firm has been slow in making payments. This may be either due to a family division of property recently in the firm which might have resulted in cash crunch for short term or some other matter unknown to the trade.

We sincerely hope, you will keep this information as strictly confidential and not divulge it for any other purpose.

We also would not be liable, legally or otherwise for sharing this information with you.

Sincerely,

(Avinash Madan)
Proprietor

LETTER REPLYING TO CREDIT VERIFICATION
(Unfavourable Reply)

Raghunath Trading Co.

E 149, Kamla Nagar,
Delhi-110007
Ph. 011-65057733

Dated : 23rd October, 2009

M/s Adam-n-Eve Garments (P) Ltd.
31F, Gaffar Market,
Karol Bagh,
New Delhi-110055

Sub. : Credit verification vide your letter dated 16.10.2009

Dear Sir,

Reference your above letter wherein you have enquired about the credit information of M/s Nirmal Boutique, we may mention that we have been in business with the said firm for the past two years only. Whereas, initially their business dealing were praiseworthy, we have found them lacking in many aspects of trade during the last 6 months.

Not only that the firm has been deferring payments for long periods on one pretext or the other, we also had a dispute with them regarding supply of stock of Rs. 1,10,000/- approximately which dispute has resulted in a loss of Rs. 40,000/- to us.

In view of the above, we have reduced our dealings with them to a bare minimum level and supplying them goods only on C.O.D. basis. We suggest a line of caution in dealing with them.

Please treat this information as strictly confidential. Further, we donot accept any liability/ responsibility for sharing this information with you.

Sincerely,

(Ravi Shankar)
Manager

LETTER GRANTING CREDIT

Adam-n-Eve Garments (P) Ltd.

31F, Gaffar Market,
Karol Bagh
New Delhi-110055

Tel. : 011-32695684, 32695685

Dated : 25th October, 2009

The Proprietor
M/s. Nirmal Boutique
M-75, Greater Kailash Part I,
New Delhi.

Sub. : Your Purchase order dated 23rd September, 2009

Dear Sir,

We take pleasure in executing your order no. 135 dated 23rd September 2009 for supply of readymade garments worth Rs. 75,000/- and opening your account in our books.

The Trade references given by you have all talked appreciatively of your business dealings with them.

We are very happy to extend you the best line of credit. We offer to our preferred dealers of long standing 30 days credit with no interest. The period may be extended to 60 days with payment of interest for one month at only 1% interest.

We are sure, you will be completely satisfied with our excellent quality and most competitive prices and continue to select us for your regular purchases.

We are appreciative of your order and hope the opening of your account in our books will be the begining of a long and happy association with you.

Sincerely

(Vineet Sachdeva)
Marketing Manager

LETTER REFUSING CREDIT

Adam-n-Eve Garments (P) Ltd.

31-F, Gaffar Market
Karol Bagh
New Delhi-110055
Tel. : 011-32695684, 32695685

Dated : 25th October, 2009

The Proprietor,
M/s Nirmal Boutique
M-75, Greater Kailash Part I,
New Delhi.

Sub. : Your purchase order dated 23rd September, 2009

Dear Sir,

We think you for providing us the names of firms for obtaining necessary information required for having a credit account in our books.

While all the firms referred to in your letter talked very high of you as a successful businessman and a man of good reputation in trade circles, we could also infer that perhaps due to family engagements or other matters, better known to you, your commitments have led to excessive liability. We assume this may be a very short-term phenomenon and a passing phase.

We would be pleased to consider your request after a couple of months, by when you will certainly have squared off the excessive liablities and obligations.

In the meantime, we would suggest you deal with us on C.O.D. terms and avail of Cash discount as well.

Looking forward to your confirmation of the above order on cash basis.

Sincerely,

(Vineet Sachdeva)
Marketing Manager

LETTER COMPLAINING DELAY IN THE EXECUTION OF ORDER

"Cool Foam" Mattresses

(Manufacturer & Wholesalers of Mattresses)
321, Panchkuin Road,
New Delhi-110001
Tel. : 011-27354142, 27355152
e-mail : coolfoam@indiatimes.com

Dated : 19th September, 2009

The Proprietor
M/s Foam (India) Suppliers
K-31, Urban Estate, Phase II,
Panipat (Haryana)

Sub. : Delay in Execution of our order dated 3rd September, 2009

Dear Sir,

It is over two weeks now, when we placed our order for the supply of 1800 pcs. of 6′ × 3′ coir sheet of 2″ thickness of grade 15 with you at your listed price.

In the past, your supplies had been very prompt and we seldom had to remind you about that. However, this time, we fail to understand why such an extraordinary delay is taking place. Also that the supplies form a full truckload, the despatch does not require formalities to be completed with Transport Company etc.,

You have also not intimated us any reason for the occurance of delay so that we could have made alternate arrangement of supplies.

You are aware that coir sheets form a prominent part of the end product 'cool foam' and without this, the entire production comes to a halt resulting in huge losses to us.

Kindly ensure supplies within next 72 hours as we are fast running out of our stock of this item for production.

Looking forward to hear from you soon.

Sincerely,

(Sunil Bhardwaj)
Purchase Manager

Encl.: Copy of our order
dated 3rd Sept., 2009

REPLY TO COMPLAINT OF DELAY IN EXECUTION OF ORDER

Foam (India) Suppliers

K-31 Urban Estate Phase II,
Panipat (Haryana)
Tel. 95120-7295381, 7295382
e-mail : foamindia@sify.com

Dated : 20th September, 2009

To,
The Purchase Manager
"Cool Foam" Mattresses
321, Panchkuin Road,
New Delhi 110002

Sub. : Execution of your order dated 3rd September 2009

Dear Sir,

While we regret that you had to take the trouble of writing to us, but we are pleased to inform that we had dispatched the entire quantity of stock of raw material as per the specification in your order.

We are sure, you must have already received the stock. We wish to make it clear that your valued orders receive our utmost attention and it is only this time, due to large quantity of pending orders, that the supply got somewhat delayed.

Assuring of our best services at all times.

Sincerely,

(Proprietor)

LETTER ABOUT SUPPLY OF WRONG GOODS

Mount Kailash Aqua Industries

86 F, Industrial Area, Phase II,
Rishikesh (Uttrakhand)
Tel. : 3745921, 3745789

Dated : 15th September, 2009.

The Proprietor
Aqua Bottle Manufacturing Co.
Industrial Area II,
Raja Ki Mandi,
Agra (U.P.)

Sub. : Supply of stock not ordered by us.

Dear Sir,

Kindly refer to our order no. 239 dated 2nd September, 2009 for the supply of 500 cases of one Dozen each of Empty Bottles with our brand name 'Mount-Kailash' printed on 1 litre bottles.

While we have received the supplies of 500 cases yesterday, we find an unusual mix-up of stock with stock of some other purchasers from you. Out of the lot, 50 cases consist of the following :

(i) 20 cases of 1 ltr. empty bottles with 'Pure' brand name printed on it.
(ii) 15 cases of 1 ltr. empty bottles with 'Aqua-Good Health' brand name printed on it.
(iii) 15 cases of 1 ltr. empty bottles without any name printed on it but not matching our design.

These 50 cases of stock not ordered by us is lying in our godown. You are requested not only to send us 50 cases of our ordered stock but also to instruct us how to deal with this stock.

On receiving instructions from you, we shall dispatch these to whatever destination, you require, at your cost and expense.

An urgent action would be welcome.

Sincerely,

(Sunil Kapoor)
Purchase Manager

LETTER FOR GOODS RECEIVED IN A DAMAGED CONDITION

Alpha Hoseiry Ltd.

F 22, Sunder Nagar Industrial Area
Ludhiana-141002
Ph. 0161-7259651, 7259652
e-mail : alphahosiery@indiatimes.com

Dated : 10th September, 2009

The Manager
M/s India Wool Mart
74, Main Market,
Sadar Bazar,
Ahmedabad (Gujarat)

Sub. : Supplies received in damaged condition.

Dear Sir,

We have taken delivery of the stocks supplied by you from M/s. Golden Transport Co. against our order no. 372 dated 28th August 2009.

While the quantity received matches with that ordered, we wish to inform you that two sacks of woollen balls were received in wet and damaged condition. While the fact was brought to the notice of the Transport Co. and a written compaint was given to them and an acknowledgement received for the same.

The damaged stock is worth Rs. 13,750.00 which was also listed in the complaint letter to the Transport Co. We strongly feel that the damage was caused by negligence of the Transport Co. which failed to properly protect the stock from rains during transit.

The stock may be disposed of at 50% of list price, or re-despatched to you at your cost and expense, for which we need your instructions.

Kindly also replace the stock at the earliest.

We are enclosing the following documents with this letter so as to enable you to file necessary claims with the Transport/Insurance company :

(i) Copy of invoice
(ii) Copy of transport receipt
(iii) Acknowledged complaint letter (in original)
(iv) List of damaged stock.

Assuring you of our best co-operation at all times.

Sincerely,

(Suman Hans)
Manager, Stores

Encl. : 4 (As above)

LETTER INFORMING DEFECTIVE SUPPLIES

Bharat Emporium

36/9, Kakodkar Road
Ahmedabad (Gujarat)
Ph. : 3279625, 3279626
e-mail : bharatempo@sify.com

Dated : 29th November, 2009.

The Proprietor,
M/s Nitin Handlooms
B-46, Nangloi,
New Delhi-110047

Sub : Intimation of supply of defective goods

Dear Sir,

We thank you very much for the timely execution of our order no. BE/179/2009 dated 2nd November, 2009. The stock delivered matched with the quantity and description as per our order except the following:

'Aristo' Recron Pillows with white cotton covers weighing 325 grams each in sigle piece poly packing as ordered by us was in fact weighed 275 grams each in weight.

We believe, the stock supplied by you must be of different price tag due to difference in weight.

We have two options. Either to reject the stock and return it to you to Delhi by Road Transport at your cost and expense. in such a case, you will send us a new invoice for the remaining stock.

Another option is that we accept the stock provided you allow us a credit note of the difference in prices of 325 grams and 275 grams variety of Recron Pillows. We believe, this option is in the interest of both of us.

Since the matter is very urgent, we would like you to intimate us so that we may act accordingly. We are withholding payment of the invoice till we hear from you.

Please treat the matter as Most Urgent.

Sincerely,

(Bharat Bhushan)
Proprietor

LETTER CLAIMING REPLACEMENT OF DEFECTIVE GOODS

Indian Book Agency
3461, Nai Sarak, Delhi-110006
Ph. 011-26354747, 26355151

Dated : 10th October, 2009.

The Manager,
M/s Asian Electronics Ltd.
B-25, Bhagirath Place,
Chandni Chowk,
New Delhi-110006

Sub. : Complaint about Malfunctioning of Air-conditioners

Dear Sir,

We purchasd two 1.5 Tons 'Asian' Air-conditioners from your company's showroom at Chandni Chowk vide invoice no. 3752 dated 16th July 2009.

We regret to state that one of the Air-conditioners has not been properly functioning since installation. It neither make the office room any cooler, nor functions at less than 25°C, which makes it a useless piece of wall hanging.

We had earlier made a telephonic complaint at your showroom on 12th August and an Engineer came to inspect the air-conditioner but no workable rectification could be made.

Since we are fed-up with the non-working air-conditioner, we would like you to replace the Air-conditioner, since it is within the warranty period.

An early action in this regard will be solicited.

Sincerely,

(Jagdish Chander)
Proprietor

REPLY TO LETTER CLAIMING REPLACEMENT OF DEFECTIVE GOODS

Asian Electronics Ltd.

(Manufactures of 'Asian' Air-conditioners)
B-25, Bhagirath Place,
Chandni Chowk,
New Delhi-110006
Tel. : 011-64392525, 64392526

Dated : 15th October, 2009

The Proprietor
M/s Indian Book Agency
3461, Nai Sarak,
Delhi-110006

Sub. : Your complaint about non-working of air-conditioner

Dear Sir,

We are in receipt of your complaint regarding malfunctioning of the Air-conditioner supplied by us under our brand name.

While our air-condioners are warranteed for two years for any manufacturing deflect, we are sure our air-conditioners conform to international standards for impeccable quality, durability, style and finish. It is very rare that we receive a complaint of the type lodged by you. We will be sending our engineer to your office to check and rectify the defect, if any, in the air-conditioner.

As a matter of caution, may we suggest you to kindly switch off your air-conditioners during power-cuts, because most of the inverters or generators can't carry the load required for air-conditioners, which causes severe damage to the compressors. Our engineer will inspect this aspect also and suggest you accordingly.

Assuring you of our best services at all times.

Sincerely,

(Akash Sethi)
Manager, Engineering Deptt.

LETTER CONVEYING DELAY IN EXECUTION OF ORDER

Yonex Sports Industries

(Specialist in Cricket Items)
N-37, Industrial Area-Phase II,
Jallandhar Cantt. (Punjab)
Ph. 0181-6206952
e-mail : yonex@yahoo.com

Dated : 4th December, 2009

The Proprietor
New Delhi Sports House,
Arunanchal Bhawan,
Barakhamba Road,
New Delhi-110 001

Sub. : Intimation of delay in execution of order

Sir,

We thank your for your valued order for the supply of 500 Willow Cricket Bats and 2000 Cricket Balls marked with your brand name 'ARISTOCRAT' imprinted on them.

Since the variety ordered by you for Bats is of excellent quality wood imported from Kashmir and presently in short supply and hence costly, we express our inability to supply the stock at Contracted Price.

However, we expect the price to come down in next 15 days since three truck loads of the Willow Wood have been despatched from Kashmir and would be reaching the market in next 7 to 10 days.

Since the stock will be manufactured with your brand name, it would be of no use to us in case you donot accept the deliveries. As such, unless you confirm allowing us additional two weeks time after the deadline set by you, we would not be able to execute the order.

In case you need urgent supplies, kindly let us know so that we work out the prices on the basis of prevailing market price of raw materials and intimate you accordingly.

Your response will initiate our prompt attention.

Sincerely,

(Ahsan Ahmed)
Proprietor

LETTER REFUSING ORDER DUE TO LOWER PRICES

Gulab Sweets (India) Ltd.

M-36, Pitam Pura (West)
New Delhi-110015
Tel. : 011-35926758, 35926756
e-mail : gulabsweets@yahoo.com

Dated : 15th November, 2009

The Proprietor
Sardar Stores
37, Lawrence Road,
Amritsar.

Sub. : Inability to Execute Order

Dear Sir,

We thank you very much for your order for the supply of 500 Boxes of Roasted Almonds (400 grams each) of 'A' quality @ Rs. 250.00 per box.

Please note that the rate quoted by you belongs to our price list dated 15th August 2009, which has since been revised due to rising price of inputs on accounts of the ongoing festival season.

According to new price list, the rates of the product ordered by you is Rs. 280.00 per box. Again, the prices are subject to change anytime depending on the market price fluctuations taking place very frequently, sometimes on day-to-day basis.

We would be unable to supply your order, unless your order is revised at prevailing prices.

Please note that the supplies will be made at prices on the date, the order is confirmed. Our today's price list is enclosed.

We are withholding your advance cheque till confirmation of your order.

Sincerely,

(Madan Mohan)
Proprietor

LETTER REFUSING SUPPLY UNLESS OUTSTANDINGS ARE PAID

National Trading Co. Ltd.

(Suppliers of Computer Periphrals)
32, 7th Floor, Ansal Towers,
Nehru Place, New Delhi-110035
Ph. 011-66352727, 66353636
e-mail : ntc@indiatimes.com

Dated : 25th September, 2009

The Proprietor
Dynamic Computers,
82, Local Shopping Centre
DDA. Market, Shastri Nagar,
Delhi.

Sub. : Your order dated 16th September, 2009

Dear Sir,

We thank you very much for your order no. 217/2009 dated 16th September, 2009.

While we value our business relations with you, we would be unable to execute your order due to an overdue outstanding of Rs. 65,000/- in your account, which is Rs. 25,000/- more than the limit allowed Moreover, we have not received any payment in the account since last 3 months, which in itself is a serious matter.

We, therefore, request you to immediately clear the overdue amount to enable us to execute your order at the earliest.

In the meantime, I am sending the order to the despatch section to keep the goods ready for prompt despatch on receipt of payment from you.

Kindly arrange to send a minimum of Rs. 30,000.00 to keep the account open and running.

Assuring you of our best co-operation at all times.

Sincerely,

(Saurabh Sabharwal)
Proprietor

Encl. : Statement of Account

LETTER DECLINING DIRECT ORDER TO COMPANY

Moser-Baer (India) Ltd.

197, Okhla Industrial Area,
Phase II, Okhla,
New Delhi-110027
Tel. : 011-35674950-56
e-mail : moserbaer@yahoo.com

Dated : 19th September, 2009

The Manager,
Double-Edge Infotech services
36, Aggarwal Towers,
Netaji Subhash Place, New Delhi.

Sub. : Your order no. 369 dated 17th September, 2009

Dear Sir,

We thank you for your above order and appreciate your interest in our products which are considered of excellent quality even by our competitors.

However, we express our inability to excute your order as our products are marketed only through authorised dealers. As a general policy, we donot accept any direct order and even our big and regular customers are serviced through our authorised dealers.

The Authorised dealer nearest to your location is M/s Bharat Computers, Rani Bagh Market, New Delhi with tel no. 011-64279250.

We have directed your order to M/s Bharat Computers who would get in touch with you shortly. You may also contact the dealer at the phone no. given above for quick supply of your order.

In the meantime, we are sending you an illustrative catalogue and the latest price list alongwith a list of our authorised dealer in the NCR region.

We are sure you will continue to receive excellent quality of products and services through our Authorised Dealers.

Sincerely,

(Ravi Malhotra)
Regional Marketing Manager

Encl. 3 (As above)

LETTER OFFERING SUBSTITUTES OF BRANDS ORDERED

Home Town

(The Home Furniture Store)
136, Mehrauli Gurgaon Road,
New Delhi
Tel. : 011-29256565, 29257576

Dated : 19th November, 2009

The Manager,
Gulati Furniture House,
Punchkuin Road,
New Delhi . 110001

Sub. : Your order for supply of 'Neelkamal' dining tables.

Dear Sir,

We thank you for your order for the supply of 135 sets of 'Neelkamal' Dining sets (Plastic Table and 6 Chairs per set) @ Rs. 1350.00 per set. While we appreciate your interest in 'Neelkamal' brand which represents excellent quality and designs, we are sorry to say that we would not be in a position to supply the required quantity.

The reason being that these items are manufactured at Ahmedabad and transporting them to Delhi entails huge cost and time due to the bulkyness of the Boxes in which they are supplied. As a result, we donot keep such large quantity of stock of this item.

May we suggest you a better and more economical **'Supreme'** brand being locally manufactured at Noida with excellent quality and designs comparable to and even better than 'Neelkamal' brand. Not only the prices are lower for 'Supreme' brand, their strength, durability and eye-catching designs are very appealing and moreover, they are available in ready stock.

May we request you to personally visit or send your representative to our showroom to view the latest design and range of 'Supreme' products and make an informed decision.

We assure you that you will not be disappointed.

Sincerely,

(Paresh Rawal)
Manager

Encl. : Catalogue & Price List of Supreme Products

D

Given below are some suggested topics under Alphabat 'D'

Debt Collection letters

- First Reminder : Remind a customer that payment is due.
- Second Reminder : Remind the customer that a payment is overdue.
- Third Reminder : Appeal to a customer's Interest to pay an overdue bill.
- Fourth Reminder : Demand payment on a delinquent account.
- Fifth Reminder : Announce your intention of taking appropriate action, if the customer fails to make the payment by a stipulated date.
- Reply to collection letter.
- Reply to collection letter : Explaining Delay in Payment.
- Letter making part payment & explaining for Balance.
- Letter allowing extension of time for payment.
- Letter disputing the amount mentioned in collection letter.
- Reply to the above letter.

QUICK TIPS FOR WRITING DEBT COLLECTION LETTERS

- The Debt collection letter should be written remembering the principle, *"It is easy to lose a customer than to make one."*
- The aim of writing a collection letter is to make the defaulter pay.
- Collection letters are also called, **"Dunning letters"**.
- The number of collection letters written vary in different situations from one to four or five.
- As far as possible, care should be taken to see that the customer is not lost by use of offensive language.
- The aim of writing a collection letter should be *"to collect the dues and not to pick-up a quarrel"*.
- The sender of a collection letter should try to ascertain the reason for late payment default, before writing it. The reasons may be either of the following:
  — misunderstanding of terms & conditions,
  — neglect through careless attitude,
  — financial tightness of a temporary nature,
  — lack of honesty,
  — habitual delay in payment,
  — permanent shortage of money
  — accident/bereavement in the family etc.
- As far as possible, collection letter should be drafted depending purely on the circumstances of each case.

- The tone of the collection letters changes everytime from pleasant to aggressive to threatening.
- The collection letter must contain all information above the payment and how it is falling overedue such as :
  — Customer's order no, and date
  — Supply date & Inoice no.
  — Contract no. and date
  — Credit policy of the Company and Credit Term allowed
  — Reminders should be numbered
- Every collection Letter must contain the reference to earlier reminders with their numbers and dates.
- As an option, the sender may, wherever possible, consider allowing some discount to the customer to motivate him to make early payment.
- As another option, the sender may, where possible, reschedule the payment plan for a customer having difficulty in paying an overdue bill.
- The final collection letter must state the penal action, if the customer does not pay the bills immediately.
- The letter must not contain empty threats. No further letter be sent asking for payment. The threat should be implemented, if payment is not received.
- If a customer is habitually delinquent or does not pay, a letter stating the withdrawl of his credit account/facility be written to him stating the reasons for such withdrawls.
- The contents and style of the collection 'Letter should be determined with an eye on the customer's usual conduct and his circumstances.
- The 'you' attitude may be used to convince the debtor that it is in his own interest to pay.

REQUEST FOR PAYMENT

Silverline Trading Co.

B-2 Aggarwal Plaza,
Bhikaji Cama Place,
New Delhi-110035
Tel. : 011- 29328888

28th November, 2009

Mr. Suresh Kashyap
Proprietor
India Stationery Mart,
Sardar Bazar,
Delhi 110006

Our Ref. : Invoice no. 522 Dt. 12.03.2009

Sub. : Outstanding Invoice

Dear Sir,

Our record shows that your account with us have a debit balance of Rs. 22,500.00 with respect to our invoice no. 522 dated 12.03.2009 for which we have yet to receive the payment. A copy of the invoice is being enclosed.

If you have already paid this amount, please ignore this notice, but do send us a copy of the receipt so that we may amend our records. Otherwis, please forward the amount immediately as it is long overdue. If you make the payment within next 7 days, we shall waive the 2% interest on late Payment, as a very special case.

Thank you in advance for your co-operation.

We look forward to continuous business with you in future.

Yours Sincerely

(Madhur Sain)
Manager - Accounts

Encl. : Invoice No. 522

DEBT COLLECTION LETTER : FIRST REMINDER

Cosco Sports (India) Ltd.

(Sports Goods Manufactures & Suppliers)
B-37, Industrial Area,
Jallandhar Cantt. (Punjab)
Ph. 0181-6543237, 6543238
e-mail : cosco@indiatimes.com

Dated : 1st October, 2009

The Accounts Manager
M/s Fastrack Sports
B-37, Lajpat Nagar, Part II,
New Delhi-110037

Sub. : Overdue Balance

Dear Sir,

We value our customers and always try to improve our services. It has always been our endeavour to keep our customers satisfied with our products and services.

We find it uncomfortable to remind you that an amount of Rs. 37500/= has been overdue in your account for over 2 months now. This is beyond our one month' term of credit.

We had been co-operating with you fully and in the same understanding would like you to clear your account as soon as possible.

As a gesture, special to you only, we would waive the interest on late payment, if the payment is received in full in the next 7 days.

We do believe, you would extend your co-operation in countinuing with the most cordial business relations, we enjoyed since last several years.

Sincerely,

(Atam Parkash Madan)
Manager, Accounts

DEBT COLLECTION LETTER : SECOND REMINDER

Cosco Sports (India) Ltd.

Sports Goods Manufacturers & Suppliers
B-37, Industrial Area,
Jallandhar Cantt. (Punjab)
Ph. 0181-6543237, 6543238
e-mail : cosco@indiatimes.com

Dated : 10th October, 2009

The Accounts Manager,
M/s Fastrack Sports,
B-37, Lajpat Nagar, Part II,
New Delhi-110037

Sub. : Long Overdue Balance

Dear Sir,

We value our customers and always endeavour to satisfy them with our quality products and services. In return, we expect full co-operation from our valued customers.

We are unable to understand why there has been such a delay in the payment of your long overdue account, which remains unpaid even after our reminder dated 1st October 2009 remained unaswered.

Despite the fact, that you have ignored our previous reminder, you can no longer delay payment if you wish to keep your account running and open with us.

We have repeatedly phoned your office to remind for the payment. As a business person, you must understand that we also have a business to run for profit.

We expect a payment of Rs. 37,500.00 (being the amount outstanding since long) from you on or before 20th of this month.

We do expect your co-operation in this matter at the earliest.

Yours Sincerely,

(Atam Parkash Madan)
Manager, Accounts

REPLY TO COLLECTION LETTER : DISPUTING CLAIM

Indian Leather Store

(Makers of Quality Shoes)
32, Mittal Market,
National Road,
Kanpur (U.P.)
Tel. : 3279444, 3279555

Dated : 15th November, 2009

The Proprietor,
M/s Punjab Shoe Co.
Railway Road,
Bhatinda (Punjab)

Sub. : Your letter dated 10th November, 09 for overdue Payment of Rs. 75,000.00

Dear Sir,

We are in receipt of the copy of the statement of our account alongwith your letter mentioned above.

At the very outset, we reject the statement for several mistakes, irregularities and wrong entries. Kindly check for the following :

- Entry for Invoice no. 1335 dated 15/4/09 is recorded at Rs. 53,875 instead of Rs. 35,875 (An excess debit of Rs. 18,000)
- Entry for Invoice no. 1642 dated 30/5/09 does not belong to us. (A wrong debit of Rs. 23,715)
- A debit entry for interest charged Rs. 3750 for the months of May, June & July. If the above corrections of entries are made, no such interest would be charged from us. (A difference of Rs. 3750)
- Our payment of Rs. 15,000 made by us on 10th October, 2009 has not been credited in our account (Another difference of Rs. 15,000)

Adding up all these corrections which are required to be made in the statement, a total of Rs. 60,465 will be credited leaving a balance of less than Rs. 15,000 in the debit of our account which does not deserve a reminder for payment.

May we also suggest you to revamp your Accounts Department, so that such silly situations donot arise again.

Sincerely,

(Vivek Kapoor)
Proprietor

REPLY TO COLLECTION LETTER : EXPLAINING DELAY IN PAYMENT

Planet XXX

(House of Modern Wears)
36, IInd floor, Shoopers Stop,
Defence Colony Extn., New Delhi.
Tel. : 011-26953233, 26294243

Dated : 15th September, 2009

The Manager : Accounts
Provogue (India) Ltd.
Regd. Office : Mirza Ismail Road
Jaipur (Rajasthan)

Sub. : Your letter no. 2379 dated 10th September, 09 for payment of Rs. 1,25,000/-

Dear Sir

We are extremely sorry that we made you to write a reminder asking us to clear our outstanding bills.

You might have learnt that a huge fire broke out at one of our showrooms resulting in substantial losses to our firm. The incident took place on 3rd August, 2009 and we are still in the process of renovating our showroom at very high costs. Our insurance claims has also not been settled and the entire business is in a mess at present.

As we are eagerly awaiting receipt of compensation from insurance company, we are also in the advanced stage of raising a loan of Rs. 25 crores from State Bank of India, Jaipur.

In the meantime, we are requesting our creditors to bear with us by allowing us an extension of one month time to start making payments of our outstanding bills. In case, we receive the insurance claim or bank loan, the remittances will start even earlier than the expiry of the extended time.

You are also requested to allow us extension of time and also to waive penal rate of interest on delayed payments.

Our previous record of makinq timely and regular payments will certainly enable you to accept our request.

Thanks in anticipation,

Sincerely,

(Vineet Kapoor)
Manager : Sales

LETTER : MAKING PART PAYMENT & EXPLAINING FOR BALANCE
(Reply to Collection Letter)

Indian Leather Store

(Makers of Quality Shoes)
32, Mittal Market, National Road,
Kanpur (U.P.)
Tel. : 3279444, 3279555

Dated : 15th September, 2009

The Proprietor
M/s Punjab Shoe Co.
Railway Road,
Bhatinda (Punjab)

Sub. : Your letter dated 10th September 09 for overdue Payment of Rs. 75,000/-

Dear Sir,

We are in receipt of the copy of the statement of our account alongwith your above mentioned letter.

Please fund enclosed a cheque of Rs. 30,000/- drawn on Canara Bank, Post Office Branch, Bhatinda, vide dated 15th September, 09.

The Balance of Rs. 45,000/- in our account now represents only the purchases made during the month of August 2009, which is perfectly within the terms of credit agreed between both of us.

May we assure you that we would be remitting regular payments.

Sincerely,

(Vivek Kapoor)
Proprietor

Encl. : Cheque (as above)

LETTER ALLOWING EXTENSION OF TIME FOR PAYMENT

Provogue (India) Ltd.

Regd. Office :
Mirza Ismail Road
Jaipur, (Rajasthan)
Tel. : 3279561-69
http://www.provogueindia.com

Dated : 21st September, 2009.

The Manager
Planet XXX
36, IInd Floor, Shoppers' stop,
Defence Colony Extn.,
New Delhi-110027

Sub.: Your request letter asking for Time Extension for payment.

Dear Sir,

We are extremely sorry to learn from your letter about the outbreak of a massive fire in one of your showrooms resulting in heavy losses.

We realise the enormous difficulties you are facing in your trade, but hope that these are just temporary and you will soon be able to tide over them.

Though, we normally donot allow more than 30 days credit, however, in extra ordinary circumstances like yours, we are always ready to co-operate with our valued clients like you.

We, therfore, would allow your account to remain in present position till 31st October, 2009, by which time, we are sure, you would resume normal trading and making remittances. We have also instructed the accounts department not to levy penal rate of interest for the late payment as a very special case.

We look forward to continue business relations with you shortly.

Sincerely,

(Vineet Kapoor)
Manager : Sales

COLLECTION LETTER INDICATING LEGAL ACTION FOR NON-PAYMENT

Prateek Enterprises
Vani Road
Bangaluru (Karnataka)
Tel. : 7945257, 7945258
e-mail : prateek@rediffmail.com

Dated : 23rd September, 2009

The Proprietor
New Delhi Garment Store,
72, Ashok Gali,
Gandhi Nagar, Delhi.

Sub. : Fourth Reminder for Payment

Dear Sir,

Kindly refer to our earlier reminders dated 10/8/09, 27/08/09 and 10/09/2009 on the above subject.

The payment of Rs. 45,750 against the supply of goods by us vide your order no. 352 dated 15th July 2009 remains outstanding till date.

Since our trade terms require payment within 15 days of invoice, it is already over 2 months that we have not received the same. You are requested to make the payment in full together with Interest @ 18% p.a. from 1st August, 2009 within 3 days from the receipt of this letter failing which we shall be constrained to place the matter in the hands of our lawyer to file a suit for the recovery of our dues.

We earnestly believe such a situation would not arise. Looking forward to an immediate response.

Sincerely,

(A.N. Raghwan)
Accounts Manager

E

E-MAIL

E-mail is an important means of communication with the help of computers using internet. E-mail is the elecrtonic mail which includes sending/receiving of messages/letters electronically. One can also transfer pictures, graphs, charts, databases, statements, videos, copies of documents, reports and any material that has been saved as computer file and which can be used as an attachment, through E-mail, that is being sent.

Format of e-mails : Format of E-mail comprises the following on the *'Compose mail'* page :

1. From : *(Sender's name & e-mail ID)*
2. To : *(Receiver's e-mail address)*
3. CC : *(e-mail addresses of persons to whom copies of e-mail are to be sent)*
4. BCC : *(Blind Copy, recipient's e-mail ID which is not to be disclosed)*
5. Subject : *(Subjectline of the message)*
6. Text Box : *Text of the Message (with or without Attachments).*

How e-mail works ?[1]

The software that moves the message from one system to another is called the 'Transport'. If the message sent from one system must get to a user on another system, it must pass through a geteway to be delivered. A gateway is an application programme that translates between two protocols of different E-mail systems. Value-Added Networks (VANs) are publie telecommunication companies, such as AT&T or MCI, that handle E-mail services to users, As a user, one can access a directory that contains names, addresses and sometimes other information about each user to find the E-mail address needed to send a message.

Using E-mail

With E-mail one can reach individuals, groups or other computer anywhere in the world to share information, files of data, spreadsheets, videos, music and anything else that can be stored on a computer file. E-mail combines some of the characteristics of writing and speaking. As a user, one has the immediacy of communicating directly to the receiver along with the advantages of being able to compose and revise a written message. E-mail can save user time in printing, copying and distributing the messages. One can use e-mail to send and receive faxes and relax. E-mail is also useful in personal communication with friends and family any where in the world.

E-mail Safety

The following steps[2] are recommended for the safety and security of your E-mail:

1. The password should be *combination of numbers and alphabets*, so that it is not easy to break.

---

1. See also Effective Business Communication : Herta A. Murthy, Herbert W. Hilderbrandt, Jane P. Thomas, McGraw Hill, 7th Ed. p. 120, 121 (Adapted).
2. Adapted from Greenill's Tips for a safe, secure and saavy e-mail user.

2. The password should be *frequently changed.* This helps in securing your e-mail.
3. The *password should not be shared with anyone.* It should never be disclosed to any caller or sender of e-mail. This is a well-known trick designed to fool e-mail user into sharing his password.
4. Never open '*attachments*' from unknown sources. They may contain '*Viruses*' which may damage your laptop/PC.
5. When not using, the e-mail account should not be kept open. 'Log out' as soon as you are done. It is very easy and quick and saves your account from trespassers.
6. When using a *public terminal* or '*Cyber Cafe*', it is advised to close the browser as soon as you are closing the 'internet session'.
7. *Never reply unsolicited messages* (Spam mail). 'unsubscribe' all unwanted e-mails.
8. Make sure that you use the latest (most up-to-date) internet software browsers (such as Microsoft or Netscape) which offer enhanced security and protection.
9. Always use a '*secure*' network which act to protect users from '*Hackers*'.
10. Maintain common sense, use caution, maintain skepticism when revealing personal information with anyone you meet through the *internet*.

DO'S AND DON'TS IN E-MAIL MESSAGES

Do's

- Do check to see what your organisation's e-mail policy is. Also if your e-mail is monitored or screened.
- Do make sure that the recipient reads your e-mail, by making it relevant to him. No one likes to receive junk e-mail.
- Be polite. Harshness can be mis-interpreted.
- Be patient. You may be familiar with e-mail etiquette, but the recipient might not be.
- Do remember to delete or trim irrelevant items from the message.
- Use emphasis by using a star * on either side of the word instead of using capital letters.
- Check your e-mail regularly and respond promptly.
- Always give a 'title' or 'subject line' of the message to reflect message content.
- Read, Re-read and proof-read for grammar and spelling before sending e-mail.
- Be succint in your message.
- Give Phone & Fax Numbers also, so that recipient could contact you.
- Always respond to received e-mail preferably in 48 hours.

Don'ts

- Donot reply an e-mail while you are angry, as you may regret it later. The 'message' once sent can't be recovered.
- Donot type the message in '*Capital letters*' as this is considered as 'Shouting.'
- Donot overuse punctuation marks (!!!) or full stops (........) especially when e-mail is a formal one.

- Donot (i) send excessive e-mail postings of the same message;
  (ii) criticise people in e-mail messages;
  (iii) conduct arguments in public (e.g., on a mailing list);
  (iv) infuriate people by using abusive language;
  (v) make personal remarks about third persons (avoid sexist language);
  (vi) post your e-mail address on websites.
- E-mail should not be used as a regular substitute for letters/messages requiring 'personal touch'.
- Avoid Irrelevant details in E-mails.
- Avoid using e-mail abbreviations in business letters.
- Avoid sending unsolicited e-mail that could be considered 'Junk' or 'spam' e-mail.
- Don't make a message 'urgent' unless it is actually so.
- Avoid 'humour' in message lest it may be termed 'taunting' or 'sarcasm'.
- Never send 'confidential' messages via e-mail.

QUICK TIPS FOR WRITING E-MAIL MESSAGES

Kitty O. Locker & Stephen Kyo Kaczmarek[3] gives the following guidelines for writing e-mail messages :

- Although e-mail feels informal, it is not private, as a conversation might be. Your employee may legally check your messages. And a message sent to one person can be printed out or forwarded to others without your knowledge or consent . Don't be indiscreet in e-mail.
- All the principles of good business writing also apply with e-mail. Remember 'You-attitude' , 'positive emphasis', use 'Reader benefits' when they are appropriate, use the pattern that fits the purpose of the message.
- Check your message for grammatical correctness and to be sure that you have included all the information.
- Re-read and proofread the message before clicking the 'send' Button.
- E-mail messages have to interest the reader in the subject line and first paragraph. If E-mail message is longer than one screen, the first screen must interest the reader enough to make him or her continue.
- E-mail message to people who report directly to you are easy because people will read anything from their superiors. But writing to people who are not in direct reporting line or to people outside writer's unit or organisation takes more care.

A printout of an actual E-mail format is reproduced on the next page.

3. Business Communication : Building Critical Skills, McGraw Hil, Ed. 2004 p. 258 (Adapted)

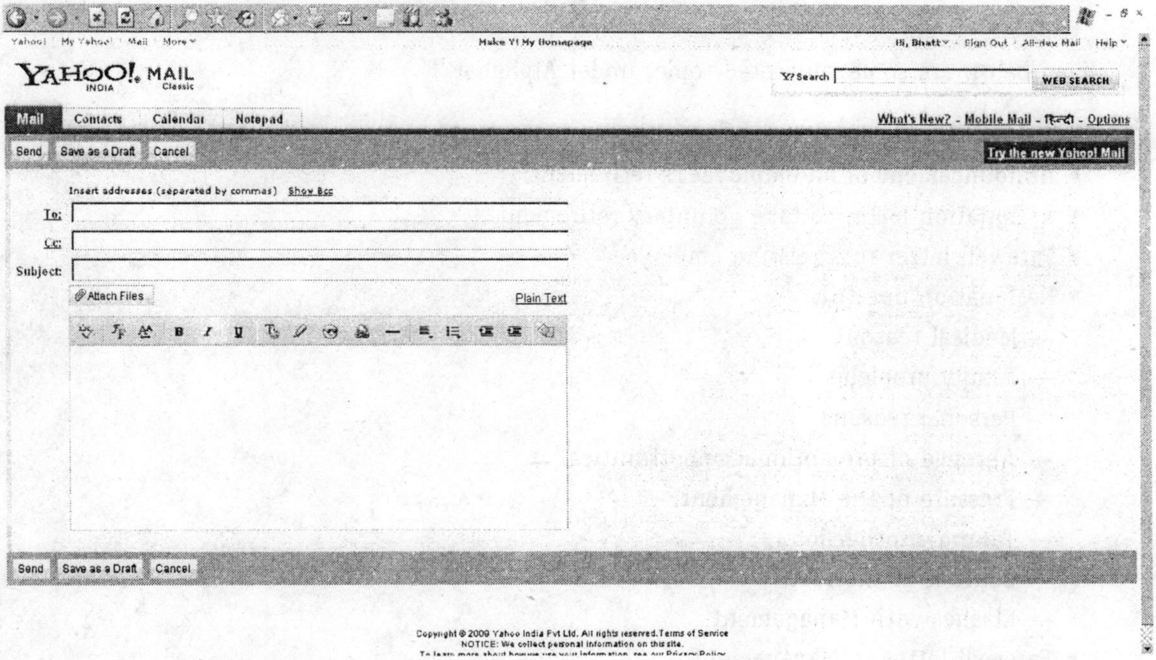

Encouragement Letters

These letters are also called as motivational letters and are generally written to sub-ordinate staff or clients. The purpose of writing these letters is to boost the morale, raise confidence, create goodwill and motivate the employees to do better or persuade a customer to take advantage of a new opportunity/scheme/promotional idea etc.. Some of the business situations that require writing of encouragement letters are given below :

- Encourage an employee to keep up good work.
- Encourage an employee after a set back.
- Encourage a customer to take advantage of a new opportunity.
- Encourage a colleague to take up new challenge.
- Write a persuasive letter to an employee
- Persuade someone to take an insurance policy.
- Write a persuasive sales letter

For Tips for Writing encouragement/persuasive letters and examples of such letters, see "sales letters" and " Insurance Letters".

F

Given below are some suggested topics under Alphabet 'F'.

Farewell Letters

- Announcement of an employees's retirement.
- Resignation letter to take voluntary retirement.
- Farewell letter to a retiring employee.
- Resignation due to :
  — Medical reasons
  — Family problems
  — Personal reasons
  — Absence of promotional opportunities.
  — Pressure of the Management.
  — Taking another job.
  — Conflict of Interest.
  — Clashes with Management.
- Farewell letter to Management.
- Farewell letter to colleagues, co-workers.
- Farewell letter to clients and customers.
- Letter of Termination (lay-off).

QUICK TIPS FOR WRITING FAREWELL LETTERS

- The farewell letter should be in friendly and positive tone, always.
- It should be written in a positive tone with well meaning appreciative words.
- The farewell letter must contain
  — Positive & Fond memories of time spent;
  — time enjoyed with colleagues & co-workers;
  — appreciation of organisation culture;
  — gratitude for opportunities received;
- The farewell letter must not contain :
  — negative remarks about management, co-workers or sub-ordinates;
  — sarcastic comments about someone;
  — cutting jokes on seniors/juniors;
  — description of bad habits of co-workers;
  — negative prophecies about the organisation; etc.
- The farewell letter should offer 'Best wishes', 'Warm regards', 'Success and happiness in future' type of closing sentences for the reader.

Few Examples of such letters are given in the following pages:

RESIGNATION LETTER

Parveen Hans

N-12, Dr. Mukherjee Nagar
Delhi - 110009

Dated: 20th August, 2009

The Manager : Human Resources
M/s Hindustan Thomson Advertising Co. Ltd.
Udyog Bhawan,
Gurgaon-NCR

Dear Mr. Manoj,

I am writing to give you a formal notice of my resignation from HT Advertising Co. Ltd. As per the terms of my employment, the 15 days notice will start from today till the 4th September, 2009.

I trust that during the two weeks period, you would find a replacement of my position. I would be pleased to help train the selected individual to take my place.

I would like to thank you for providing me an opportunity to work in the company in various positions and my stint at the company will prove very valuable in my career in future.

I express my deep sense of gratitude to my colleagues, seniors and your goodself.

Kindly acknowledge,

Yours Sincerely.

(Parveen Hans)

TERMINATION LETTER/LAY-OFF LETTER

National Computers (India) Ltd.

Regd. Office : Charminar Road
Hyderabad (India)
Tel. : 022-2737091, 2737092

Dated: 29th August, 2009

Dear Mr. Suman Verma

As you are aware, the recent economic slowdown have created a profound effect on almost all industries and service sectors alike. The sales of our company have dropped 40% in past six months. Though we donot expect this to be very long term phenomenon, we donot expect our sales to return to normal level in the next one year or so.

Due to the loss in business, we regret to inform you that we are closing our service and maintenance section at Delhi which employs approximately 85 employees. We deeply regret that your services shall also be terminated.

As per the conditions of employment, you will be entitled to one month's salary, which will be paid in full along with your next pay cheque and other benefits.

We appreciate your hard work and dedication at National Computers (India) Ltd, and will be glad to consider you for appointment, whenever the need arises.

Sincerely,

(B.K. Bhatt)
Manager: H.R.

G

Given below are some suggested topics under Alphabet 'G'

Goodwill Letters

- Announcing an employee health scheme.
- Announcing a company saving/investment plan.
- Announcing ESOPs (Employee Stock options).
- Announcing completion of important projects.
- Keeping employees informed of company's progress.
- Keeping customers informed of company's future plans.
- Invitation to clients & staff for Business Associates meeting.
- Invitation letters to dealers to visit company's plants.
- Announcing exceptional/best achievement performance by an employee or a department and offering a reward.

QUICK TIPS FOR WRITING GOODWILL LETTERS

Goodwill letters are either announcement letters or congratulating letters. They are most effective to build and enhance business relationships, provided :

- A goodwill letter should always be written in positive tone.
- A goodwill letter should be honest and sincere in approach.
- A goodwill letter should focus on the recipient (whether employee or client or business associate). Self (or company's) appreciation has no place in a goodwill letter.
- A goodwill letter should be clearly distinguished from a sales letter. Its sole objective is to spread goodwill, create confidence and enhance loyality towards the company.
- The letter should be specific and accurate in detail. Any type of generalisation should be avoided.
- Goodwill letters are solely written for :
  - — expressing gratitude,
  - — appreciating performance/achivements,
  - — recognition of good work/job well done,
  - — offering awards or rewards (optional)
- The goodwill letter should be carefully worded, professional and result-oriented.

Govenment letters

There may be innumerable situations originating in business necessitating the writing of letters to Government organisation, Government Deparment or Government Agencies. Some of these are listed below :

- Write a letter to Income Tax Officer for I.T. Refund.

- Write a letter to Income Tax Officer for Income Tax Clearance Certificate
- Application for grant of REP licence.
- Application for allotment of PAN.
- Application for issue of a Passport.
- Application for refund of TDS.
- Application for enhancement of Powerload (To Electricity Department).
- Application for Registration as a Small Scale Industry.
- Application for exemption from Octroi Duty on Imports (Inter-state).
- Application for exemption from Customer Duty on Imports.
- Application for grant of 'Export House' status.
- Application for the listing of shares of the company at the stock exchange.
- Letter providing required information to a Government Department.
- Letter requesting a Government Department or Agency for Prompt action.
- Requesting information from a Government office (under The Right to Information Act).
- Disputing a demand made by a Government Agency.
- Filing an appeal against Penal action by a Government Department.
- Complaint letter about ineffciencies of a Government Department.
- Complaint letter regarding excessive electricity bill.

QUICK TIPS FOR WRITING GOVERNMENT LETTERS

Government letters should be very carefully written, as they may be used as legal documents in future. After writing, these must be checked and re-checked for contents, facts, details and the purpose they serve.

- A Government letter should :
  - — Clearly state the purpose for which it is written
  - — Clearly intimate sender's name, address, status/position in the company, he/she represents
  - — Clearly state reference no./date/subject line of Government office's letter which is being replied.
- A Government letter should be addressed to a particular individual stating clearly his designation/position & address of the department concerned.
- A Government letter should be brief, concise, to the point and straight forward. Phraseology or flowery language is a strict NO-NO.
- If the letter contains a complaint, substantiate your claim by relevant facts, documents, reports and other relevant material.
- If the letter disputes the claim made by the Government Department, provide complete details of your version on the subject.

- Before writing Government letters, sender should do adequate research and present his arguments in logical and legal manner.
- If the sender disputes a Government claim, he/she should also indicate what action/ adjustment he anticipates through action on his letter.
- The sender may also request, through the letter, permission for personal audience with the Government officer/department concerned.
- A follow up letter may be sent, a few days after the original letter is sent to a Government office to evince response.
- Letter should be written in polite and positive tone. It should remain courteous and respectful.
- A copy of every government letter received or written should be kept as permanent record of the organisation.
- A Government letter should inverıably be written in a formal style. Informal style may be used for some other types of letters.

A few examples of "Goodwill" and "Government Letters" are given in the following pages :

LETTER TO POST MASTER COMPLAINING ABOUT NON-DELIVERY OF A SPEED POST/REGISTERED ARTICLE

Hare Krishna Industries

39, Baba Kharag Singh Marg,
Connaught Circus,
New Delhi-110001
Tel. : 011-26459062-63
e-mail : harekrishna@gmail.com.

Dated : 15th October, 2009

The Head Post Master
General Post Office,
Gole Dakkhana,
New Delhi-110001

Sub. : Non-delivery of a speed post article

Re. : Speed Post mail no. 01234 dt. 3rd oct. 2009

Dear Sir,

We had sent an article containing valuable documents on 3rd Oct. 2009 via speed post from your post office to M/s. Kewal Krishan Enterprises, Gomti Road, Lucknow (U.P.) we have been telephonically informed by the said party that the speed post has still not reached them. It is causing us great anxiety and fear of loss.

You are earnestly requested to make necessary enquiries to trace the whereabouts of the above speed post envolope and arrange for its delivery to the addressee at an early date.

Sincerely,

(Proprietor)

Encl.: Copy of Speed Post Receipt.

LETTER TO STATE ELECTRICITY BOARD FOR CHANGE OF NAME AND LOAD ENHANCEMENT

Yogesh Kumar Mongia

BXlX - 529, Rishi Nagar,
Income Tax Colony
Ludhiana (Punjab) 141009
Tel.: 0161-6549352

Dated : 18th November, 2009

The Accounts Manager
Punjab State Electricity Board,
Kitchlu Nagar,
Ludhiana (Punjab)

Sub. : Request for change of name and load enhancement.

Dear Sir,

I have recently purchased this property in my name and want to get the name of owner changed in your records. I am enclosing the following documents for this purpose, alongwith this letter :

1. Agreement of Sale of House Property in my favour.
2. N.O.C. from previous owner to ger the name changed.
3. Application form prescribed for the purpose completed and signed.

In addition, I would also request you to enhance the electricity load on my meter from 2KW. to 5KW., as I am interested in installation of Two 1.5 tonne Air Conditioners at my home. Kindly add the conversion charges in the electricity bill for next billing cycle.

Thanking in anticipation,

Sincerely,

(Yogesh Kumar Mongia)

Encl. : 3 (As above)

LETTER TO INCOME TAX OFFICER FOR ISSUE OF I.T.C.C.

Ashok Kumar Malhotra

232, Ist Floor, Block PW,
Pitam Pura, (East)
New Delhi 110015
Tel. : 011-64294119

Dated : 20th November, 2009

The Income Tax Officer
Ward 45 Circle (2)
Aayakar Bhawan,
I.T.O., New Delhi 110001

Re : My PAN CN35P9052E

Sub. : Request to issue I.T.C.C.

Sir,

I am planning to visit my brother, an American citizen at Virginia City, Texas state in the United States, with my wife to attend the marriage of my Nephew in the month of January, 2010.

I need foreign exchange of US $ 5,000 and a U.S. visa from the Consulate General, Embassy of U.S. in India. For both the puproses, I need I.T.C.C. (Income Tax Clearance Certificate) issued by your office.

Please note that my I.T. returns have been filed and have also been assessed uptodate.

Kindly issue the I.T.C.C. at an early date to facilitate the formalities of Visa, foreign exchange etc.

Thanks

Sincerely,

(Ashok Kumar Malhotra)

LETTER TO RAILWAY AUTHORITIES COMPLAINING ABOUT DAMAGE OF PARCEL IN TRANSIT

Rakesh Sehgal

B-22, New Moti Nagar,
Ludhiana (Punjab)
Tel. : 0161-6429527

Dated : 29th September, 2009

The Station Master
Ludhiana Main Railway Station,
Near Clock Towers,
Ludhiana. 141001

Sub. : Damage of Parcel in Transit.

Re. : Railway Receipt No. 03597Y dated 4th Sept. 2009

Dear Sir

I have just taken delivery of the parcel containing damaged watches and watch parts vide R.R. No. 03597Y dated 4th September, 2009 sent by Mr. R.K. Gupta from New Delhi Rly. Station.

As I have taken open delivery duly signed by the Delivery clerk in whose presence the parcel was opened, I estimate the value of loss to the tune of Rs. 6,500.

I am submitting a claim form duly completed and signed for Rs. 6,500/- alongwith a copy of Railway Receipt duly authenticated by Railway clerk on the back side in witness of open delivery and damaged stock.

As the stock was duly insured, you are requested to process the claim at the earliest.

I shall be ready to produce the stock before Railway authorities for inspection and assessment of damage in connection with settlement of claim.

Kindly acknowledge receipt.

Sincerely,

(Rakesh Sehgal)

Encl. : 2 (As above)

LETTER APPLYING FOR REPLENISHMENT LICENCE

Pearl Auto Accessories Ltd.

Regd. Office :
3rd Level, Tribhuwan Towers,
Worli-Kurla Road,
Mumbai - 400093
Tel. : 022-70925694
http : //www.pearlauto.com/India

Dated : 29th November, 2009

The Controller of Imports & Exports
Ministry of Commerce,
Govt. of India
Worli (East),
Mumbai . 400079

Sub. : Replenishment Licence for Imports

Sir,

Our company is a registered exporter with your office and we export large quantities of Auto Accessories under our brand name 'PEARL' to several countries in the South-East Asia. During the last three months, we have exported stocks worth Rs. 1.50 corers (equivalent U.S. $ 3,00,000 approximately) we are therefore entitled to 30% Replenishment licence for import of goods which amounts to US $ 90,000 approx. worth of import licence for actual users category.

We are submitting you following documents, as required under the rules for processing of our import licence :

1. Application form for import licence duly completed and signed.

2. Copies of our export invoices for the last 3 months totalling Rs. 1.50 crores Approx. (Equivalent US $ 3,00,000)

3. Statement of Bank A/c as a proof of deposit of foreign currency worth US $ 3,00,000 in State Bank of India, Worli (West) Branch, Mumbai.

4. Certificate from State Bank of India certifying the deposit of above amount of foreign currency with them.

5. A bank guarantee of Rs. 50 lacs for making payment against the Replenishment licence.

6. An undertaking that the Rep-licence shall be used for our own purposes and not for resale.

7. An indemnity bond, as specified.

Kindly process the application on an urgent basis as we wish to place confirm order with our foreign suppliers.

We would be ready to complete any pending formalities, as and when required.

Sincerely,

(Director : Exports)

Encl. : 7(As above)

REQUEST LETTER FOR OCTROI-EXEMPTION

Neelgagan Stationers (P) Ltd.

Regd. office;
F- 37, Model Town (Main Road)
Panipat (Haryana)
Tel. : 95124 : 7259351-53

Dated : 15th November, 2009

The Commissioner,
Panipat Municipal Corporation,
Panipat (Haryana)

Sub. : Request for exemption letter (Octroi charges)

Dear Sir,

We are manufacturers of school note books, diaries, drawing registers, drawing sheets, typing papers, and other paper products for use in schools, Colleges and offices. We import raw paper from Mysore, Baroda and Pune.

We understand that paper and paper products like note books, diaries, pads, drawing sheets etc. are exempted from levy of octroi charges in the state of Haryana via State Government Circular no. Octroi/1356/26/8/09

We, therefore, request you to issue us exemption certificate for payment of octroi charges on paper and paper products imported by us from outside Haryana, so that the consignments from Mysore, Baroda, Pune etc. may be brought in by carriers free of octroi.

Sincerely,

(H.K. Dua)
Manager : Purchase

I

Given below are some suggested topics under Alphabet 'I'

Inquiry letters

The following are some of the business situations when inquiry letters are written.

- Requesting information on a subject/product or service
- Sending information
- Requesting information of any type under the Right to Information Act,
- Requesting a copy of an official document,
- Requesting information through a mailed questionnaire.
- Requesting information from a Government office
- Requesting sending of samples of products
- Requesting estimates, bids, tenders etc.
- Reply/Response to any of the above Enquiry Letters.
- Follow up of an Inquiry Letter, if no response is received in reasonable time.

Types of Inquiry letters

Inquiry (Enquiry) letters are basically of the following types :

1. Solicited Inquiry
2. Unsolicited Inquiry
3. Credit Inquiry (or Status Inquiry).

1. Solicited Inquiry: During competition every seller tries to approach prospective buyer directly or indirectly. Direct approach may mean through travelling salesmen or sales representative. Indirect approach may mean collecting the names and addresses of buyers and contacting them. In the process, the buyer may enquire from the seller the detailed terms and conditions for buying the product. This secondary approach by the buyer is called ***'solicited enquiry'***.

2. Unsolicited Inquiry: Sometimes, a buyer, in need of a product, may collect the names and addresses of different sellers through different sources (e.g., advertisements, trade journals etc.). In case he wants to know the details of the product or terms and conditions for buying the product, he may send an inquiry letter to such sellers. This primary or direct approach by the buyer is called ***'Unsolicited Inquiry'***.

3. Credit Inquiry: When a new buyer wants to buy a product on credit basis, the seller, before giving credit, may try to find out buyer's credit-worthiness and/or status in the market. The seller may write to the buyer asking him to provide names and addresses of some businessmen, with whom he has business dealings. Letters written to these business (called credit-references) about the credit-worthiness of the buyer are called 'Credit Inquiry' letters.[1]

1. Also see business Communication: R.C. Bhatia; Ane's Student Edition. 2007.

QUICK TIPS FOR WRITING INQUIRY LETTERS

Since inquiry letters are request letters to elicit information, they should, under all circumstances be courteous. The reply/response to an enquiry letter necessitate spending of time and resources by the recipient, the following guidelines should be adhered to by the sender of an inquiry letter.

- Inquiry letter should not elicit information that is easily available through other sources e.g., business directories, corporate websites, internet etc.
- An inquiry letter should :
  - — be short, brief and concise
  - — be long enough to explain what is being enquired about.
  - — assure the recipient that the information supplied will be kept confidential
  - — assure the recipient that the information supplied will not be put to any commercial use, without authorisation by the supplier.
- The sender of inquiry letter should enclose either postal stamps or self addressed envelope or reimbursement of recipient's costs of typing, photocopying or mailing of information. or, atleast offer to compensate him as a courtery measure.
- Any questionnaire, blank forms, particular formats or other documents should also be properly enclosed with the inquiry letter to enable the response quick and fast.
- The sender should also provide his complete contact information so that the receiver may respond on phone, via e-mail or otherwise, instead of writing letters.
- The inquiry letter should indicate the time factor, i.e; the date by which the reply is expected by the sender.
- The sender should also send a 'Thank you letter" on receipt of the required information.
- The sender should wait for a few days or a week for response after which a polite reminder letter may be sent.
- Business Ethics demand that one should not openly ask for anybody's financial position, dealings, networth etc.
- A 'Status' inquiry letter should essentially contain the following:
  - — A request to provide information (opinion as well) about the prospective customer's dealings, standing etc.
  - — An assurance of keeping the information 'confidential'.
  - — An expression of thankfulness.
  - — A self-addressed stamped evelope for reply.
  - — Marking of ***"Confidential"*** or ***"Private & Confidential"*** on the envelope of the letter.
- A reply to a 'Status' inquiry letter should essentially contain the following:
  - — A reference of the 'Status' inquiry letter.

— The period of dealings with the concerned firm or party.

— A general information (without responsibility) about the firm's dealings, payments, turnover, goodwill etc.

— The present position of Assets/Liabilities of the firm (if known).

— An opinion about the limit of credit, period of credit etc. which may be allowed by the seller to the buyer firm.

— A mention must be made that the opinion/information being supplied is without liability or recourse and should be kept secret and confidential.

QUICK TIPS FOR RESPONDING TO AN INQUIRY LETTER

- The response letter should specify the reference number and subject line of the inquiry letter.
- If possible, the receiver should personally respond to the letter.
- It is advisable not to give any advice or recommendation in response to an enquiry letter to avoid any future legal consequence.
- If the recipient can't personally reply/respond to an enquiry letter, he should:

  — express regret being unable to help;

  — provide contact information of the person who can provide information ; or

  — delegate someone to provide information
- A response letter should expressly absolve the writer of any legal liability arising out of providing such information.
- The response letter should close by saying :

  — That you would be happy to help the reader again in the future, if he/she needs any further assistance ; or

  — Wish the applicant well in his endeavour/effort/project etc.

Insurance Letters

Just like Banking letters, Insurance letter are a category of its own, Both are needs of every business enterprise. Innumerable situations may arise in business to write insurance letters, some of which are stated below :

- Request for issue of a fire/Marine/General Insurance Policy
- Request for Medi-claim policy for the staff .
- Reply of Insurance Company for Medi-claim Policy
- Entertaining Medi-claim of an Employee.
- Rejecting a claim under Medi-claim Policy.
- Request for life insurance.
- Request for loan against surrender value of a Life Policy.

- Letter to insurance company for Marine claim.
- Reply of Insurance Company on above letter.
- Intimation of fire claim.
- Under-insurance (plea) raised by Insurance Co.
- Settlement of claim.
- Request for issue of a floating Insurance Policy.
- Reply to the above.
- Motor car Insurance-disputing claim.
- Application for Insurance Agency.
- Reply to the above application.

QUICK TIPS FOR WRITING INSURANCE LETTERS

- Letter to or by the Insurance Company should be carefully written.
- The tone of the letter should be positive, language simple and straight forward.
- The Reference must indicate the Policy No. or your relationship with the Insurance Company.
- The subject line must clearly state the subject for which the letter is being written, e.g., request for issue of a policy, payment, claim under the policy, settlement of claim etc..
- The letter must contain complete detail about the subject matter e.g., in a fire claim letter, the policy number, date of policy, amount of policy, the outbreak of fire (with date, time) the efforts taken to mitigate the loss, the expected loss, the probable reason (if any) of the fire and so on.
- The letter must specify clearly what is expected of the receiver; e.g.

  — to appoint surveyor,

  — to make assessment of loss,

  — to settle claim,
- Similarly, in the case of a medi-claim, the sender must specify when and where (date, time and place) the claiment fell sick, the nature of sickness, the diagnostic tests undertaken, details of hospitalisation, expense vouchers, net claim under the policy and so on.
- In a reply by insurance company, if the claim is not admissible or is outside the purview of the policy, the insurance company must state the reasons of rejection, specifying the terms and conditions of the policy leading to such rejection etc..
- An insurance letter must be carefully worded as it may become a legal document in case of future disputes.
- A copy of every insurance letter should be preserved for future records.

Introduction Letters

Introduction letters are written to introduce a company, organisation, product ro service. They serve the purpose similar to that of the Sales Letter. A few out of the numerous situations that may arise in business for writing Introduction letters are mentioned below :

- To introduce a business, product, service or a professional contact.
- To introduce a new employee in the organisation.
- To announce the opening of a new store, branch, office or showroom
- To introduce a new partner in the firm.
- To introduce someone to the organisation.

'Introduction Letters' and 'Announcement letters' often caters to the same or similar situations in business. Please refer to the Tips for writing 'Announcement Letters' for writing 'Introduction Letters' as well.

Invitation Letters

On many occasions in business, invitation letters are issued to clients, customers, employees, acquaintances, business associates and the like. On many occasions either printed cards are used or Cards/Letters are specifically printed for a particular occasion when invitation letters are to be sent. An invitation may be extended to an individual, a group of persons/organisation/employees/ associates etc. Some of the situations when invitation letters are issued, are given below :

- Extend a formal invitation to someone.
- Invite a customer(s) to a sales exhibition organised by the company.
- Invite business associates for a business presentation.
- Invite someone for a sales appointment.
- Invite someone for a product demonstration.
- Invite prospective customers to a product exhibition.
- Invite someone for a business appointment.
- Invite someone for a training session of employees.
- Invite someone to a business event/conference/meeting/seminar etc.
- Invitation to attend a business anniversary.
- Invitation to attend a business award function.
- Invitation to attend the opening of a new showroom.
- Accepting Invitation (any of the above invitations).

QUICK TIPS FOR WRITING INVITATION LETTERS

- When someone is invited, he becomes a guest and should be treated like that, honourably, respectfully and cordially.

- The invitation letter should clearly explain the event (name of the event, date, day, time, venue, entry/admission/registration formalities required, etc.
- If the event is a special purpose (e.g., celebrating a business anniversary, or honouring someone), it should be stated clearly in the letter.
- The tone of the invitation letter should be positive and respectful (always).
- If the event is a retirement, anniversary or honouring someone, state clearly if gifts are not expected. Otherwise, don't mention.
- If the event requires invitees to follow a dress code, it must be mentioned.
- Request attendance of the recipient at the event/function/presentation/exhibition, as the case may be.
- The invitation letter should be sent sufficiently in advance to the date of the event. A 10-15 days gap would be reasonable.
- The invitee may be requested to confirm his attendence by a specified date.
- If the event would be followed by a lunch or dinner, it must be clearly indicated in the letter with a request to the invitee to stay back for it.
- If gift hampers are to be given to those attending the event, a printed coupon (preferably numbered and signed) should be enclosed with the letter, to facilitate easy distribution.

A few sample letters covering Inquiry Letters, Insurance letters, Introduction letters, Invitation Letters etc. are given in the following pages:

LETTER REQUESTING INFORMATION

Hitech Services Pvt. Ltd.

B-2/375 Aggarwal Bhawan
Bhikaji Cama Place,
New Delhi-110035
Tel. : 011-47592732 Fax : 011-55792732
e-mail : info@hitech.com

Dated : 22nd December, 2009

To,

M/s Perfect Systems
2/17 Hari Nagar,
New Delhi-110089

Sub. : Brouchure and Price list

Dear Sir,

I should be grateful if you would send us your brochure and price list about the services provided by you in respect of development and maintenance of website, on an annual and long term basis.

We are dealing with providing technology Consultancy Services to a large section of industries in different sectors. We are currently developing our web-sites and are intersted in awarding long term contracts for its development and maintenance.

Looking forward to hearing from you.

Yours faithfully,

(S.K. Srivastava)
Manager : Information Technology.

LETTER SENDING INFORMATION

Perfect Systems

2/17 Hari Nagar,
New Delhi-110089
Tel. : 011-65359870
Fax - 011-65359877
e-mail : psystem@yahoo.com.

Dated : 25th December, 2009

Mr. S.K. Srivastava
Manager (Information Technology),
M/s Hitech Services Pvt. Ltd.
B-2/375, Aggarwal Bhawan,
Bhikaji Cama Place,
New Delhi-110035

Sub. : Our Services & Fees

Dear Mr. Srivastava,

Thank you for your letter of 22nd December, 2009 enquiring about our services and fees etc.

Perfect systems offer a full range of web related services to help you in the development of your own websites and their subsequent maintenance. I have pleasure in enclosing our latest brochures and price list. You will find our prices to be most competitive and our services highly reliable.

Looking forward to further communication from you.

Yours Sincerely,

(Parveen Hans)
Sales Manager

Encl. : 2

LETTER OF INVITATION

Home Town Stores
(House of Furniture & Accessories)
Mehrauli-Gurgaon Road
New Delhi-110017
Tel. : 011-29325656

Dated: 27th November, 2009

Dear Valued Customer,

You are one of our frequent customers, who have been patronising us since last several years. We greatly value our association with you and invite you to the GRAND Exhibition Cum sale being organised by us in the month of December.

The Grand Exhibition-cum-sale shall be a 7 days event from 15-12-2009 to 21-12-2009 (Both days Inclusive). The Exhibition-cum-sale shall be held at Pragati Maidan, Hall no. 7 in the 12000 sq. feet area which shall be fully air-conditioned. The entry shall be from Gate no. 5. Timings being 9:00 A.M. to 9 P.M.

As a gesture, we are sending you a gift certificate of Rs. 1,000 which you may use with your purchase of Rs. 5,000 onwards.

A Free Parking sticker is also enclosed.

We look forward to seeing you at the Grand event. Please bring this invitation for free entry.

Yours Sincerely

(Sheila Chauhan)
Sales Manager

Encl. : 2

LETTER INDICATING EXPRESSION OF INTEREST

Fit-outfits (India) Ltd.

(Garments for the Fit and Young)
F-32, Naraina Industrial Area Phase I,
Naraina, New Delhi-110029
Tel. : 011-26354243, 26354244
e-mail : fitoutfits@yahoo.com

Dated : 7th October, 2009

The Advertiser
M/s Reliance Fashions Ltd.
32, Ambience Towers,
Vile Parle (West), Mumbai

Sub. : Expression of Interest in your project.

Dear Sir,

Through the Advertisement in The Hindustan Times, dated 5th October, 2009, that you are looking for regular suppliers of readymade garments under your 'Reliance' brand on a long term basis.

Our company is an established source of high quality manufacturer of readymade garments for all ages and sexes and for all occasions since last 15 years. We have been a preferred supplier for several renowned brands like 'Provogue', 'Ebony', 'Hi-life', 'Seven-days', 'Red Bull', 'Charlie Outlaw', 'Koutons' and many more for the last 8-10 years.

Our quality is unmatched. Our complaint/defect Ratio has been 0.05 percent as against the Industry average of 0.35 per cent. We follow the policy of *'Instant replacement-No questions asked'*. Our installed capacity is to produce 1500 units per day, i.e. 4.50 lacs pieces per annum. We may raise the capacity to double at a short notice.

We would be highly interested in being on your penel of 'Preferred Suppliers' of high quality garments under a long term contract.

As a gesture, we offer you to send a team of your purchase department to inspect the quality and quantity, we can offer.

Looking forward to doing business with your company.

Sincerely,

(Vijay Kumar Malhotra)
Director : Marketing

INSURANCE LETTER: INTIMATION OF FIRE & FIRE CLAIM

Clairmont Supplies
(Electrical & Electronics Stores)
Bhikaji Cama Road, Goregaon (East)
Mumbai-400063
Tel. : 022-62423759-60

Dated : 17th October, 2009

The Manager
Oriental Insurance Co. Ltd.
Matunga Branch, Matunga (West),
Mumbai-400049

Ref. : Our Fire Policy, No. KY094732107 Dt. 12th July 2009 for Rs. 75 lacs

Sub. : Intimation of Fire and Fire claim

Sir,

We regret to inform you that a fire broke out at our electronics showroom at Bhikaji Cama Road, Goregaon (East) on the night of 13th & 14th October, 2009 at approx. 11.50 p.m. Our security guard immediately phoned the Fire Brigade and the Police which reached within 12 minutes.

In the process of extinguishing fire, heavy dose of water was pumped at very high pressure into the showroom after breaking and removing the shutters. Due to fire and water, almost entire stock lying at the showroom was gutted and became only a debris of waste.

The initial investigation by the Fire Department point to the 'short circuit' as the most probable cause of fire. Apparently, there is no reason to suspect any sabotage causing the incident.

According to our books of accounts, the value of stock lying in the showroom on the date of fire, amounted to Rs. 29,71,000/- which amount is fully covered under the above policy.

We are enclosing a claim form duly filled in alongwith a report of the fire department and a copy of our Insurance Policy with your company.

You are requested to process our claim so as to enable us to restart our business.

Sincerely,

(Shri Ram Chaudhary)
Partner

Encl. : 3 (As above)

REQUEST FOR THE ISSUE OF A POLICY

Black, White & Colour Printers,
Progressive Lane, Station Road,
Worli (West), Mumbai - 400019
Tel. : 022-42197979-80

Dated : 30th September, 2009

The Manager,
United India Insurance Co. Ltd.,
Keshav Patil Road, Worli (West)
Mumbai - 400019

Sub. : Proposal for Fire Insurance of Stock

Dear Sir,

Please refer to our telephonic conversation on the above subject. Your representative Mr. Vilas Rao Patil visited us and inspected our godowns and showrooms. As per his instructions, we are sending the following documents with a request to issue insurance cover of Rs. 25 lacs on our stocks, furniture, fitting, equipments & accessories at our showroom and Godown.

1. Proposal form for Insurance Cover
2. Stock Statement as on 31-03-2009
3. Audited Balance Sheet and P&L Account for the year ending 31st March, 2009
4. A cheque for Rs. 15,675/= being the Premium for the fire Insurance.

You are requested to issue a cover note with immediate effect.

A line in confirmation shall be solicited.

Sincerely,

(R.K. Deshmukh)
Partner

Encl. : 4 (As above)

REPLY TO THE ABOVE LETTER

United India Insurance Co. Ltd.

Keshav Patel Road
Worli (West), Mumbai-400019
Tel. : 022-42193141-46

Dated : 4th october, 2009

Mr. R.K. Deshmukh
Partner,
M/s Black, White and Colour Printers,
Station Road, Worli (West)
Mumbai-400019

Sub. : Insurance Cover for fire

Dear Sir,

Kindly refer to your letter dated 30th September 2009, we are pleased to a cover note for fire Insurance over your stocks, furniture, fittings, equipment and accessories in your showroom and godown upto a limit of Rs. 25 lacs, subject to realisation of cheque.

The cover note no. 2890 dated 3rd October 2009, effective from midnight of 3rd/4th October 2009 and valid till the midnight of 2nd/3rd October 2010, is enclosed with this letter.

While we appreciate you understand the desirability of getting an insurance cover for stock etc., we caution you against the risks of under-insurance.

While reviewing your stock statement and the balance sheet as on 31st March 2009, we find that your stock alone values Rs. 35 lacs at cost. Add to this the value of your furniture, equipment and accessories, the total value exceeds Rs. 40 lacs. Surely, you are under-insured to the extent of Rs. 15 lacs at the least.

One of the major risk of under-insurance is that, in the unforeseen event of loss, the insurance Co. will only be liable to the extent of actual insurance as a ratio of total value of goods insured. In our case, your loss, if it arises, will be covered in the ratio of 25 lacs: 40 lacs (i.e. 5/8th). In simple terms, if you suffer a loss of Rs. 10 lacs by fire, Insurance Co. will pay you a claim of Rs. 6.25 lacs only (being 5/8th of actual loss).

May we suggest that you, in your own interest avoid under-insurance of your goods and act accordingly.

We assure you of our best services, at all times.

Sincerely,

(Vishesh Patel)
Manager

Encl. : Cover Note

SETTLEMENT OF CLAIM (FIRE INSURANCE)

Oriental Insurance Co. Ltd.

Matunga Branch, Matunga (West)
Mumbai-400049
Tel. : 022-32914141, 42, 46

Dated : 2nd November, 2009

Mr. Shri Ram Chaudhary,
Partner
M/s Clairmont Supplies,
Bhikaji Cama Road,
Goregaon (East), Mumbai-400063

Re : Fire Policy no. KY 0934732107 Dt. 12th July 2009

Sub. : Settlement of your Fire Claim

Dear Mr. Chaudhary,

Kindly refer to your letter dated 17th October 2009, regarding a fire claim of Rs. 29,71,000 submitted by you alongwith necessary documents.

We have received a report of our surveyors, who have valued your loss estimated at Rs. 22,50,000 which includes the value of stocks (at cost) at Rs. 19,75,000 and the depreciated value of your furniture, equipment and accessories at Rs. 2,75,000. We are also adding Rs. 1,20,000 since your policy also covered consequential loss clause arising out of loss by fire. A draft for Rs. 23,70,000 being in full and final settlement of your claim is enclosed herewith. Kindly acknowledge receipt.

Sincerely,

(Hari Parsad Dhotiwala)
Manager

Encl. : Draft No. 324569 Dt. 1st Nov. 2009, for Rs. 23,70,000
on Dena Bank favouring yourself.

RAISING LOAN AGAINST SURRENDER VALUE OF A LIFE POLICY

Satish Bhatia

291, Sakshra Apartments,
Mayur Vihar,
New Delhi-110029
Tel. : 011-64902325

Dated : 3rd November, 2009

The Manager,
Life Insurance Corp. of India
PNB Building, Parliament Street
New Delhi 110001

Re : My life Policy no. 5035729143 issued by your Branch

Sub. : Request to grant loan against Assignment of Policy

Dear Sir,

I had taken the above policy for Rs . 5 lacs for 20 years, during the year 1995. My enquiries from your branch have revealed that the policy has a surrender value of Rs. 2,65,000/- as of now. According to the terms of the policy, the policyholder can take a loan upto 90% of the surrender value of the policy upon assignment of the policy in favour of LIC of India.

I need an urgent loan of Rs. 2 lacs, for the purpose of meeting educational expenses of my son, who is pursuing engineering course at I.I.T. Delhi. The amount of loan is within the permissible limit of allowable loan.

I am surrendering the original policy duly assigned in favour of LIC of India alongwith a request form duly filled in alongwith copies of my I.D. Proof and Residence proof required for the purpose.

Kindly process the application at the earliest under intimation to me.

Sincerely,

(Satish Bhatia)

Encl. : 2 (As above)

REQUEST FOR ISSUE OF FLOATING MARINE POLICY

NUMERO UNO Apparels
(Exporters of Designer Wears)
Lalbhai Mills Compound,
Borevali (West),
Mumbai - 400059
Tel. : 022-42993271-76
http. : //www.numerouno.com

Dated : 15th November, 2009

M/s United India Insurance Co. Ltd.
Mahatma Gandhi Road,
Mumbai-400001

Sub. : Request for Floating Marine Policy

Dear Sir,

Our Exports Divison has been able to penetrate into Scandenevian Markets of Europe. We have received substantial export orders from firms in **Norway, Sweden, Denmark, Estonia, Finland** and **St. Pitts Berg** for our quality designer wears.

In the next two weeks, we would be exporting huge quantities of stocks to these countries. We, therefore, need to have a floating marine policy for an annual value limited to Rs. 10 crores.

Kindly arrange to send your representative with necessary proposal forms and also quote your lowest rate fot the above policy on F.A.A. (free of all average) and A.A.R. (against all risks) basis and outline the working of such a policy.

An early execution of Policy will be solicited

Sincerely,

(N.R. Subramaniam)
Exports Manager

REPLY TO THE ABOVE

United India Insurance Co. Ltd.

Mahatma Gandhi Road,
Mumbai - 400001
Tel. : 022-42914437-40

Dated : 18th November, 2009

The Exports Manager,

M/s Numero UNO Apparels,
Borewali (West),
Mumbai - 400059

Sub. : Your request for floating Marine Policy

Dear Sir,

We thank you for your proposal to obtain a floating Marine policy for your export stocks.

Please be informed that the rates of floating marine policy varies from 2.75% to 3.50% (Per Thousand) depending upon following parameters :

(i) Port of Destination (Efficient vs Inefficient Port)
(ii) Distance covered.
(iii) Value of lot consigned.
(iv) Container load or loose consignment
(v) Nature of Packing (Wooden boxes or bags, waterproof packing or otherwise)
(vi) Frequency of consignment.
(vii) Perils covered.
(viii) Total Value of Policy.

An additional load factor of 0.25% for F.A.A. and 0.50% for A.A.R clauses will be added. Service Tax is added on the Total amount of Premium.

Our representative Mr. B.K. Pandey will be visiting your office within next 2 days (with prior appointment), to complete the formalities and explain to you the working of a floating marine policy.

Kindly feel free to ask for any queries.

Sincerely,

(Avinash Chander)
Manager.

LETTER TO INSURANCE CO. FOR MARINE CLAIM

Suzlon Energy Equipments Ltd.

Regd. Office :
Vani Road, Bangaluru (Karnataka)
L-32, Express Building,
Lala Lajpat Rai Marg,
Mumbai -400039
Tel. : 022-66224841-45
http : //www.suzlonenergy.com

Dated : 20th September, 2009

The Manager,
M/s New India Assurance Co. Ltd.,
37, Raheja Chambers,
Bhulabhai Desai Road,
Mumbai - 400029

Re : Our Marine Policy No. K094573019 Dt. 15th July, 2009

Sub. : Intimation of Marine Loss

Dear Sir,

Kindly refer to our letter no. 1235 dated 10th August, 2009 for endorsing of our consignment of Energy Equipments vide Invoice no. PX/0395/2009 to Spain Ex Madrid for the value of INR. 3,50,00,000 (Rs. 3.50 crores), under above policy shipped via S.S. Seaqueen shipped on 12th August Ex Mumbai Port.

We have received an intimation from our consignees at spain that the stocks have been badly damaged in Transit. He has refused to take delivery of the stock resulting in Total loss to us.

The stocks are lying at MADRID Port, which may be inspected by your surveyors/agents. We are enclosing the following documents for processing of our claim under the above marine policy :

1. Copy of our Insurance Policy issued by your office.
2. Authority letter on our company's letterhead for allowing inspection of damaged stock to Port Authorities at Spain.
3. Copy of our Invoice.

4. Copy of Bill of lading.
5. Packing list
6. Copy of Bill of entry
7. Claim from duly filled in.
8. Damage Report by the consignee.

Kindly depute your surveyor for the assessment of damage or loss for an early settlement of claim.

Please acknowledge receipt.

Sincerely,

(Sudhanshu Mittal)
Manager, Exports

Encl. : 8 (As above)

REPLY TO THE ABOVE LETTER

New India Assurance Co. Ltd.

Regd. Office :
87, Mahatma Gandhi Road, Mumbai
37, Raheja Chambers, Bhulabhai Desai Road,
Mumbai-400029
Tel. : 022-47329501-06

Dated : 7th October, 2009

The Exports Manager,
Suzlon Energy Equipments Ltd.,
L-32, Express Building,
Lala Lajpat Rai Marg,
Mumbai-400039

Re : Your Marine Policy No. K0934573019 dt. 15th July, 2009

Sub. : Your claim under the policy Dt. 20th September, 2009

Dear Sir,

We are in receipt of a Report from our surveyors who have inspected the stock shipped by you at Port Madrid, Spain vide your Invoice no. PX/0395/2009 of the value of INR 3.50 crores on Dated 12th August, 2009 from Mumbai Post.

We are enclosing a copy of our surveyor's report which in brief states as follows :

1. Out of 115 wooden cases shipped by you, 42 cases were damaged, leaving the remaining in perfectly deliverable condition.
2. The value of 42 wooden cases, reportedly damaged, stands at Rs. 91,37,500 according to invoice value.
3. The damaged stock may be disposed of in the local market at Madrid at 40% less than the Invoice value. This means a sum of Rs. 55 lacs Approx. may be recovered leaving a balance of Rs. 36 lacs as irrecoverable loss.

We are sending you a fresh claim form to enable you file your claim afresh.

Assuring you of our best services at all times

Sincerely,

(Sudhir. K. Patil)
Manager.

Encl. : Copy of Surveyor's Report

LETTER REQUESTING FOR MEDI-CLAIM POLICY

Modern Retail Point (P) Ltd.

(A Unit of Future Business Solutions)
Regd. Office : 632 East Park Road, Delhi-110007
F-23, IInd Floor, Shoppers Stop,
Fort, Mumbai- 400023
Tel. : 022-42973211-16

Dated : 15th October, 2009

The Branch Manager
United India Insurance Co. Ltd.
Divisional Office No.3,
Fort, Mumbai - 400023

Sub. : Request for issue of Medi-claim Policy

Dear Sir,

Ours is a company dealing in Retail trading of all kinds of household goods through our company's owned retail outlets at prominent locations in all major towns of Maharashtra. We have 16 outlets employing more than 750 employees in different employment categories.

We are interested in obtaining a Group Medi-claim policy covering all of our employees and approach you to provide one such blanket policy.

Kindly send your representative to complete all formalities for the said purpose. The Representative may fix an appointment with our M.D. on Telephone before coming.

Sincerely

(Public Relations officer)

REPLY OF INSURANCE CO. FOR MEDI-CLAIM POLICY

United India Insurance Co. Ltd.

Divisional office No.3
Fort, Mumbai 400023
Tel. : 022-47939011-16

Dated : 18th October, 2009

The Public Relations Officer
Modern Retail Point (P) Ltd.
F-23, IInd floor, Shoppers Stop,
Fort, Mumbai - 400023

Sub. : Your Proposal for Medi-claim Policy for your staff

Dear Sir,

Thank you for your proposal to obtain Mediclaim Policy for your staff from our office, we would like you to make the following preparations at your end to facilitate us to issue such a policy.

1. A complete list of your staff containing the following information :
   - (i) Name, in full of each employee
   - (ii) Father's Name
   - (iii) Date of Birth & Age
   - (iv) Complete Residential Address.
   - (v) Employed with the Co. since
   - (vi) Present Designation
   - (vii) Monthly Gross & Take home Salary
2. Medical History of each employee
3. A Medical Fitness Certificate of each employee by a certified Medical Practitioner registered with Indian Medical Association.
4. Medi-claim limit for each employee (on annual basis)
5. A Medi-claim Proposal form duly filled in and signed by at least 2 directors of the company, duly authorised to do so.

Upon completion of these formalities, we would be in a position to give you our best quotation for such a Policy.

We would get in touch with you in a few days to proceed further in the matter.

Sincerely,

(S.K. Bakshi)
Administrative Officer

Encl. : Mediclaim Proposal form

ENTERTAINING MEDI-CLAIM OF AN EMPLOYEE

United India Insurance Co. Ltd.

Divisional Office No. 3
Fort. Mumbai, 400023
Tel. : 022-47939011 - 16

Dated : 7th December, 2009

Mr. Akshay Malhotra
Accounts Assistant
M/s Modern Retail Point (P) Ltd.,
F-23, IInd Floor, Shopper's Stop,
Fort, Mumbai-400023

Sub. : Your claim against Medi-claim Policy No. P04392781 issued to M/s Modern Retail Point (P) Ltd.

Dear Sir,

We are in receipt of your claim for reimbursement of Medical Expenses of Rs. 7,935 incurred by you in getting medical treatment for your illness as stated in your letter.

Please note that for reimbursement of your claim, you need to provide us the following documents in original :

1. Claim form (enclosed) duly filled in and signed by you.
2. Attending Doctor's Prescription slip.
3. Receipt of consultation fees charged by Doctor.
4. Receipt of all Medicines/Pathological Tests/X-Rays/Physiotherapy etc. issued by Hospital/ Chemist.
5. In case of Hospitalisation, Discharge slip and Bill for Hospitalisation Expenses.
6. Certificate from Surgeon/Anaesthetist, as the case may be.
7. Certificate of Medical fitness after Treatment, showing the exact period of absence from Duty.

Kindly comply these formalities to enable us to process your claim promptly.

Sincerely,

(S.K. Bakshi)
Administrative Officer.

Encl. : Claim Form.

MOTOR CAR INSURANCE — DISPUTING THE CLAIM

United India Insurance Co. Ltd

Mahatma Gandhi Road, Mumbai - 400001
Divisional Office No. 4
Backbay Reclamation,
Mumbai - 400069
Tel. : 022-45920312-16

Dated : 15th November, 2009

Mr. Bindeshwar Nath Joshi
13th Floor, Mehta House,
Nariman Point (West),
Mumbai-400063

Sub. : Your Motor Insurance claim against Policy no. P-03927125 issued by our office.

Dear Sir,

We have received your claim for reimbursement of accidental repairs of your Motor car no. Mx 03A 4397.

We wish to advise you as under :

1. Our Surveyor's Report estimates the amount of loss to Rs. 13,500 against your claim for Rs. 18,60C.

2. You have charged the MRP of the parts fitted in the vehicle, whereas a depreciation rate of 60% is to be charged due to the vehicle being five years old, as per norms of our company.

3. You have not supplied the photographs of the accidented vehicle, which are mendatory for settlement of claim.

We are withholding your claim till the completion of the above formalities at your end.

Looking forward to hear from you soon.

Sincerely,

(G.P. Pandey)
Branch Manager

APPLICATION FOR AGENCY

Bharat Stationers (P) Ltd.

Regd. Office : 56, Main Bazar,
Chandni Chowk, Delhi 110006
Ph. : 011-65093674
e-mail : bharatstationers@yahoo.com

Dated : 19th November, 2009

The Managing Director,
M/s Today Writing Instruments (P) Ltd.
M-32, Connaught Circus,
New Delhi-110001

Sub. : Proposal for Distributorship

Dear Sir,

We are one of the leading wholesale dealers of stationery products in Delhi. We are Distributors of prominent brands of stationery items like, Neelgagan Note Books, Apsara Pencils, Kores Carbon Papers, Power and BILT Writing Papers, Cello writing Instruments, Bittoo Stationery Items, Camlin Drawing Materials and several other Stationery Products.

We are having strong presence in the market with our distribution network spread across Delhi, New Delhi, East and South Delhi and Noida. We are in the business in this line for the last 15 years and have built a customer base of 600 retailers in all areas.

Our turnover exceeds Rs. 15 crores per annum with an annual growth of around 20 per cent for the last 3 years. We feel interested in the distribution of your most popular brand of 'Todays' Pens for the state of Delhi. Our unblemished track record of the last 15 years provides confidence in us to make our business relations, a major success story.

Awaiting your favourable response.

Sincerely,

(Prakash Chander)
Proprietor

REPLY TO THE ABOVE : OFFER OF AGENCY

Today Writing Instruments (P) Ltd.

M-32, Connaught Circus,
New Delhi 110001
Tel. : 011- 27554601 - 06
http : //www.todaypens.com

Dated : 28th November, 2009

The Proprietor,
M/s Bharat Stationers (P) Ltd.
Regd. Office : 56 Main Bazar,
Chandni Chowk, Delhi 110006

Sub. : Your proposal for Distributorship for Today Pens.

Dear Sir,

We thank you for your letter dated 19th November 2009 While we are considering several other proposals, we find your proposal quite interesting. Very shortly, we would be inviting you to our office for further deliberations on the subject.

In the meantime, we are sending you an MOU (Memorandum of Understanding) as a first step to intimate you the requirements for the contract of distributorship with our company. These may be briefly stated as under :

1. An upfront investment of Rs. 10 lacs in stocks.
2. Stock deliveries by us on 'COD' terms.
3. Distributor's margin of 4.5% of Invoice value of stock alongwith dealers margin of 17.5% of invoice value at M.R.P.
4. Appointment of atleast 3 sales staff at your level.
5. A minimum sales target of Rs. 5 crores for the current year.
6. All promotional schemes for onward distribution in the market.
7. Re-imbursement of all out-of-pocket marketing expenses on actual basis after verification by our staff.
8. Implementation of Company's policies and instructions at your end.

If these terms are acceptable to you, kindly complete the M.O.U. and send to us for proceeding further in the matter.

In case of any queries, please donot hesitate in directly telephoning me during business hours.

Looking forward to hear from you soon.

Sincerely,

(Managing Director)

Encl. : (as above)

BUSINESS INTRODUCTION LETTER

Nav Bharat Publications (P) Ltd.

B-54 Sector 96, Surajpur Road,
Greater Noida (U.P.)
Tel. : 3527987, 3527988
e-mail : navbharat@rediffmail.com

Dated : 16th October, 2009

The Manager,
Indian Book Store,
M-39, Connaught Circus,
New Delhi-110001

Sub. : Introducing our Business

Dear Sir,

We, at Nav Bharat Publication (P) Ltd. wish to introduce ourselves as one of the most reputed publishers of General and Academic Books in the Country.

While we take pride to mention that we publish quality university and professional courses books at under and post graduate levels apart from professional courses like C.A., C.S., L.L.B., I.C.W.A., M.B.A. etc., we also publish books on General Knowledge, Short stories, Novels, Fiction and Competition Level Books etc.. We have over 1500 titles on the first category of knowledge.

As you are one of the prominent book stores in Delhi and New Delhi and are located at a very prominent location at Connaught Place, we would like to start doing business with you.

As a first step, we are enclosing our latest catalogue alongwith handouts of our new releases which includes books by most famous authors. We would shortly be sending our marketing executives with samples of books for your consideration.

We wish to assure that our terms of business are most lucrative and better than competition.

Looking forward to serve you.

Sincerely,

(M. Wasnik)
Managing Director.

LETTER INTIMATING LAUNCH OF A NEW PRODUCT

Ajanta Time Machines Ltd.

(World's No. 1 manufacturers of wall clocks)
New Market, Sanders Road, Ahmedabad,
Ph. 4597357, 4597358
e-mail : ajantaclocks@indiatimes.com

Dated : 25th September, 2009

The Manager,
M/s India Times,
88, Janpath,
New Delhi-110001

Sub. : Launch of new range of wall clocks

Dear Sir,

We are pleased to announce the launch of a new range of wall clocks under our brand 'Ajanta'. The new range shall be called under the sub-brand name, 'WAVE' and shall have the following unique features

- Available in 7 different pleasing colours
- Having a 'sweep second' in lieu of 'second hand'.
- Noiseless
- Facility of Alarm
- Lighting Dial at Night (Auto on-off every 12 hours)

These wall clocks will be available at very economical price range (M.R.P. between Rs. 350/= to Rs. 575/=).

We are launching this range on 5th October, 2005. Since you are one of our valued dealers, we would like you to place an advance order for the entire range of the wall clocks.

Your order before 30th September, 2005 will enable us to include your name in the list of dealers in the press advertisement realeased on the eve of launch of the new range.

We look forward to your bulk order, asap.

Sincerely,

(Akshay Kumar Jain)
Marketing Manager

Encl. : (2) As above

J

JOB (EMPLOYMENT) LETTERS

Employment related letters form an important and integral part of every organisation, firm, company or business enterprise. The erstwhile 'Personnel' department has been transformed to 'Human Resources' department. An extremely large number of H.R. situations may arise in business which necessitate writing of letters both by the prospective employees/staff member and the employer. A few instances of such letter are given below :

Job Application letters

- Application for the post of an Assistant/a Manager/or any post in the organisation.
- Application in response to an advertisement.
- Application requesting for an interview.
- Cover letter to introduce a resume.
- Letter requesting recommendation for a job.
- Request for employment.
- Letter in search of a job.
- Sending a resume in anticipation.
- Follow up during a job search.
- Accepting a job offer.
- Negotiating a job offer.
- Negotiating a higher salary.
- Negotiating job conditions.
- Confirming the acceptance of a job offer.
- Request letter for a raise or promotion.
- Decline a job offer/transfer or promotion.

Job offer letters

- Announcing a job offer.
- Declining/rejecting a Job Application.
- Extending a job offer.
- Writing interview letter for a job.
- Write an appointment letter with detailed terms & conditions.
- Appointment letter.

Resignation Letters

- Writing a resignation letter.
- Resigning to take voluntary retirement.
- Resigning in protest.
- Resigning due to family problems.
- Resigning under management pressure.

- Resigning due to personal reasons.
- Resigning to take a better job opportunity.
- Resigning due to conflict of interest.
- Accepting a resignation.
- Announcing the retirement of an employee.

Promotion/Transfer/Relocation Letter

- Letter announcing promotion of an employee.
- Letter giving raise to an employee.
- Letter transferring an employee from H.O. to Branch office or *Vice Versa*.
- Letter announcing Promotion with Transfer of an employee.
- Letter relocating an employee.

Termination Letters

- Letter announcing retrenchment.
- Letter announcing Lay-off.
- Letter of termination of an employee's services.
- Termination letter on the ground of poor/below average performance.
- Termination on the ground of bad behaviour.
- Termination on the change of sexual harassment.
- Termination on charge of embezzlement of funds.
- Termination on the ground of fraud.
- Termination on business closure/merger/acquisition etc.
- Termination on the ground of conflict of Interest.

QUICK TIPS FOR WRITING JOB (H.R.) LETTERS

Job Applications

- An application for a job must be written in simple, polite and positive language.
- A job application should clearly state the following :
  — the advertisement which is responded.
  — the nomenclature (name, designation etc.) of the job applied for.
  — proper and complete address of the advertiser.
- A job application letter is a request letter, therefore, it must be written in a requesting and respectful tone.
- The resume or bio-data of the applicant should be carefully drafted/worded to highlight :
  — career objectives of the applicant.
  — complete name, address and contact information of the sender.
  — how the senders qualifications match the job requirements.
  — details of correctly stated qualifications (academic and professional), experience, personal traits etc.

- A job application must :
  — state only the facts,
  — avoid irrelevant details;
  — be thorough but concise;
  — express enthusiasm for the job applied
- Generally, copies of testimonials, qualifications, experience are enclosed with the resume.
- The copies should preferably be attested or atleast self-attested for authentification.
- The enclosures should clearly state the number of documents attached.
- Advisably, the job applicant should not impose his own conditions to accept the job offer, as these may jeopardise his chances of appointment.

QUICK TIPS FOR WRITING JOB OFFER LETTERS (EMPLOYER'S)

- A job letter should clearly state the title of the job, the designation offered, the remuneration package, the allowances, the responsibilities related to the job.
- The job offer letter must offer only that what can actually be offered by the organisation
- Clarity of details in Job offer letter eliminates misunderstandings in future legal implications.
- Job offer letter should be direct and encouraging to the applicant.
- A job offer letter should also detail the following :
  — date of joining the job,
  — location of the job, the designation
  — starting salary & other allowances
  — privileges attached to the job
  — how and when to join the job

QUICK TIPS FOR WRITING RESIGNATION LETTERS

- There may be several reasons for resigning a job, *viz.*, personal reasons, health problems, family reasons, frustration, lack of career opportunities, management pressure, voluntary retirement etc. These letters should be carefully worded as not to offend anyone.
- A resignation letter should be graciously written, polite in tone, without use of sarcastic language or in bad taste.
- A registration letter should, preferably, appreciate the time spent at the organisation, express gratitude to colleagues, co-workers and juniors.
- A resignation letter must not contain irrelevant facts, discuss family problems or project future plans after resignation.
- A resignation letter should not attempt to or result in ending relationships. It should aim at continuing it, for, sometimes, the new employer may want to enquire about the employee from the old employer.

QUICK TIPS FOR WRITING PROMOTION/ TRANSFER/ RELOCATION LETTER

- A promotion or promotion with transfer letter is a type of congratulatory letter and should be written in enthusiastic and motivational language which should be simple and clear.
- Like an appointment letter, the promotion letter should contain the details about :
  — the new job position (The title/designation)
  — date of joining the new position
  — location of the job.
  — the pay package & other allowances;
  — privileges attached to the new job;
  — the responsibilities of the new job.
- A transfer or relocation letter should preferably state the reasons necessitating transfer or relocation. Such a letter should state the following :
  — the location of the job
  — the date of joining
  — the relocation benefits offered to the employee
  — motivational and positive language.

QUICK TIPS FOR WRITING TERMINATION LETTER

- A termination letter should be as brief as possible but at the same time clear and complete in contents.
- A termination letter may express sorrow or grief by using the words 'Regret', 'Sorry', 'under the circumstances' etc..
- A termination letter should not result in ending the relationship.
- A termination letter should also specify the following details :
  — the reason for termination decision.
  — the date from which job stands terminated, or
  — 'with immediate effect' termination ; or
  — 'notice period' or 'salary in lieu of' the notice period of termination
  — the procedure to be followed
- A termination letter should be very carefully worded as it may become a legal document in future.

A few sample letters of job applications, job offers, resignation, termination etc. are given in the following pages :

LETTER OF REFERENCE

Inter Communications Ltd.

27, Max Buildings,
Netaji Subhash Place,
New Delhi-110015
Tel. : 011-23795151

Dated : 27th December, 2009

To Whom It May Concern

Reference for Mr. Satish Bhatia,

Mr. Satish Bhatia joined our company in July 2006. Since then he has proved to be a most reliable and effective member of the marketing department of the company.

Mr. Satish is very sincere, professional and hard working in his approach to work and is liked and appreciated by his colleagues and executives as well as the company clients. He is able to work both independently as well as a team member. He has always over achieved sales targets and received performance bonus every year without fail.

I have no hesitation in recommending Mr. Satish for a responsible position in any organisation. I however, regret his decision to move on.

We wish him all success in life.

Yours Sincerely,

(Ashish Chopra)
Managing Director

WELCOME E-MAIL TO NEW STAFF MEMBER

To : "Mr. Vinay Sharma" <vinay@electronicity.com>

CC : All staff

BCC : "Ankit Kapoor" <ankit@electronicity.com>

Dear Vinay Sharma

It is a pleasure to welcome you to the staff of Electronicity Ltd. We are excited to have you in our team, and hope that you will definitely enjoy working with our company.

We are holding a special staff meeting (followed by staff lunch) on 1st January, (Monday) to welcome you and also enable you to meet all our senior staff and any other new staff who has joined us this month. Please make sure to attend the meeting at 1.00 p.m. in the conference Room. Mr. Ankit will give you details of the meeting.

If you have any queries in the meantime, please do not hesitate to e-mail me at my e-mail address given below or reach me at my office line extn. 222.

Warm regards

Amit Aggarwal

Manager : H.R.
<amit@electronicity.com>
16.12.2009

THANK YOU LETTER FOR JOB OFFER

Pramod Jain

B-32 Alaknanda Appartments,
New Delhi-110017
011-29354445

Dated 30th November, 2009

Mr. Manoj Malhotra
Director, Accounts
Best Indian Advertising Co. (Pvt.) Ltd.
745, Chiranjeev Towers,
Nehru Place,
New Delhi-110019

Dear Mr. Malhotra,

Thank you for offering me the Senior Accounts Executive Position in your esteemed company and for taking the time to meet with me yesterday.

As I mentioned in my interview, after having graduated from the Prestigious Shri Ram College of Commerce of the University of Delhi and MBA in Finance & Banking from Faculty of Management Studies, University of Delhi, I had the work experience at the Finance Department of M/s Global consultant Pvt. Ltd. as Assistant Finance Manager, since 2006 till date. I hope and am confident that the experience I gained during these years will make a valuable contribution at your esteemed company.

I would like to join your company from 21st December, 2009 after getting relieved from my present position.

Thanking you once again,

Yours Sincerely

(Pramod Jain)

LETTER ACCEPTING A JOB OFFER

Ashutosh Jha
237, Gandhi Nagar,
Delhi (East)-110043
Ph. : 011-35978181

Dated: 25th October, 2009

Mr. Bhaskar Bhatt
Director, Human Resources
Pure Aqua (India) Ltd.
314, Ansal Towers,
Nehru Place,
New Delhi-110019
Ph. 011-29377474

Dear Mr. Bhatt,

I am delighted to confirm my acceptance of the job of Marketing Executive for your esteemed company. I have received your letter of offer and am very pleased with the remuneration package offered to me. I am planning to join the work on November, 1st, 2009.

I am confident that I will be able to contribute to the Marketing Department with my experience, expertise and education.

Thanking you once again and looking forward to working under your guidance and supervision.

Yours Sincerely,

(Ashutosh Jha)

LETTER DECLINING A JOB OFFER

Anirudh Goswami

374, Parmanand Colony,
Delhi-110009
Tel. : 011-2765 9293

Dated: 9th December, 2009

Mr. Anil Kapoor
Manager ; Marketing,
Stretegic Consultants Pvt. Ltd.,
715, Ambica Towers,
Nehru Place,
New Delhi-110055

Dear Mr. Kapoor,

Thank you for offering me the position of Senior Networking Consultant with your company. I highly appreciate your taking time to meet me and discuss the details of the position and the compensation package and giving me time to consider the offer.

Although the job offer is very encouraging and tempting in many aspects, the only hitch is the requirement to move to Chandigarh from Delhi, the place of my residence. As I have family responsibilities with my aging parents, I find it difficult to move out and to accept the offer.

Through this is a very difficult decision for me, but one that is appropriate for me at this point of time. I appreciate your consideration and courtesy and look forward to working with you some other time.

Yours sincerely

(Anirudh Goswami)

COVERING LETTER FOR RESUME (CV)

Surinder Singh
35, University Apartments
Reeds Line,
Mall Road,
Delhi-110009
Tel. : 011-27609876
e-mail : black_rose@yahoo.com

Dated: 10th September, 2009

The Marketing Manager,
Ion Exchange (India) Ltd.
Regd. Office : B-32,
Connaught Place,
New Delhi 110001

Dear Sir,

Sub. : Application for the Post of Sales Officer

Reference advertisement dated 3rd September, 2009 for the above post in your esteemed company, I wish to apply for one of these positions. I am presently employed as a Sales Representative with Medica India Ltd. since July 2007.

My present responsibility include meeting with new prospects, demonstrating product features and gaining sales for the company. In addition, I have my weekly, monthly, quarterly and annual targets, that I have always over achieved.

As a sales officer, I would bring a focus on customer relationship management and sales development to your company. Further, I have an inherant quality of team building and development.

I am enclosing for your purusal and consideration, my resume as a first step in exploring the possibilities of employment with your esteemed organisation.

I would appreciate, if the application is kept confidential. I offer myself for an iterview on any date, time and place suitable to you.

Thank you for your consideration

Yours faithfully,

(Surinder Singh)

Encl. : Resume

COVERING LETTER FOR JOB APPLICATION

Kamal Sethi

365, 7th Floor,
Himadri Appartments,
Indira Puram,
Ghaziabad (U.P.)
Ph. 095120-3272541
e-mail : jaiho@rediffmail.com

Dated : 20th December, 2009.

The Manager,
Human Resource Department
Lintas (India) Ltd.
7th Level, Antriksha Bhawan,
Barakhmba Road,
New Delhi 110001

Sub. : Application for the post of Executive Secretary

Dear Sir,

In responce to your advertisement that you have a vacant position of an 'Excutive Secratory', I would like to apply for the position.

My resume is enclosed here and as you will see, my education, experience and wide range of skills, could be an asset to your company. Briefly stated, I have excellent communication skills, I am computer literate and my work experience in three different companies over the last 15 years speak out my capabilities and competence.

May I have a personal interview at your convenience ? I may be contacted at the telephone or e-mail mentioned above.

Anticipating a positive response.

Yours sincerely,

(Kamal Sethi)

Encl.: Bio-data

LETTER OFFERING APPOINTMENT

Home Products (India) Ltd.

25, Esplanade Road,
Calcutta
Tel. : 35916729, 35925929
e-mail : hpil@indiatimes.com

Dated : 17th September, 2009

Mr. Ravinder Kumar Malhotra
E-42, Arya Samaj Road,
Uttam Nagar,
New Delhi. 110059.

Sub. : Appointment Letter

Dear Mr. Malhotra,

I am very pleased to inform you that our company has selected you for the covered post of Regional Marketing Manager of our Electonics Division. Your resume and subsequent interview were commendable to make the selection process easier for our H.R. Department. We congratulate you for that.

If you accept this offer, the company will provide the following compensation package :

Basic Salary : Rs. 60,000 per month.
H.R.A. : Rs. 15,000 p.m. or company accommodation in lieu thereof.
Company car plus Rs. 1,500 per month for Petrol and Maintenance.
Car Driver : on company payroll.
Medical, Leave travel, P.F., Group Insurance and
Bonus : As per Company Norms

Please confirm by phone or e-mail, when would you be joining our company, latest by 25th September, 2009.

Looking forward to your joining our team.

Sincerely,

(Parveen Hans)
Director : Human Resources

A LETTER OF PROMOTION

Beauty Aid Products (India) Ltd.

Regd. Office : 32, Ring Road,
South Extension Part I,
New Delhi - 110003
Tel. : 011-62984545, 46, 47
e-mail : beautyaids@sify.com

Dated : 20th November, 2009

Mrs. Sarabjeet Kaur
B-66, Hardev Nagar,
Outer Ring Road,
Delhi-110084

Sub. : Promotion Letter

Dear Madam,

I have pleasure in breaking the news that you have been promoted to the post of Assistant Manager, Cosmetics Department of the Co. at its Head Office at Antriksh Bhawan, Barakhamba Road, New Delhi with immediate effect. You are requested to take charge of the new position within next 2-3 days. While taking this decision, the Management has been guided by your efficiency, sincerity and experience during the last 5 years of service at this company.

Please accept my hearty congratulations on your promotion.

Your salary will be fixed in the pay-scale of Rs. 25,000 - 1,000 - 35,000 - 1,500 - 50,000 plus all admissible allowances as per company norms. Other conditions of service remain unchanged.

Kindly acknowledge receipt by signing the second copy of this letter.

Sincerely,

(General Manager : Operations)

Encl. : One

A LETTER OF TERMINATION

Bharat Jashion Works Ltd.

Regd. Office : 56, Main Road
Dalton Ganj, Kolkata
Tel. : 29655741 - 45
http : //www.bharatfashionworks.com

Dated : 28th November, 2009

Mr. V.B. Bose
Accounts Executive

Sub. : Notice of Termination

Dear Mr. V.B. Bose,

I regret to inform you that your services will stand terminated 30 days from the date of this letter.

The Management has given this onerous task of informing you that inspite of several reminders and issue of Three Memos served upon you have shown no improvement in your punctuality and sincerity towards work. Your work always remained pending and caused great embarrassment to seniors time and again. Your lack of punctuality became a laughing stock and demotivating for the entire office staff. Hence the management is compelled to give this one month's notice to you as per terms of your appointment. You may even opt for one months salary in lieu of the period of notice.

Sincerely,

(Manager : Accounts)

M

MEMORANDUM

The word 'Memorandum' has been derived from the Latin word 'memorare' or 'memorandus' and means literally 'to mention' or 'tell'. In short form, a 'Memorandum' is known as 'Memo' and is singular in number. Its plural forms are 'memorandums' or 'memoranda'. By definition :

" A 'memorandum' is a written statement that is prepared specially for a person or persons in order to give them information about a particular matter."

In large organisations, a memo is used for internal communication between executives and subordinates or between officers/executives of the same level. It is never sent outside the organisation. Large companies need an efficient system by which colleagues can communicate with each other either in the same building/office or in departments or sections situated in different locations. Though telephone offers a method of immediate and convenient communication, yet in many situations, a written record is often necessary for future reference. For such types of written communication, memorandums are used. They may be for the attention of one person only or in the form of a circular for attention of several people.

A memo can be used to :

(i) issue instructions to the staff
(ii) communicate policy changes in the organisation
(iii) give/seek suggestions/opinions
(iv) confirm & communicate a decision to staff
(v) elicit information on a subject
(vi) granting/withholding permission on a subject
(vii) warn employees on specific type of conduct/misconduct
(viii) seek explanation on a subject.

A copy of the memo may be retained for filing purposes for future reference.

QUICK TIPS FOR WRITING MEMOS

The standard Memo format is similar to Block Format of Business Letters but has no salutation, close or signature. Kitty O. Locker & Stephen Kyo[1] lists the following guidelines for Writing Memos :

- Memos omit both the salutation and the close.
- Memos never indent paragraphs.
- Subject lines are required in Memos, but headings are optional.

1. Op. Cit. p. 159 (Adapted)

- Each heading must cover all the information until the next heading.
- Never use a separate heading for the first paragraph.
- Memos are usually initialled by To/From block. Initialling tells the reader that Memo had been proof-read and prevents someone's sending out your name on a memo you did not infact write.
- Some organisations have special letterhead for Memos, where Date/ To/ From/ subject are already printed on the form.
- Some organisations ask employees to sign memos rather than simply initialling them. The signature goes just below the last line to prevent anyone adding unauthorised information.
- If the Memo runs two or more pages, use a heading at the top of second and subsequent pages.
- Since many of the memos go to the same people, putting a brief version of the subject line will be more helpful than just using "All Employees."

A few sample memorandums are given on the following pages.

MEMO FORMAT (ON PLAIN PAPER)

October 7th, 2009

To : All Employees

From : The Manager, Accounts Department

Subject : Personal Telephone Calls : Keeping Check on

It has been brought to my notice that the Telephone at The Reception office is often being misused for making personal calls by the employees.

While the management has no objection to the use of the Office Telephone by employees in an emergency, the unusally high telephone bill of the Reception Office can't be overlooked in the context of the cost cutting measures taken by the company to combat the economic slowdown and its effect on the company's finances.

As part of the economy drive, the Reception Office incharge is directed to maintain an exclusive Call Register wherein any employee making a call is expected to enter the details in respect of telephone no., date, time, duration, name of caller, purpose of call (official/personal) etc..

This memo is issued for immediate compliance.

Sd/-

Manager (Accounts)

MEMO FORMAT (ON PRINTED MEMO LETTERHEAD)

Sapient (India) Ltd.

Dated : November 15th, 2009

To : All Heads of Department

From : Human Resource Department

Subject : Department Meeting on 21st November, 2009

All Heads of Department are informed that a joint meeting of all departments has been fixed for 21st November, 2009 at 10.00 A.M. at The Seminar Room (7th floor) Main Building, to discuss the recent changes in "Leave Rules" as per G.O.I. notification dated 1st November, 2009.

All relevant papers relating to the Agenda have already been circulated.

Please do consult all colleagues in your department, prior to the meeting, to form common opinion.

In case of inability to attend, the next in seniority may be deputed to represent the department.

Sd/-

Manager (H.R.)

O

ORDER LETTERS

Order related letters are the backbone of every business. The volume of 'order' related letters far exceed any other category of business letters. Order letter are necessary 'Purchase' letters and hence should be distinguished from 'Sales' letters. There may be hundreds or even more situations in business for writing order letters, a few of which are listed below :

- Placement of order.
- Acknowledgment of an order.
- Cancellation of order.
- Complaint about delay in an order.
- Confirm the receipt of an order.
- Confirm the shipping of an order.
- Decline to accept an order.
- Decline an order without advance payment.
- Decline an order but offer substitute product.
- Inform about delay in shipment.
- Inform about shortage in supplied order.
- Inform about damaged goods.
- Inform about incorrect merchandise.
- Request for rush supplies of an order.
- Request a discount for damaged goods.
- Request part payment before despatch of goods.
- Request for Price list, Catalogue, bids etc.
- Reply to an inquiry about product or service.
- Thank a customer for prompt payment.
- Request to send a statement of Account.
- Informing about bouncing of a customer's cheque.
- Writing Collection Letters for delayed payment.
- Disputing entries in the statement of Account.
- Requesting for better trade terms.
- Letter offering better trade terms.
- Letter enclosing samples of products.
- Supply of a catalogue, brochure or other literature.
- Request for advance payment before despatch of an order.
- Request for favourable terms & conditions.
- Request for extended term of credit.
- Request for a credit line against supplies of goods.
- Returning unwanted or incorrect supply received.
- Letter for a credit note against damaged supplies.

QUICK TIPS FOR WRITING ORDER LETTERS

- Order letters are important business letters. In many cases, they are pre-printed form letters, having blank spaces for the following :
  - — Reference order no. and date.
  - — Name and address of the recipient.
  - — Complete description of goods/products ordered.
    - * Quantity of goods ordered.
    - * Quality /specification of goods.
    - * Name of Brand.
    - * Description of goods.
    - * Price (per unit/dozen/hundred or by weight etc).
    - * Other Terms
  - — Shipping or despatch Instructions.
  - — Delivery schedule (By what date supply is required)
  - — Any other Information.
- If the order letter is to be typed individually, the following points may be kept in mind :
  - — all the above information.
  - — no irrelevant details or facts.
  - — it should be brief, concise but complete.
- Order letters are written in direct and straight forward manner, therefore tone, language, positivity, politeness etc. are irrelevant in such a letter.
- A copy of every order letter should be preserved for future reference & legal implications.
- In case defective/damaged or incorrect supplies are received against an order, a letter informing the fact should be *immediately written* to the supplier, so that he may initiate the matter with the Transport company or Insurance company for filing of claim etc.,
- Any such letter informing of defect/damaged/incorrect supply must include the following details :
  - — Stock ordered vs. stock supplied.
  - — The extent of damage clearly indicating the damaged quantity and its money value calculated at the rate per unit plus taxes plus shipping charges etc.
  - — The letter should indicate the intention of the receiver, in clear terms, about :

    (i) Returning the stock at suppliers' cost & risk :

    or (ii) accepting the stock if a credit note for the amount of loss is issued by the supplier and (iii) request the supplier to replace the damaged/incorrect/defective stock; and (iv) withholding of the payment of invoice.

A few sample order letters are given in the following pages:

LETTER FOR PLACING AN ORDER

Hindustan Computers (International)
B-212, Okhla Industrial Area
Okhla-Phase II
New Delhi-110047
Ph. 011-65973251-65976532

Dated : 27th September, 2009

The Marketing Manager,
M/s Techno-Systems Network,
A-37, Lawrence Road,
Amritsar (Punjab) 181003

Sub. : Order for the Purchase of Hard Disc Drives etc..

Dear Sir,

We are pleased to place an order for the purchase of following items :

1500 Nos. 80 GB Hard Disc Drives–Transend VT 1.
1000 Nos. 200 GB Hard Disc Drives–Sony W 7
1000 Nos. 250 GB Hard Disc Drives–Impex B 9
3500 Nos. Total

The order is based on the Price list Dated 1st August, 2009, supplied by you, for price and other terms. We will greatly appreciate it, if you transport all the supplies in one consignment as soon as possible via Golden Transport Co., so as to reach us on or before 5th October, 2009. Any delay in delivery must be intimated in advance and approved by us. Payment terms and conditions shall be just like the previous purchase orders.

A line in confirmation shall be appreciated.

Sincerely

(Winston Jacob)
Purchase Manager

LETTER ACCEPTING THE ORDER

Techno-Systems Network

A-37, Lawrence Road,
Amritsar (Punjab) 181003
Ph. 0181-7252371, 7253961

Dated : 29th September, 2009

The Purchase Manager
M/s Hindustan Computer (International)
B-212, Okhla Industrial Area,
Okhla-Phase II,
New Delhi, 110044.

Sub. : Acknowledging Receipt of the Order

Dear Sir,

We gratefully acknowledge having received your valued order and are in the process of arranging despatches of the same.

In order to meet the deadline of 5th October, 2009, We are making special arrangement for sending it through a special truck assigned for the purpose, of M/s Golden Transport Co., as desired by you. We hope the consignment to reach the destination (same as earlier supplies) latest by 3rd October, 2009. In case of any change of destination, kindly inform us immediately.

We always feel obliged in serving valued customers like you.

Please feel free to call us for further assistance.

Sincerely,

(Vijay Kumar Patni)
Marketing Manager

LETTER DECLINING TO ACCEPT AN ORDER

Techo-Systems Network
A-37, Lawrence Road,
Amritsar (Punjab) 181003
Ph. 0181-7252371, 7253961

Dated : 29th September, 2009

The Purchase Manager
M/s Hindustan Computers (International),
B-212, Okhla Industrial Area,
Okhla-Phase II
New Delhi-110044.

Sub. : Inability to accept your Order

Dear Sir,

We acknowledge having received your valued order, but express our inability to accept the same due to the following reasons :

1. The prices of all the items in your order have gone up from 5-15% since 1st August, 2009 (our last price list). We are enclosing our new price list dated 15th September, 2009.

2. Sony Hard Disk Drives continue to be in short supply since last 2 months due to shipment and other problems. We have no stock of these, which can be supplied.

3. Kindly also take note of our new payment terms in our Price list dated 15th September, 2009.

In view of the above, we would request you to modify your order.

We would be very pleased to serve you, always.

Sincerely,

(Vijay Kumar Patni)
Marketing Manager

LETTER ASKING FOR BETTER TRADE TERMS

Asian Electronics Ltd.

F-36, 7th Level, Omaxe Towers,
Backbay Reclamation Road,
Mumbai.
Tel. : 022-64296666, 64296667
e-mail : asianelectronics@sify.com

Dated : 15th September, 2009

The Marketing Manager,
Naveen Electronics Ltd.,
4th Floor, Ansal Towers,
Bhikaji Cama Place,
New Delhi. 110035

Sub. : Your Catalogue Dated 15th September, 2009

Re : Trade Terms

Dear Sir,

We are in receipt of your Catalogue and Trade Terms referred to above and wish to submit as follows :

- You offer 12% Trade Discount and 2% cash discount for payment in 15 days of Invoice date. However, several other competing firms offer as 15% Trade discount in addition to usual cash discount.
- We are getting F.O.R. Destination prices for all our orders with competing firms whereas your prices are ex-godown, that makes huge difference when orders are heavy and quantities huge.
- Further, we have been enjoying credit facilities equivalent to our average quarterly orders from some of our suppliers, whereas your catalogue is silent about it.

In view of these, it would not be possible for us to place orders with your company.

Would you please consider the trade terms to match with the competitors, we would consider having business relations with you.

Looking forward to a better response from you.

Yours faithfully,

(Naresh Patil)
Purchase Manager

LETTER OFFERING BETTER TRADE TERMS

Naveen Electronics Ltd.

4th Floor, Ansal Towers,
Bhikaji Cama Place,
New Delhi. 110035

Dated : 20th September, 2009

The Purchase Manager,
Asian Electronics Ltd.
F-36, 7th level, Omaxe Towers,
Backbay Reclamation Road,
Mumbai.

Sub. : Trade Terms

Dear Sir,

We are in receipt of your letter dated 15th September, 2009 regarding trade terms, and thank you for your interest in dealings with us.

May we point out that our catalogue contained most competitive prices taking into account the quality and variety of our products and the most efficient after sales services provided by our company. You have indicated the difference in discount and F.I.R. prices which is more than offset by our lower prices of similar products.

However, to honour your interest in us, we shall be pleased to allow you additional 3% Trade discount on orders above Rs. 1 lac.

Other Terms (Cash Discount. Ex-Factory Price etc.) shall however remain the same.

As for credit facilities, it is our company's policy to provide such facilities after 6 months of uninterrupted trade.

We are sure, you will now find our prices and terms most favourable and patronise us by sending you valued order to us.

Looking forward to hearing from you.

Yours Sincerely,

(A.P. Madan)
Marketing Manager

LETTER ENCLOSING SAMPLES OF PRODUCTS

Vikas Udyog Ltd.

(Manufacturers of Car Accessories)
Udyog Vihar, Gurgaon (Haryana)
Ph. 95120-2735937, 2735938
e-mail : vikasudyog@gmail.com

Dated : 20th December, 2009

The Manager,
M/s Carzone
Gaffar Market Block B,
Karol Bagh,
New Delhi-110015

Sub. : Dispatch of Samples of Car Accessories

Dear Sir,

We introduce ourselves as one of the leading manufacturers of car upholstry and car accessories catering to different models of car manufacturers such as Maruti, Hyundai, Tata Motors and Chevrolet. Our range include leather and foam products in seat covers, mattresses, mudguards, steering covers, gear locks and a host of other accessories.

We are pleased to note that you have a huge showroom for the sale of car accessories in the most prominent location for marketing of such items in the capital.

We would be interested in initiating business dealings with your firm. As a first step, we are sending you 24 samples of different products manufactured by us, which we would like you to place at appropriate visible spaces in your showcases so as to evince customer's interest.

We are also enclosing our catalogue and price list including trade terms in detail to make you believe how lucrative doing business with us would be.

Our representative shall also be visiting you shortly.

Looking forward to hear from you soon.

Sincerely,

(Alok Jain)
Manager Marketing.

Encl. : As a above (24)

LETTER PLACING AN ORDER RESERVING RIGHT TO REJECT

Bharat Emporium

36/9, Kakodkar Road,
Ahmedabad (Gujarat)
Ph. : 3279625, 3279626
e-mail : bharatempo@sify.com

Dated : 20th November, 2009

The Manager,
Nitin Handlooms,
B-46, Near Rly. Station,
Nangloi,
New Delhi-110065

Sub. : Order for purchase of goods with conditional delivery

Dear Sir,

Please find enclosed with this letter our order No. BE/179/2009 which, we, hope, you will execute without delay, since all the items ordered have been selected from your latest catalogue dated 1st November, 2009.

We may specifically mention here that time of delivery is the essence of this purchase order. Since we require the goods urgently for the purpose of exports, we must receive the delivery on or before 30th of November, 2009.

We, therefore, reserve the right to reject the goods if received by us later than 30th November, 2009.

If you think, you are unable to meet the delivery deadline, kindly inform us immediately so that we may make alternate arrangements in time.

Looking forward to hear from you soon.

Sincerely,

(Bharat Bhushan)
Proprietor

Encl. : Detailed Purchase Order.

ORDER FORM

Tel. : 3279625
3279626
e-mail : bharatempo@sify.com
Ref. No. BE/179/2009

Bharat Emporium
36/9, Kakodkar Road,
Ahmedabad (Gujarat)
Dated : 20th November, 2009

M/s Nitin Handlooms,
B-46, Nangloi,
New Delhi-110065

Dear Sir,

Kindly supply the following items so as to reach us on or before 30th November, 2009.

S.No	*Description*	*Quantity*	*Per Unit Rate*	*Remarks.*
1.	'Sleepwell' Double Bed Sheets (Assorted Colours)	500	Rs. 325	Single Piece Box Packing
2.	'Aristo' Recron Pillows with White Cotton Covers Weighing 325 Grams each	1000	Rs. 195	Single Piece Poly Packing
3.	'Bharat' Double Bed Covers (Assorted Colours)	300	Rs. 275	Single Piece Poly Packing.
4.	'Indian Art' Single Bed Sheet (Assorted Colours)	200	Rs. 195	Single Piece Poly Packing.
	Total	2000		

Please send the goods by road transport through M/s Golden Transport Co. deliverable at our godown at Transport Nagar, Ahmedabad during working hours.

Sincerely,

(Purchase Manager)

LETTER CONFIRMING DISPATCH OF GOODS

Nitin Handloons

B-46, Near Rly. Station,
Nangloi,
New Delhi-110065
Tel. : 9891424091, 26359264
e-mail : nitinhandloom@in.com

Dated : 25th November, 2009

The Proprietor
M/s Bharat Emporium,
36/9, Kakodkar Road,
Ahmedabad (Gujarat)

Sub. : Confirming dispatch of goods

Dear Sir,

We thank you for your valued order no. BE/179/2009 for the supply of 2000 pieces of ordered stock, vide your enclosed order.

We are pleased to inform you that we have today dispatched the entire stock through Golden Transport Co., as desired by you. We are sure, you will receive the deliveries within 3 days, *i.e.*, by 28th November 2009, (before the deadline set by you)

We are sure, you will be pleased to see the excellent quality and packing of the stock.

For any further information, you may phone our sales executive Mr. Ravinder Gupta at Ph. no. 98101-27274, at any time as per your convenience.

We will be glad to serve you in any matter concerning the supply of our products.

Kindly acknowledge receipt of goods.

Sincerely,

(Nitin Madan)
Manager

PLACING AN IMPORT ORDER

Hindustan Computers Ltd.

B-11 Noida Industrial Estate-Part II,
Noida. (U.P.) India
Ph. : 95120-42379501-06
http : // www.hindustancomputers.com

Dated : 20th November, 2009

The Asia Manager,
M/s Johnson, Thompson & Co. Inc.,
Asia Agents : Microsoft Inc.,
35, Oxford Street,
London (U.K.)

Sub. : Placement of order for purchase of computer parts

Dear Sir,

Kindly refer to the e-mail sent by you on dated 18th November, 2009 regarding your price list, illustrated catalogue and terms and conditions of your company.

As indicated earlier via e-mails sent by us, we are desirous of having a long term contract for the supply of Hard Disc Drives of different makes and configurations on a regular basis, with your company.

We place with you the very first order for supply of the following on immediate basis :

S.No.	Description of Item.	Qty.	Your Quotation (C.I.F.)
1.	200 GB HDD 'SONY'	3000	£ 2.95 P/P
2.	250 GB HDD 'SONY'	2500	£ 3.75 P/P
3.	500 GB HDD 'SONY'	500	£ 7.30 P/P
4.	250 GB HDD 'Microsoft'	2500	£ 3.95 P/P
5.	500 GB HDD 'Microsoft'	1500	£ 7.75 P/P

Since we require the stocks urgently, kindly send them in a 'Container Load' by Air Freight.

Please ensure the consignment reaches us latest by 10th December, 2009.

In the meantime, we are opening an L/C (Letter of credit) at State Bank of India, New Delhi in your favour.

Please acknowledge acceptance and receipt of this order.

Sincerely,

(Surinder Kumar Bakshi)
Director : Purchase

REPLY TO THE ABOVE

Johnson, Thompson & Co, Inc.

Asia Agents : Microsoft Inc.
35, Oxford Street, London (U.K.)
Tel. : 69532879-84
http : // www.johnsonthompson.com/uk

Dated : 28 November, 2009

Mr. Surinder Kumar Bakshi,
Director : Purchase
M/s Hindustan Computers Ltd.
B-11, Noida Industrial Estate-Part II
NOIDA (U.P.) INDIA

Sub. : Your Purchase order dated 20th November, 2009

Dear Sir,

We thank you for placing your valuable order mentioned above and accept the same.

As mentioned by you, you are fully aware of our terms and conditions for sale, yet for transparency in business dealings, we reiterate them briefly here :

1. Acceptance of order subject to availability of stocks.
2. Our prices are NETT on C.I.F. basis at London.
3. Our products carry one year International Warranty of the company concerned.
4. Full payment on shipment of stock *i.e.*, on receipt of original Bill of lading by Importer.
5. Our rates include *shipping freight*. In case of *air transport* desired by you, the difference in freight shall have to be paid by you.
6. We guarantee shipment prior to delivery date. We shall not be responsible for delay in transit for any reason, whatsoever.

In the absence of any communication from you within a reasonable period of time, we shall presume your acceptance of the above terms.

We look forward to long term business association with your firm.

Sincerely,

(Brian Adams)
Director : Exports.

SHIPPING ADVICE BY EXPORTER

Johnson, Thompson & Co. Inc.

Asia Agents : Microsoft Inc.
35, Oxford Street,
London, (U.K.)
Tel. : 69532879-84
http : // www.johnsonthompson.com/uk

Dated : 5th December, 2009

Mr. Surinder Kumar Bakshi
Director : Purchases,
M/s Hindustan Computers Ltd.
B-11, Noida Industrial Estate, Part-II,
NOIDA (U.P.) INDIA.

Sub. : Shipping Advice for your purchase order dated 20th November, 2009

Dear Sir,

We are pleased to inform you that one container load of stocks, exactly as per your orders have been despatched by us per Scandenavian Airways from Heathrow Airport, London today, to reach New Delhi Airport by tomorrow night.

We have faxed all the documents including Invoice, Air Consignment note, Certificate of origin, Consular invoice etc. and are sending them by courier also to reach you within next 48 hours.

As per the terms of contract, kindly arrange to send the letter of credit immediately to our Bankers, The Bank of England, Oxford Street, London towards the payment of our Invoice no. 01729 dated 3rd December, 2009

Looking forward to repeat orders from you.

Sincerely,

(Brian Adams)
Director : Exports,

Encl. : 5 (As above)

LETTER TO CLEARING AGENT : REQUESTING TO ARRANGE CLEARANCE OF GOODS

Hindustan Computers Ltd.

B-11, Noida Industrial Estate, Part II
NOIDA (U.P.) India.
Tel. : 95120-42379501-06
http : //www.hindustancomputers.com

Dated : 7th December, 2009

The Manager,
M/s Bipin Das & Co.
Clearing & Forwarding Agents,
Airport Road, Bijwasan,
New Delhi.

Sub. : Request to arrange the clearance of our Goods

Dear Sir,

We have been informed by our exporters M/s Jhonson, Thompson & Co., London, U.K. of having despatched a container load of computer hardware vide their Invoice No. 01729 dated 2nd December, 2009 through Scandinavian Airways. The consignment must have reached New Delhi Airport (IGI Airport) by yesterday.

Please, arrange to clear the above consignment on our behalf. We are enclosing the following documents, in original, to facilitate custom clearance of the goods :

1. Invoice no. dated 2nd December, 2009
2. Consular Invoice
3. Air Consignment Note
4. Transit Insurance Policy
5. Certificate of origin.
6. Packing list
7. Authority letter in your favour.

Please return these documents after the goods have been cleared from the Cargo Terminal.

Kindly send the container through Golden Transport Co. to our Noida Godown immediately on clearance.

Kindly raise your bills through State Bank of India, Sector 11, Noida Branch. (U.P.)

Sincerely,

(Surinder Kumar Bakshi)
Director : Purchase

Encl. : 7 (as above)

R

Recommendation Letters

Some of the situations for writing recommendation letters are given below :

- Letter of recommendation for a job.
- Recommendation letter for a policy change.
- Recommendation letter for a new method or procedure.
- Recommendation letter for Technology Adoption.
- Recommend a product or service.
- Recommend promotion of a staff member.
- Recommend transfer of a staff.
- Recommend Penal action against a staff.
- Recommend a particular course of action.
- Request to write recommendation letter.
- Recommendation letter for supporting a decision.
- Recommendation for grant of credit.
- Recommendation for an award/reward to an employee.
- Thank you letter for writing recommendation letter for you.
- Recommend use of an alternate system/method or procedure.
- Acknowledging a recommendation.

QUICK TIPS FOR WRITING RECOMMENDATION LETTERS

Recommendation letters are of great variety, hence every letter should follow different guidelines. However, every recommendation letter should :

- detail the subject-matter being recommended
- state the reasons why it is being recommended
- give your judgement in clear and single-meaning words.
- be precise and to the point. Sacrifice brevity for completeness.
- provide your contact information for enquiry/follow up.
- while recommending an individual for a job, avoid mentioning his/her race, religion, disability or marital status.
- recommendation letter for policy change, technology adoption etc. should try to convince the staff about its positive effect on their services and about protection of job opportunities and improvement of working conditions etc.
- every recommendation letter should close with a sentence re-emphasising the subject of recommendation.

- In a recommendation letter for a job, avoid generalised praise of the individual. Better to give specific examples of his qualifications, qualities, traits and character.
- Avoid undue praise as it may be viewed as biased.
- List the applicant's exceptional skills and qualities e.g., communication skills, academic achievements, reliability, qualities of leadership and control, specific experience etc.
- Avoid restatement of employee's resume, rather elaborate key points of it.
- Proof-read the letter of recommendation as it represents both you and the applicant.
- If you can't write a positive recommendation letter, decline respectfully.

S

SALES LETTERS

Order letters and Sales letters are the two pillars of any business. Innumerable types of sales letters, sales promotion letters etc. are written in day-to-day business. Some of these situations are listed below :

- Announce a sales quiz or contest.
- Announcing a price decrease.
- Announcing the launch of a new product/service.
- Announcing a sales promotion scheme.
- Motivating a sales force.
- Announcing the appointment of a new distributor.
- Announcing a complimentary gift with every sale.
- Announcing a special sale/discount sale.
- Write a recommendation letter for promoting sale.
- Using a reference in a Sales Letter.
- Requesting a change in Sales Agreement.
- Announcing a Sale exhibition/Demonstration.
- Inviting to attend a Sales exhibition/Demonstration.
- Inviting to attend a seminar/conference to promote sales.
- Motivating Company's Sales personnel.
- Letter intimating Sales Targets to Staff.
- Sales Promotion letters for special occasions, e.g., festivals like Diwali, Holi, Raksha Bandhan, Id etc.,
- Sales Promotion letters for specific days, e.g., Valentine Day, Mothers Day, Chocolate Day, Sisters Day, Grand parents Day, X-Mas, New year.
- Letter offering something new, e.g., more information or new product launch or offer of a special discount or credit/instalment terms etc.
- Follow up letter after a Sales Demonstration or Presentation.
- Follow up of a Sales Interview (should he within 48 hours and not later).
- Second letter after a follow up letter (indicating how important the customer/response is to you.
- Write an insurance sales letter.
- Follow up sales letter after telephonic conversation.
- Follow up after sales exhibition/presentation/product demonstration etc.
- Follow up of a special sales offer.
- Write sales letter to old customers.
- Write sales letter to potential customers.
- Write a thank you letter on completion of a sale.

- Write collection letter for recovery of overdue payment.
- A sales letter writer (Sales correspondent) should have thorough knowledge of the 3P's ; such as :

  (i) Product[1] : The sales correspondent must have through knowledge of the product he is selling and must know it perfectly well. Then only he can :
  — educate the customer in the use of goods,
  — convince the customer about the superiority of product,
  — arouse interest in the customer's mind.

  (ii) Prospect : understanding the prospect means understanding their needs and offering products (goods & services) to satisfy their needs and demands. A sales letter is like an 'uninvited guest' which may not receive a 'warm welcome'. Therefore it should speak in *'you'* terms to arouse reader's (prospect's) interest in the product.

  (iii) Preposition : A preposition is a complete package *e.g.*, product, price, warranty, discounts, performance, after sales services, customer care etc., Every prospect weighs these offers and terms carefully and in comparison with competitive products, decides about making a purchase or not.

- A sales correspondent must put himself in the prospect's shoes so as to understand his psyche and elicit positive response for the letter.

QUICK TIPS FOR WRITING SALES LETTERS

- Sales letter should be persuasive
- Provide complete detail of the product, service, promotion scheme, special sale, discount offer etc. in the sales letter.
- Also discuss the action expected of a reader. State the deadline for a scheme, promotional sale etc.
- If sales letters are to invite a potential customer to an exhibition, product demonstration etc., clearly state the dates, timings and venue (location) of such an offer.
- If the product or service has some drawbacks, weigh them against the many benefits it offer.
- Compare the product with competitors for price, features, benefits, services, after sale services, warranty period etc. to prove the superiority of your product.

A few examples of sales letters are given in the following pages

1. Also see Essentials of Business Communication: Rajendra Pal and J.S. Korlahalli; Sultan Chand & Sons, Ed. 2008, p. 140.

SALES LETTER

Anand Hotels & Spa Ltd.

Jawaharlal Nehru Road,
Kolkata 700034
Tel. : 62350909, 62352020
e-mail : anandhotelsnspa@in.com

Dated : 20th September, 2009

Sub. : Inaugural offer on Spa Membership

Dear Valued Customer,

'A thing of beauty is joy forever', is a timeless quotation. But you can't ignore Beauty Treatment even if you are born beautiful. Beauty needs constant care and skin its nourishment. Our business is to keep you beautiful and most attractive.

At Anand Hotel, we have opened a Spa to provide beauty treatment and health services to our esteemed customers. It has always been our tradition to provide the best possible services to customers to make their stay at the hotel, a memorable experience. In the same tradition, our Spa will provide the world class beauty treatments and other services with our five star infrastructure and scientifically tested proven ayurvedic and herbal solutions applied by our most professionally trained staff to make you feel wonderful and stunningly different. As a gesture to our valued customers, we are offering an inaugural discount on the annual membership of the Spa. The special prices for this inaugural offer are as follows :

	Normal Price	Special offer Price
Silver Card Membership	Rs. 5,000 p.a.	Rs. 3,500 p.a.
Gold Card Membership	Rs. 10,000 p.a.	Rs. 6,500 p.a.
Diamond Card Membership	Rs. 15,000 p.a.	Rs. 11,000 p.a.

The inaugural offer is available till 30th September, 2009. We are sure, you will grab this opportunity immediately and add glow and charm to your skin and body throughout the year.

Looking forward to see you soon.

Sincerely,

(Arindam Chaudhary)
Manager : Spa

SALES LETTER : MODULAR FURNITURE FOR OFFICE

Bhutan Boards (P) Ltd.

Regd. Office : Raheja Towers II
Douglas Road, Ballard Estate,
Mumbai-400001
Tel. : 022-69374292-97
http : //www.bhutanboard.com

Dated : 29th September, 2009

The Manager : Purchase
Fortune Retails (P) Ltd.
Big Bazaar Outlet, Netaji Subhash Place,
Pitam Pura,
New Delhi.

Sub. : Modular Furniture for Office

Dear Sir,

Bhutan Board is a household name with the strengths of quality and superior workmanship coupled with lifelong durability and universal applicability.

We at Bhutan Board always strive to bring the best quality boards for making of office and Home Furniture and for interior and exterior purposes.

We have launched, for the first time in India, Modular Office Furniture for use in both, open and closed offices, for clerical upto director's office, for computer as well as workstation of any kind.

Modular Office Furniture offers the following unique features :

- It is light weight & easily moveable.
- It is available in variety of shades.
- It can be adjusted for height, length, breadth, depth etc.
- It can be assembled and reassembled in a few minutes time.
- It saves upon carpenters cost which are substantial.
- Entire office can be furnished in one day (saves time in traditional carpenter's work)

Modular office saves upto 40% of cost and huge amount of time. It is also very easy to transport.

Since you have very good turnover of furniture sales at your Big Bazaar Furniture Counters, we would like you to display our brand of modular office furniture at very attractive business terms.

A detailed catalogue, price list and business terms are enclosed.

Looking forward to hear from you soon.

Sincerely,

(Avinash Ghatak)
Manager : Marketing

Encl. : 3(As above)

A SALES LETTER ABOUT COLLECTION SOFTWARE

INFO SYSTEMS (P) Ltd.

DLF TOWERS, 7th level
Udyog Vihar,
Gurgaon (Haryana)
Tel : 95120 : 4439736, 4435681
http. : //www.infosystems.com

Dated : 20th September, 2009

The Manager
M/s Lotus Toys Marketing Co.
236, Chandni Chowk,
(Opp. State Bank of India)
Delhi-110006.

Sub. : Our new Software for collection of Dues

Dear Sir,

We, at Infosystems, introduce ourselves as providers of Business Solutions software to serve business enterprises in the most economical and extremely reliable manner.

We have recently launched a Debt Collection Software to help marketing companies like you in the following ways :

- It can be programmed for payment recovery in any number of days *i.e.,* 7, 10, 15, 30, 90 days etc.
- It provides a list of overdue accounts on a daily basis.
- Interest calculations on overdue accounts is automatically done.
- Different interest rates for different accounts can be programmed.
- Provides total debtors alongwith list of debtors on daily basis.

The software may be installed very easily and can be further programmed to suit your specific requirements.

The software may be franchised to you at a nominal annual fee of Rs. 3,000 only as compared to around Rs. 10,000 p.a. for similar softwares available in the market.

As a gesture, we are waiving the installation charges of Rs. 1,000 for you.

We sincerely hope you will take benefit of this most lucrative office. We can arrange for a free demo at your office.

Looking forward to hear from you.

Sincerely,

(Munish Malhotra)
Manager : Promotions

APPOINTMENT AS SOLE SELLING AGENT

Today Writing Instruments (P) Ltd.

M-32, Connaught circus,
New Delhi 110001
Tel. : 011-27554601-06
http : //www.todaypens.com

Dated : 12th December, 2009

The Proprietor,
M/s Bharat Stationers (P) Ltd.
56, Main Bazar, Chandni Chowk,
Delhi 110006

Sub. : Appointment as Distributor of Today Pens

Dear Sir,

We thank you for accepting and signing of the MOU for distributorship of our most popular Brand 'Today Pens' for the state of Delhi, and are pleased to appoint you our Distributors on the following terms and conditions :

1. The Appointment shall be for a period of 3 years, subject to renewal for a similar term at the option of both the parties.
2. The Appointment shall be terminable by any party be giving a 3 months notice of Termination to the other party.
3. You will work as a Sole Selling Agent for Today Pens in the entire state of Delhi.
4. Other Terms & Conditions as accepted and agreed in MOU shall remain the same.
5. Please note that all advertising and marketing activities shall be conducted by us (The Company) but in consultation with you and all advertisements and publicity materials shall carry your name as 'Sole Selling Agents' for Delhi Area.
6. We agree that all defective and damaged stock will be freely replaced by the company as per company's policies.
7. All disputes shall be subject to Arbitration only. Kindly sign the second copy of this letter as a token of your acceptance and mail it to us immediately.

Sincerely'

(Managing Director)

Encl. : 1 (as above)

S

SECRETARIAL LETTER

Secretaries[1] are of several types. Our concern is mainly with (i) Company Secretary and (ii) Office Secretary. Secretarial correspondence relates to a host of business situations.

A company secretary's correspondence may be directed towards :

- Directors of the company;
- Shareholders of the company;
- SEBI and Stock Exchanges;
- Tax & Regulatory Authorities;
- Government Offices;
- General Public.

Similarly, an office Secretary's correspondence may be directed towards :

- The General Manager of the Office
- The Subordinates
- The Clients and Customers
- The Government Authorities
- Other Offices

Innumerable situations in business may require the Secretary to write letters to others, some of which are given below :

- Letters to directors informing of meetings of Board of Directors.
- Letter to director supplying information demanded by them.
- Letter to request for inclusion of a matter in the agenda of a meeting (Director's Letter)
- Secretary's Reply to above
- Letter to directors on the request of chairman to communicate in connection with Board Meetings.
- Letter to director to disclose his interest in another company/contract etc.
- Letter asking the director to be present at a Board meeting.

---

1. Different types of secreteries may include (i) Company Secretary, (ii) Office Secretary, (iii) Secretary of a Society, (iv) Secretary of a Club or Association, (v) Personal Secretary etc.
2. There may be number of issues such as (i) Non-receipt of dividend, (ii) Non-receipt of bonus shares/right shares, (iii) Non-receipt of refund, (iv) non-resolution of a dispute etc.

- Notice of Board meeting to directors
- Letter of shareholders to Secretary on various issues[2]
- Reply of secretory to shareholder.
- Letter to Stock Exchange for filing of prospectus.
- Letter to Stock Exchange for listing of shares
- Letter to file different tax returns (*e.g.,* Sales Tax, VAT., CST, TDS, Income Tax, Service Tax etc.)
- Letters to Government Departments/Sections/Agencies submitting required information.
- Letter to public providing/submitting required information.
- Letter of share holder asking about progress of company's projects.
- Secretary's reply to above.
- A letter requesting conversion of Bonds into equity shares.
- Letters to employees offering ESOPs
- Letter accepting conversion of ESOPs
- A circular letter to the shareholders highlighting performance of the company.
- A letter by secretary requesting payment of call money.
- Notice for Annual General Meeting of the company.
- Circular to shareholders
- Letter to auditors to take-up audit work.
- A shareholder's letter to secretary asking for advice whether to buy company's shares.
- Secretary's reply to the above.
- Letter announcing a visit of shareholders to company's plants.
- Letter to shareholder replying to his queries (of different types).

QUICK TIPS FOR WRITING SECRETARIAL CORRESPONDENCE

- A secretary's letter represents the company, it discloses the corporate information in the public domain, answers queries of shareholders, supplies information to Government, Stock Exchanges, SEBI, Tax Authorities, Government Offices, Directors, shareholders and General public, hence it must be very carefully worded for future legal implications.
- The letter must be accurate, straight forward and state facts without any bias, prejudice or deceit.
- The tone of the letter should be positive.

- If the negative news of the company have to be disclosed, they should not be written in the opening paragraph of the letter. Such news should form a minor part of the body of the letter, without emphasising it.
- Being subordinate to Directors, Secretary's letters to them should be courteous and tactful.
- While corresponding with SEBI, Stock Exchanges, Government Authorities, Secretary must be careful of the statutory dates by which different information/documents have to be filed to avoid penal action later.
- Secretary should be practical and down to earth while corresponding with shareholders.
- *"A secretary just cannot afford to assume airs or promise castles in the air"*.

Given below are a few examples of the Secretary's Correspondence with different segments.

SECRETARIAL CORRESPONDENCE : NOTICE OF BOARD MEETING TO A DIRECTOR

OMAXE Constructions (P) Ltd.

Regd. Office :
1407, Chiranjivi Towers,
Nehru Place, Delhi-110017
Tel. : 011-29653291-97
e-mail : omaxeconstructions@sify.com

Dated : 1st November, 2009

Mr. Beni Prasad Jaipuria
104, Alaknanda Apartments,
Gulmohar Park Extn.
New Delhi-110023

Sub. : Notice of Meeting of Board of Directors

Dear Sir,

A meeting of the Board of Directors of the company has been convened for Saturday, the 7th November, 2009 at 3.00 p.m. at the Seminar Hall at the Registered office of the company to transact the business mentioned in the Agenda.

A copy of the agenda alongwith other necessary papers concerning resolutions therein, is enclosed.

Kindly make it convenient to attend the meeting.

Sincerely,

(Kapil Srivastava)
Secretary

Encl. : As above

LETTER FROM A DIRECTOR TO SECRETARY FOR INCLUSION OF CERTAIN ITEMS IN AGENDA

Beni Prasad Jaipuria
104, Alaknanda Apartments,
Gulmohar Park Extn.,
New Delhi-110023
Tel. : 011-29258435-36

Dated : 3rd November, 2009

The Secretary,
Omaxe Constructions (P) Ltd.
1407, Chiranjivi Towers, Nehru Place,
New Delhi-110017

Re : Board Meeting Dated 7th November, 2009

Sub. : Agenda for Board Meeting

Dear Sir,

I shall be grateful, if you, in consultation with the Chairman, will include the following items in the Agenda for the next Board Meeting dated 7th November, 2009, for deliberations among members of the Board.

1. Proposal to keep on hold our 'under Construction Projects' at Noida, Gurgaon and Panipat in view of the financial crunch faced by the company.
2. Proposal to lay-off atleast 20% of workforce in Construction and Administration Departments in view of the economic scenario.
3. In view of the global economic slowdown, the prices of real estate have gone down between 20 to 50% of their peak values. With virtually no offtake at even these reduced prices, the company is facing acute financial crunch to the extent that payment of salaries has become a herculean task. And the near future also appears to be equally dark. In view of this, I propose that the company may offer a discount of 20 to 25% on the Quoted prices of the Flats and Apartments which are lying ready for possession to tide over temporarily, the financial crunch faced by the company.
4. Proposal to defer Payment of Bonus to staff, in view of the grim scenario on Profit front.

I strongly believe that these proposals will find favour with the Board members.

Please confirm at the earliest.

Sincerely,

(Beni Prasad Jaipuria)

SECRETARY'S RESPONSE TO THE DIRECTOR'S LETTER

OMAXE Constructions (P) Ltd.

Regd. Office:
Chiranjivi Towers, Nehru Place,
New Delhi-110017
Tel. : 29653291-97
http : //www.omaxeconstruction.com

Dated : 5th November, 2009

Mr. Beni Prasad Jaipuria
104, Alaknanda Apartments,
Gulmohar Park Extn.,
New Delhi-110023

Re : Board Meeting Dated 7th November, 2009

Sub. : Proposals for Agenda

Dear Sir,

Thank you for your letter dated 3rd November, 2009. I had discussed your proposals with the Chairman who has requested me to inform you as follows :

- That your proposals no. 1, 3 and 4 are wholly acceptable and will form part of the Agenda for the next Board Meeting to be held on 7th November, 2009.
- That your Proposal no. 2, though very desirable and need of the time is very difficult to execute because of the following reasons :

  — Competitive companies have not laid off.
  — Large scale lay off will create panic among regular workforce of the company.
  — Loss of image of the company resulting in further lowering of share prices at the Stock market.
  — Company's 60 per cent revenue comes from Government Contracts, which will be jeopardised.

The Chairman has suggested that though your proposal no. 2 is very valid but can't be included in Agenda, yet it will be discussed informally at the meeting and such discussion will not form part of the minutes of the Board meeting.

The Chairman wishes to thank you for making such wonderful suggestions in the interest of the company.

Sincerely,

(Kapil Srivastava)
Secretary.

CHAIRMAN'S LETTER TO A DIRECTOR TO DISCLOSE HIS INTEREST IN A CONTRACT WITH THE COMPANY

Havells (India) Ltd.

(Leaders in Switchgear Technology)
Regd. Office : E 71, Sector 59
Greater Noida. (U.P.) INDIA.
Tel. : 95120-3772351-57
http: //www.havellsindia.com

Dated: 26th November 2009

Mr. R.K. Gupta
Director : Production,
172, Sakshara Apartments,
Mayur Vihar,
New Delhi.

Sub. : Disclosure of Interest u/s. 299 of the Companies Act, 1956

Dear Mr. Gupta,

As decided in the meeting of Board of Directors dated 7th November, 2009 tenders were invited for the supply of Plant and Machinery for our Pune factory.

I have been informed by the Administrative Manager that one of the Tenders received from M/s Akshay Enterprises mention my name as a partner is that firm. Incidently, the tender offers the most favourable terms and is likely to be considered for approval.

Under Section 299 of the Companies Act, 1956, a director is required to disclose his interest in any contract with the company, to the Board of Directors.

I wish to draw your attention to the above provisions of law, which if not complied with in time, may result in unpleasant situation for you, later on.

It is, therefore in your own interest to comply with the provisions of law, before the tender is approved.

Assuring you that any information supplied by you shall be treated as highly confidential.

Sincerely,

(Chairman)

SHAREHOLDER'S LETTER TO SECRETARY

Iqbal Chand

3692, Rana Partap Bagh,
Delhi-110007
Ph. 011-27453901

Dated : 15th November, 2009

The Secretary,
Indo-Asian Fusegear Ltd.
786, G.T. Karnal Road
Sonepat (Haryana)

Sub. : My Shareholding in Your Company.

Dear Sir,

I purchased 2,500 shares of your company @ Rs. 138 per share in January 2008 which are now being traded at Rs. 27 per share after the crash of stock prices worldwide.

I have lost nearly 80% of the capital invested by me in your company's shares.

May I request you to advise me how much time, I shall have to retain these shares to regain my capital and any information about the issue of Bonus or Right shares in the near future, or the possibility of increased dividend this year.

Your advice in the matter will be a morale booster to me.

Sincerely.

(Iqbal Chand)

REPLY TO THE ABOVE

Indo-Asian Fuse Gears Ltd.

Regd. Office :
3692, G.T. Karnal Road
Sonepat (Haryana)
Tel. : 95124-3292597-600
http : //www.indoasian.com

Dated : 25th November, 2009

Dear Mr. Iqbal Chand

Sub. : Your query regarding Bonus/Right Shares/Dividend Prospects of the Company

I appreciate your interest in this company. In response to your letter dated 5th November, 2009. I wish to inform you that in view of the legal position and the nature of the job, I can't disclose any such information to any shareholder which would be prejudicial to the interests of general body of shareholders.

However, I would suggest you to study and draw inferences from the following sources of information with regard to the Stock Market performance of this company :

(i) Annual Reports and Balance Sheet & Profit & Loss Accounts Published by the Co.
(ii) Press Releases issued by the Co. from time to time (Source : Co's website)
(iii) News Reports of papers like The Economic Times, H.T., ToI, Financial Express etc.
(iv) Magazines like Business World, Business India, Capital, etc. publishing corporate reports, forecasts etc.
(v) Opinions from your sharebrokers, Investment Analysts etc. regarding future prospects of the company.

Judicial interpretation of information from different sources may help to decide whether to remain invested in a scrip or otherwise, the Global meltdown of equities, notwithstanding.

Sincerely,

(S.C. Agarwal)
Secretary.

SHAREHOLDER'S LETTER TO SECRETARY—NON RECEIPT OF DIVIDEND

Rakesh Khurana

705, Ist Floor,
Dr. Mukherjee Nagar
Delhi-110009
Tel. : 011-27603609

Dated : 16th November, 2009

The Secretary
M/s GMR Infrastructures Ltd.
Regd. Office :
B-58, Charminar Road,
Hyderabad (A.P.)

Sub. : Non-Receipt of Dividend

Re : My demat A/c No. NSDL-0397521 with M/s Sharekhan

Dear Sir,

I am holding 1500 Equity shares of your company in the above demat account since last 2 years. I wish to draw your attention to the fact that I have not received the Dividend Warrant on these shares @ 20% declared by your company more than 2 months ago in the Annual General Meeting of the company.

Kindly look into the matter and arrange to send the Dividend Warrant at an early date.

Sincerely,

(Rakesh Khurana)

REPLY TO THE ABOVE

GMR Infrastructures Ltd.

Regd. Office :
B-58, Charminar Road,
Hyderabad (A.P.)
Tel. : 3947251-58
http : //www.gmrinfra.com

Dated : 24th November, 2009

Dear Mr. Rakesh Khurana,

Sub. : Non-Receipt of Dividend Warrant.

Thank you for your letter dated 16th November, 2009 regarding non-receipt of Dividend warrant for 1500 shares held by you under Demat A/c. no : NSDL-0397521 with Sharekhan.

Our record show that Dividend Warrant no. 596278 dated 30th September, 2009 for Rs. 4,500 payable at par at all Branches of Kotak Mahindra Bank was sent by courier to your address in our records on 6th October, 2009. If you have still not received it, it may be presumed to have been lost in Transit.

To receives a Duplicate Dividend Warrant, you need to send us an Indemnity Bond (proforma enclosed) on non-judicial Stamp Paper of Rs. 10 duly signed by you attested by notary public. Please also provide information about your Demat A/c No. and the company which is maintaining the account. The Indemnity Bond should accompany a request letter for the issue of duplicate Dividend Warrant.

Please also intimate if there is any change in the address in the company's records.

The Duplicate Dividend Warrant will be promptly issued on receipt of the above documents.

Sincerely,

(Vishwa Pratap)
Secretary.

LETTER TO STOCK EXCHANGE FOR LISTING OF SHARES OF THE CO.

Vagh–Bakri Tea Co. Ltd.

Regd. Office :
32, Central Market,
Darjeeling (Assam)
Tel. : 5492351-57
e-mail : vaghbakritea@yahoo.com

Dated : 15th November, 2009

The President,
M/s Bombay Stock Exchange Ltd.
Dalal Street,
Mumbai

Sub. : Request for enlistment of our Co's Equity Shares on BSE

Dear Sir,

Our company was incorporated on 1st March, 1992. During then last 17 years, we have expanded our Tea business to the whole of India through the distribution network of our parent Co. M/s National Tea Co. Ltd. We have now decided to make a public issue of the shares. Prior to that, we want our existing equity shares to be listed on BSE and NSE.

In order to meet the legal requirements for listing of shares; we are submitting the following documents :

1. A resolution of the Board of Directors, Meeting, approving the submission of application to BSE for enlistment of Co's shares.
2. Copy of the Memorandum of Association of the Co.
3. Copy of the Articles of Association of the Co.
4. One copy of the Proposed Prospectus of the Co.
5. Copy of the Certificate of Incorporation.
6. Details about Director's Names, Addresses, Shareholding in the Co. etc.
7. List of existing shareholders with their shareholdings.

Kindly arrange for the consent of the Stock Exchange for listing of the Co's shares.

Sincerely,

(Secretary)

Encl : 7 (as above)

T

THANK YOU LETTERS

Thank you letters are in the category of Compliment letters, Appreciation letters, Welcome letters etc.. Many people opt for/prefer sending of Printed Cards (available in plenty for all occasions in the market) than writing letters. However, it must be noted that a printed card can't replace a letter which contains personal touch, intimacy, genuineness of feelings and creates goodwill for the sender. Out of a very large list of Business situations requiring the writing of Thank you letters, some are listed below :

- Thank an employee for a job well done
- Thank a customer for making payment
- Thank someone for advice
- Thank someone for recommendation
- Thank someone for a response to your letter
- Thank someone for attending a meeting
- Thank someone for an appointment.
- Thank someone for a Training session for your staff
- Thank someone for supplying information.
- Thank a customer for purchasing a product or service.
- Thank a customer for showing interest in a product or service.
- Thank a retiring employee for his/her services during the tenure of employment.

TIPS FOR WRITING THANK YOU LETTERS

- Thank you letter must, as a rule, be promptly written.
- Thanking in advance is not apt and should be strictly avoided. It shows the sender is not inclined to send 'Thank you' or follow-up letters.
- Thank you letter should be clear and concise. Irrelevant details must be avoided. Only to the point writing is desirable.
- Be honest and show genuineness in Thanking someone.
- Always write thank you letter to a specified person (by name) and not to a firm or company in general.
- Thank you letters should better be handwritten than typed, so as to give a personal touch to the letter.
- Thank you letter should also be accurate, free of typing or grammatical mistakes
- A poorly written or inappropriately worded letter can do more harm than good for the sender.
- According to some authors, even a small gesture or gift should also be accompanied by a Thank you letter. Even a short e-mail to thank is considered appropriate.

GUIDELINES FOR THANK YOU LETTERS FOR JOB[1]

The thank you letter is one of the most important, yet least used tools in a job search. It is used to establish goodwill, to express appreciation, and/or to strengthen your candidacy. The basic rule of thumb is that everyone who helps you in any way gets a thank you letter. When used to follow up on employment interviews, thank you letter should be addressed to your interviewers(s). If the letter is received within 48 hours of the interview, it may help in the decision-making process. Thank you letters should also be sent to your contacts who granted you informational interviews and to people who served as your references. Keep in mind that recruiters remember those who don't send thank you letters (usually in a negative light).

Note : You may want to consider faxing or sending your letters overnight to make a positive impression of strong interest. If you wait too long to send your thank you letter, the hiring decision may already be made. If you fax, be sure to send the original copy by mail and note in the fax that original will follow by mail.

Opening Paragraph : *Purpose*

— A quick one-sentence "thank you" and a reminder of where and when the interview took place.

— Personalize it by referencing things discussed during interviews. Mention a positive aspect of your conversation, such as information for which you are grateful or agreement on a point raised by your contact.

Paragraph Two: *Skills*

— This is the reinforcement section that guides the contact in the direction you wish to go.

— Convey your understanding of the recruiter's situation, the needs of the company, and the requirement of the job.

— State or imply how much you can contribute. Include information that occurred to you after the interview that reinforces your "fit."

— Sell your skills, previous experience, Re-emphasize specific abilities related to the position for which you were interviewed.

Closing Paragraph : *Next Step You Will Take*

— Close by reiterating your interest in the position and your willingness to provide additional information.

— Thank them again for the time spent with you and tell them that you look forward to hearing from them.

1. ***Sources***: University of Indiana Stanford University, Duke University, Notre Dame, and University of Miami.

Z
ZED LIST

This list contains such types of letters, which are not frequently written. Some important categories under this list consists of :

- Agency letters
- Import-Export letters
- Public Relations letters
- Representations
- Letters to editor etc.

A few of the situations covering the above topics are listed below :

- Appointment of a Sole Selling Agent
- Letter offering franchise opportunity
- Import Trade Enquiry
- Reply to above
- Exporter informs of shipment
- Import order through clearing agents
- Felicitation on election to a public body
- Letter to bank to open letter of credit
- Congratulating on winning a national/state award
- Letter of appreciation for quick settlement of a claim.
- Letter of Representation to Management requesting for a uniform promotion policy
- Representation for extension after retirement
- Representation for inadequate canteen facilities.
- Representation for provision of better transport facilities for the staff.
- Representation for provision of better sports facilities.
- Representation to C.E.O, against transfer to a remote area.
- Letter to editor regarding rising corruption in public offices.
- Letter to editor regarding poor conditions of roads in the locality.
- Letter to the editor (Reprinted from ET 2/06/09)
- Letter to the ombudsman regarding unfair practices of a Bank.

TIPS FOR WRITING LETTERS UNDER ZED LIST

- These letters are of extreme formal category and hence must be carefully written.
- The letters must state facts only. It must be correct to the last word. Any incorrect statement might land the writer in legal troubles in future.
- The letter must not be offensive to anybody . No false/incorrect accusations or allegations should be levelled against any person by name or designation, as it may become a case under 'defamation'.

- Exaggeration should never be attempted.
- If the writer does not believe anything to be true, it should not become part of the letter.
- The letter should show restraint and respect.
- A letter to the editor should relate to a current topic of public interest.
- The most popular and perhaps the only salutation in a letter to the editor is 'Sir'.
- The letter should be capable of arousing readers interest.
- Since space in newspaper/magazines is scarce, the letters to the editor should be brief. (It should be within 100 to 300 words limit.)
- The letter to the editor should not include any personal information or advertising material to avoid rejection at editor's desk.
- A letter to the editor should provide complete contact information of the sender in the cover letter.

A few sample letters on the above topics are given in the following pages.

LETTER OFFERING FRANCHISE OPPORTUNITY

Tasty Foods (Pvt.) Ltd.

Regd. Office :
332, Chiranjeev Towers,
Nehru Place,
New Delhi-110017.
Ph. 011-65397273, 65399192
http. : // www.tastyfoods.com

Dated : 1st October, 2009

The Proprietor,
M/s Capital Ventures,
32, Model Town
Panipat (Haryana)

Sub. : Offer of Franchise Opportunity

Dear Sir,

Ours is a fast food company based in New Delhi, established in the year 2005. We have fast food outlets within the city and in other cities around Delhi, like Ghaziabad, Noida, Faridabad, Gurgaon in the NCR region. We have already opened 15 outlets and will expand to 20 by the end of 2009, and 35 by end 2010.

Our fast food outlets are extremely popular with young people. The modern ambiance and great tasting food makes our outlets ideal places for business and social gatherings. Our brand 'TASTY FOODS' has already become a household name in the NCR region.

In order to meet the expansion targets of our company, we are offering franchise opportunities to financially and managerially sound parties. This, we believe, would be a great opportunity to be part of a company with great potential for growth.

We propose to offer this lucrative opportunity to your esteemed firm. Should you feel interested, we may meet to discuss further modalities for the joint venture in greater details.

For more details on the outlet locations available for franchise and nature of contract indicating the financial requirements and managerial inputs for successful running of the outlet, please visit our website to make an informed decision.

Looking forward to meeting you in near future.

Your truly,

(Managing Director)
Tasty Foods (Pvt.) Ltd.

e-mail : tastyfoods@in.com

IMPORT TRADE ENQUIRY

Hindustan Computers Ltd.

11-B, Noida Industrial Estate, Phase II
NOIDA (U.P.)
Tel. : 95120-2876321-28
http. : //www.hindustancomputers.com

Dated : 15th November, 2009

The Country Manager : London
M/s Silicon Velley Inc. (U.S.A)
34th Avenue, Derby,
Yorkshire, England

Sub. : Trade Enquiry for Mainframe : Super Computer

Sir,

Our company, Hindustan Computers Ltd. is one of the top five companies of India dealing in Computer hardware and peripherals. We market our own 'HCL' brand of Desktops, Laptops, Leap Tops and other hardware products. Ours is a $ 2 Bn. company growing at 25% p.a. for the last 5 years.

We got to know of your company at the recently held 'International Trade Fair' at Frankfurt, Germany, as authorised supplier of Mainframe for Super Computers Developed by M/s Microsoft Inc. of USA.

We are interested in purchase of 100 pieces of Mainframes for Super Computer to be imported in India for onward supply to Government Departments in various ministries at Central as State levels.

May we except the most reasonable and competitive quotations with trade terms and conditions relevant for the purpose.

An early reply would be highly appreciated.

Sincerely,

(S.K. Kulhalli)
Director, Purchase.

REPLY TO THE ABOVE

Silicon Velley Inc. (USA)

London Office :
84th Avenue, Derby
Yorkshire, England
Tel. : 91237598-99
http. : //www.siliconvelley.com

Dated : 25th November, 2009

Mr. S.K. Kulhalli,
Director, Purchase,
M/s Hindustan Computers Ltd.
NOIDA (UP)

Sub. : Our Quotation for Mainframe: Super Computer

Re : Your request letter dated 15th November 2009

Dear Mr. Kulhalli,

Please find enclosed our latest Catalogues and Price list for our entire range of Products including those in which you have expressed interest.

Please be informed that our prices and terms of sale our uniform for whole of Asia. Kindly refer to our website where the Home Page provides you the FAQs (Frequently asked Questions) and their answers which would remove most of your queries. Should you feel interested, kindly complete the formalities as directed in our website to register your valued order to enable us to promptly execute them.

Sincerely,

(John Michel)
Manager : Marketing

Encl. : As above (2)

PUBLIC RELATION LETTER : FELICITATION ON ELECTION TO A PUBLIC BODY

Raheja Chemicals (P) Ltd.

Regd. Office : 37,
Subhash Katra,
Khari Baoli, Delhi 110006
Tel. : 011-26354747-48
e-mail : rahejachemical@indiatimes.com

Dated : 15th November, 2009

Mr. Parveen Hans
N-12, Dr. Mukherjee Nagar
Delhi 110009.

Your election as President of Delhi Chemical Traders Association Ltd. is a great news. Please accept our Hearty congratulations on this occasion.

This election is a testimony of your growing popularity in the chemical trade as a result of your decades of selfless services to the improvement of Governments, understanding of the hardships faced by general chemicals traders and striving to achieve better terms of trade from the authorities. You have always worked for the welfare of the chemical traders community and your election as President of the Association is a mark of respect for your services to the community.

We, as a member of the Chemical Traders Association are confident that under your able leadership the Association will work as a truly representative body committed to the welfare of the chemical traders as well as the society.

Sincerely.

(Pramod Kumar Raheja)
Proprietor

PUBLIC RELATIONSHIP LETTERS : CONGRATULATING ON WINNING A NATIONAL AWARD

PRIYA BOUTIQUE (P) LTD.

M-71, Main Market,
Greater Kailash, Part I,
New Delhi. 110065
Tel. : 011-32247475-76
e-mail : contact@priyaboutique.com

Dated : 7th December, 2009

Mr. Tribhovan Dass Javeri
Jewellers,
1, Janpath, Connaught Circus,
New Delhi-110001

Dear Mr. Javeri,

Please accept our hearty congratulations and felicitations on the occasion of winning a National Award of Entrepreneurship from the Ministry of Small, Medium and Micro Industries, Government of India. This has come as a great news for all of us.

This award is a true recognition of your entrepreneurial qualities and business acumen that has resulted in your acquiring a place of prominence among Jewellery Traders. Not only that your company has become one of the most trusted and reputed one in Jewellery Trade, the business and employment opportunities created by your enterprise deserves praise and commendation.

We are sure, you will be gaining many more laurels in the near future.

Congratulating once again.

Sincerely,

(Mrs. Suman Hans)
Proprietor

PUBLIC RELATIONS : LETTER OF APPRECIATION FOR QUICK SETTLEMENT OF CLAIM

Las Vegas Garments Store

332, Malik Chamber,
Sector 17, Chandigarh (U.T.)
Tel. : 3279587-88
http : //www.lasvegasgarments.com/India

Dated : 15th December, 2009

The Manager,
United India Insurance Co. Ltd.
Sector 21, Chandigarh, (V.T.)

Sub. : Our Fire Claim against Policy No. 035798 dt. 27/10/2009

Dear Sir,

When I thought of taking a fire policy for my showroom & stock, one of my friend strongly recommended the name of your company and branch. Now I realise how correct he was.

While I suffered a huge loss due to a fire at my showroom on 10th November, 2009, my sufferings were greatly reduced by the courteous behaviour and swift handling of the claim submitted by me to your office. Not only that the claim amount was sanctioned to my satisfaction, its payment was also released in a short time. The satisfactory settlement of the claim in such a short period of time has immensely helped us to renovate our showroom for the forthcoming New Year period of bumper sale.

I not only commend the quality of service offered by you and your staff but also the swiftness of dealings in handling and settlement of claims.

Like my friend, I will surely recommend your branch and company to my business friends for their insurance needs.

Thank you once again.

Sincerely,

(Ekansh Hans)
Proprietor

REPRESENTATION : INADEQUATE CANTEEN FACILITIES

Dated : 4th December, 2009
The Chief Manager
Punjab National Bank,
Regional Office,
Circular Building, Parliament Street,
New Delhi.

Dear Sir,

Sub. : Inadequate Canteen Facilities

We wish to bring to your notice, the inadequate canteen facilities in the circular building housing our Bank's Regional office and several other office of reputed companies.
We strongly emphasise the following points :

— A total of 260 members of our Bank's staff work in the Building and an equal number of staff of other companies.
— The canteen is barely sufficient to seat 12 persons. The paucity of space causes huge rush during lunch hours.
— The canteen owner does not provide table service for tea etc. It becomes embarrassing when even tea can't be served to valued clients.
— The entire staff has to depend on the roadside Rehriwallas who supply fruits, juices and eatables in very unhygienic conditions.
— The rush on the road outside the building during Lunch hours causes traffic problems and accidents.
— The staff members who bring lunch from home are not even provided hot case or heaters to warm up their food etc.
— During rains or in extreme weather conditions staff has to miss the lunch altogether.

In view of the above, we call upon the management to provide a solution to the long standing demand of the staff. We suggest the following alternatives :

A spacious canteen may be set up (after obtaining permission from concerned authorities) on the Terrace of the Top floor which can easily provide a seating capacity of 150 persons; or

The Basement, which is currently used for parking may be converted into a staff canteen. The vehicle owners may park their vehicles in the MCD parking lot across the road which is hardly 20 meters from circular building.

Please note that the provision of a canteen is an urgent necessity and a quick decision in this regard will not only help as a morale booster but also reduce frustration during lunch hours.

Awaiting an early action.

Sincerely,

Secretary
PNB Staff Association Ltd.

REPRESENTATION : PROVISION OF TRANSPORT FACILITIES FOR STAFF

To,
The Managing Director,
M/s INFOTRACKS (INDIA) LTD.
726, Vani Road,
Bangaluru (Karnataka)
Ph. : 3975237-41
http. : //www.infotracks.com/india

Dated : 15th November, 2009

Sub. : Inadequate Transport facilities for the staff

Dear Sir,

Infotracks (India) Ltd. was established in 1993 with a staff of 37 employees housed in the modest building from which it continues to operate till date, now with a staff of 220 employees. Though the building has been expanded and renovation and modernisation of infrastructure undertaken from time to time, the surrounding area has also seen a tenfold increase in population during last 15 years. This has resulted in many problems facing the staff such as

- Absolute lack of Parking facilities. The building could accommodate only 25 cars for Parking in 1993. The situation is same in 2009
- Non-Reliable public transport system.
- Most densely congested area in the town.
- Huge increase in the number of visitors to our office over the years.

The problem has become so acute that the Punctuality of our staff is severely affected creating tensions and depression among employees.

Many companies facing similar problems in the vicinity have arranged private transport facilities (Buses, Vans, Cabs, Taxis) for their staff.

We, the members of staff, urge your good office to make similar arrangements so as to relieve the staff of the tension in this regard. Infact, the company by providing Private Transport can save on the monthly Transport Allowance being paid to the staff. It might prove to be a gaining proposition to the company in the long run.

Hoping for a swift action.

Sincerely,

(Members of the Staff Association-Jointly)

REPRESENTATION : FOR A UNIFORM PROMOTION POLICY

State Bank of India Officers Staff Association Ltd.

Regd. Office,
16, Parliament Street,
New Delhi-110001
Tel. : 011-35974244-48
e-mail : contact@sbistaffunion.com

Dated : 25th November, 2009

The Executive Director,
c/o The Board of Directors,
State Bank of India, H.O.
16, Parliament Street,
New Delhi-110001

Sub. : Promotion Policy in respect of Bank Officers

Dear Sir,

On behalf of the SBI Officers Staff Association Ltd. I have been instructed to bring to your kind notice the glaring discrepancies in the Promotion policy of the Bank with regard to Officer's Grade II and III of the Bank. The Bank has always taken credit in propagating that it has a sound promotion policy but in practice it smacks of injustice and prejudice due to arbitrariness and whimsical attitude of the Management. Here are some instances :

1. In the promotion list announced in October 2009, 37 Officers grade II were promoted and allowed to continue at same branch, whereas 115 Officers of the same grade were promoted and sent to far off places, in some cases 2500 kms. from their existing branch.
2. In the same period, 25 Officers grade II were promoted after just 2 years serving, in grade III whereas 17 officers were promoted, after 6 to 8 years serving in grade III.
3. Since promotion and transfer are often linked, several members whose family circumstances does not allow them to accept transfer, have to decline promotion. Sometime, it ruin their careers as the dis-satisfaction of remaining at the junior level than the junior becoming senior by accepting promotion leads to frustration and lower motivation level of the employee.
4. A distant or out of state transfer of an Officer on promotion uproots him from his residence and also interrupts the education of his children which in certain cases create haveoc in the life of the promotee.

In order to evolve a more comprehensive and uniform policy on Promotions, the Association makes the following suggestions for Management's consideration and implementation.

1. Time bound Promotions should be awarded to all officers in grade II and III
2. Officers once posted to a branch should not be moved out for a minimum of 5 years (3 years at present)
3. Out-of-state transfers should be made in rare cases only.
4. Promotion Policy should have a human touch. In case of genuine domestic problems, the officer should be given a second option. The aim is that no officer should be compelled to decline promotion.
5. Total number of Transfers faced by an employee should not exceed 3, and by an officer, 2.
6. Officers above the age of 50 years should not be subjected to transfer at the time of promotion.

We strongly urge that the promotion policy should be uniform and fair to all. It should not only be just and equitable, it must be transparent as well. There should be no place to the arbitrariness and whimsical attitude of some members of the Management Board. Moreover, human considerations should always prevail. A balance between organisational needs and human hardships caused by it should be maintained.

With regards,

Sincerely,

(SBI Officers' Staff Association)
President.

REPRESENTATION : EXTENSION AFTER RETIREMENT

United India Insurance Officers' Association Ltd.

Regd. Office : United India Building
26, Asaf Ali Road,
New Delhi-110002
Tel. : 011-27559291-96
e-mail : contact@UIIofficersasociation.com

Dated : 20th November, 2009

The Managing Director,
C/o. The Board of Directors
United India Insurance Co. Ltd.

Sub. : Extension after Retirement

Dear Sir,

After deliberating on the above issue, in several brain storming sessions, the Association has decided to put forth the following representation for your consideration.

In view of the fact that the life expectancy of Indians living in towns (big or small) has increased during last 2-3 decades due to several reasons like access to better health services, drinking water wholesome food and social security coupled with financial independence, a normal person retiring at the age of 60 from active working life appears to be a punishment. Many a people enjoy decent health which can be productively utilised for a few more years.

In view of the above, the Association suggests that every employee retiring at the age of 60 should be offered an extension of employment for a period of 2 years, to begin with.

However, in order to be fair to the interests of the organisation, we suggest the following exceptions :

- Extension of employment may not be offered to the following :
  - — officers who have opted for voluntary retirement,
  - — officers whose record of past performance is bad,
  - — officers whose integrity is proven doubtful,
  - — officers whose health donot permit to accept such extension, or
  - — any other just and equitable reason.

- Officers who express their unwillingness to work post-retirement may also be excluded from this scheme.
- The management may fix the remuneration package for each level of officers. The Package must be uniform for one set of individuals and so on.

We sincerely hope you will place our Associations suggestions on the above subject as an item in the Agenda of the Next Board meeting, for favourable consideration.

Sincerely,

President,
UII Officers Association Ltd.

LETTERS TO THE EDITOR : STATE OF ROADS IN THE LOCALITY

1. COVERING LETTER

P.K. Bajpai
B-8, SFS Flats,
R.K. Puram,
New Delhi-110003
Tel. : 011-29566363

Dated : 25th November, 2009

The Editor,
Hindustan Times,
Bahadur Shah Zafar Marg,
New Delhi-110001

Sir,

I shall be grateful if you publish the enclosed letter in the 'Reader's Column' of your esteemed daily at an early date.

Sincerely,

(P.K. Bajpai)

Encl. : The Letter.

2. LETTER TO BE PUBLISHED IN HT

25th December, 2009

Sir,

You have, yesterday, very prominently published the remark of the newly Sworn Union Minister of Road Transport Mr. Kamal Nath which he made while talking to his Ministry officials that, "I need roads on land, not on Papers'. This remark by none other than a Union Minister speaks volume of the most deplorable state of Indian Roads and the extent of corruption engulfing all the major departments of the Government of India.

His remark reminds me of the most deplorable state of Roads and by-lanes in my locality—R.K. Puram, which is one of the Poshest colonies of South Delhi. The New Delhi Municipal Corporation has only one work left with itself of charging taxes, fines and penalties only. It appears that the entire funds of the corporation are spent in payment of salaries (of the highly excess staff employed by it) enhanced by the Sixth Pay Commission.

In private conversation, people talk that the roads in the area have been built thrice (on paper) and payment made for it. Our corporator is never available and considers such complaints as petty things not worthy of his time and attention. Even the NDTV had televised a half-an-hour programme on the state of roads in our locality and the hardships faced by the Residents.

At times, we consider ourselves so helpless that we feel like Boycotting payment of all taxes to the corporation. Perhaps fighting the British rulers was easier than now fighting our own Indian rulers of Independent India.

We dream of Mr. Kamal Nath, the Hon'ble Minister to drive through the lanes and roads of our colony, some day, and set the things right, at least once.

Yours truly,

(P.K. Bajpai)

LETTER TO THE EDITOR : PUBLISHED IN THE ECONOMIC TIMES, 2ND JUNE, 2009

Improve faculty

This refers to your edit 'Fix education and roads' (ET, May 30). Immediately after assuming office, HRD Minister Mr. Kapil Sibal announced that he would bring in necessary reforms in the education sector. This is a welcome step. However, creation of 1,500 universities does not serve any purpose without proper infrastructure.

There is dearth of quality faculty in most of Indian universities and it is suggested that an institution similar to the Administrative Staff College of India can be created for faculty development and training in different parts of the country. Also, let us hope that Minister for Road Surface Transport Mr. Kamal Nath will give necessary impetus to the development of roads, which is the backbone for the economic development of the country.

KNVS Subaramanyam
Hyderabad, June 1.

TESTIMONIAL BY A COLLEGE PROFESSOR

Dr. P.K. Taneja
Associate Professor
Shaheed Bhagat Singh College,
University of Delhi,
Triveni, Sheikh Sarai,
New Delhi-110017
Tel. : 011-29267777, 78
e-mail : sbscollegedu@indiatimes.com

Dated : 18th November, 2009

To Whom it may concern

I feel pleasure in certifying the credentials of Mr. Umesh Nagpal who was a student of B.Com. (Hons.) Course at this college during 2005-2008. He was a brilliant student of the college and graduated with a good First Class with Finance and Marketing as his specialised subjects.

During his stint at this college, he showed academic merit and keen interest in sports and cultural activities of the college. He was Vice President of the College Students Union during his final year and represented the college in various inter-college events and activities very successfully.

Mr. Umesh Nagpal also attended two Summer Camps of the N.C.C. unit of the college and demonstrated good qualities of leadership and organisation. He was, throughout, a very popular student with class mates, teachers and others alike.

I can happily vouch for his excellent character, enthusiastic behaviour and motivational approach.

I wish him all success in life.

(P.K. Taneja)

Appendices

WRITING BETTER ENGLISH

CONTENTS

APPENDIX I

BUSINESS JARGON SIMPLIFIED

Very frequently, writers of Business Letter make use of Business Jargon[1]. Sometimes it consists of garbage words and expressions,[2] which may be replaced by simple words or dropped altogether.

Garbage words & expressions	*Substitute words(s)*
above mentioned	above
accompanied by	with
acquire	get, buy
affix your signature	sign
afford an opportunity	allow
all concerned	everyone
alternative	choice, possibilities
amend	change
amongst	among
anticipate	expect
approximately	about
are in agreement	agree
as soon as	when
ascertain	learn, find out
assist	help
at all times	always
at an early date	soon
at this moment	now
attached hereto/herewith	attached
aware of the fact	aware
beneficial	helpful
by means of	by
cheque for the amount	cheque
concerning	about
consequently	so, accordingly
consider	feel, think
currently prevailing	present
Dear Sir/Madam	Dear (Name)
detailed information	details
determine whether	find out

1. The word 'Jargon' means, 'specialised technical language of a particular subject, e.g. Arts, Science, Profession etc.
2. Miss Susan Roberts has invented 'Garbage words and expression', in the Bankers' Magazine of Australasia, Vol. 92 No. 2 (National Mutual Life Association of Australia Ltd.)

disclose	show, tell
said order	your order
dispatch/shipped	send
due to the fact	because
during the period	when
Please find enclosed herewith,	enclosed is, here is
enclosed herwith	enclosed
encounter	meet
endeavour	try
please be informed	(omit)
expiration	end
facilitate	make easy
facilities	services
finalise	complete, end, finish
firstly	first
please donot hesitate	(omit)
forward	send
please be advised	(omit)
hereby acknowledge the receipt	thank you
hereunder	below
immediate requirement	current needs
inconnection with	about
indicate	show
initial	first
initiate	start, begin
in order that	so, to
inter alia	among other things
in the event of	if
in the sum of	for
in view of	therefore
it appears	apparantly
it is anticipated	I expect
it is essential	must
it is important	must
it is required	must
it is suggested	I suggest
it will be necessary	must
it would appear	apparently
it would be appreciated	please
kindly	please
locate	find
Madam (in salutation)	(use name)
namely	that is
necessity	need

number of occasions	often
penultimate	second last
practically	nearly, almost
prima facie	on first consideration
prior to	before
provided that	if
rectify	correct
regarding	about
reject	cannot accept, decline
requirement	need
resolve	settle
secondly	second
Sincere apology	apology
Sir (in salutation)	use name
So that	so
subsequently	later
sufficient	enough
thanking you	thank you
together with	with
under separate cover	separately
utilise	use
verification	Proof
whilst	while
will be obliged, if	please
with a view to	so
with regard to	about
with respect to	about, on, with
will have a duration of	will last

Some of the Garbage words and expressions[3] which should be dropped altogether and the sentence should be re-written, are given below :

- acknowledge receipt
- as regards
- as soon as possible
- do not hesitate
- effective immediately
- for your information
- further to your
- fot the purpose of
- hereto
- in accordance with
- in due course
- in reply
- in respect to
- in the case of
- in this matter
- in this regard
- refer to your letter/memo
- it is in order
- it is intended
- not to your satisfaction
- per
- please be advised
- please be guided
- accordingly

3. Ibid (Adapted)

- relative to
- such that
- sum of
- take this opportunity
- thank you for your attention
- this is, to inform you
- undersigned
- with kind personal regards
- with kindest regards
- with personal good wishes
- with reference to
- on the occasion of
- with a view to
- in the neighbourhood of
- in the meantime
- at the present moment
- in the event of
- in spite of the fact
- in the near future
- just in case
- just sometime ago
- for the purpose of
- supposed to be
- please be advised
- please be informed

APPENDIX II

FRENCH & LATIN WORDS AND EXPRESSIONS USED IN BUSINESS CORRESPONDENCE

As a general rule, the writer of a business letter should avoid the use of the following words and phrases etc. of French or Latin origin. It is because any use of these at a wrong place or in a wrong manner can completely alter the meaning and essence of the latter. These are illustrated here to make the reader understand their context and meaning.

a fortiori	— all the more so
a la mode	— in fashion
a priori	— self evident
ab initio	— from the beginning
ad hoc	— for this purpose.
ad infinitum	— endlessly
ad nauseam	— to the point of disgust
ad valorem	— according to value.
addenda	— list of additions (to a report).
alma matar	— one's old school, college or university
appropos	— relevant to
avant-garde	— ahead of the times
bete-noire	— disliked person or thing
bizarre	— unusual
bon voyage	— happy journey (wish)
bonafide	— genuine "in good faith".
Carte blanche	— free hand (unconditional authority)
caveat emptor	— 'Let the buyer beware'.
circa	— about
cliche	— out of date idea/expression
consensus ad idem	— agreeing on the same thing in the same sense.
corrigendum	— list of errors
coup de-grace	— death blow, final stroke
coup-d-etat	— violent attempt by a small group to dethrone head of a state
'curriculam vitae'	— resume, outline
de 'mode'	— out of date
de facto	— actual, real.

debacle	— sudden failure
defacto	— in reality
deja vu	— experiencing something for the first time
dejure	— in accordance with the law.
ditto	— the same
en bloc	— as a whole.
en masse	— collectively, in a body.
entourage	— delegates travelling with a V.I.P.
errata	— list of errors
esprit de corps	— sense of loyalty shared by a group
etc	— etcetera
ex officio	— by virtue of one's office.
ex-gratia	— out of goodwill
ex-parte	— one-sided.
faux pas	— an embarring situation, blunder
feit accompli	— an established fact.
ibid	— previous reference
ignorantia juris non excusat	— Ignorance of law is no excuse.
Impasse	— deadlock
In Memorium	— in memory of
in toto	— as a whole, entirely, wholly or entirely.
incognitio	— hiding one's identity
inter alia	— among other things
ipso facto	— by that fact, virtually.
laissez faire	— free (the principle of non-interference), non-interference
locus standi	— the right to interfere.
mala fide	— in bad faith; treacherously.
millenium	— a period of 1000 years
modus operandi	— "way of working", way of doing a thing.
modus vivendi	— "way of living".
nota bene	— take notice (N.B.)
nouveau riche	— newly acquired richness
nouveaux riches	— persons who have become lately rich.
op. cit	— cited in an earlier (not previous) reference.
paparazzi	— sensational photo journalist
par excellence	— eminently, to the highest degree
passe	— out of date
per capita	— per head.
per diem	— per day
per se	— by itself

prima facie	— on the face of it, on first consideration
pro rata	— in proportion to.
proviso	— a modifing clause in a contract
Q.E.D.	— what was to be demonstrated
Quid-pro-quo	— 'something in return'.
raison d'etre	— purpose of existence
rapport	— close understanding
resume	— curriculam vitae (C.V.)
sans recourse	— without liability
sine die	— "without a day", at no set data, indefinitely
status quo	— the existing condition.
sub-judice	— under consideration of a judicial body
sui generis	— of its own kind
tele-a-tete	— intimate conversion
ultra vires	— beyond one's powers.
vendatta	— long lasting dispute
verbatim	— word for word
versus	— against.
via media	— a means to carry the point
vice versa	— in the opposite way
vide	— indicates reference to something
vis-a-vis	— compared with, in relation to, opposite.
viva-voce	— by oral testimony/interview
volte-face	— about turn, policy reversal
volte-face	— taking a completely different position (U-turn)
Vox Populi	— public opinion

APPENDIX III

ENGLISH SYNONYMS

The word *'Synonym'* comes from Ancient Greek *syn* ("with") and *onoma* ("name"). Synonyms are different words (or phrases) with identical or very similar meanings. Words that are *synonyms* are said to be *synonymous*, and the state of being *synonym* is called *synonymy*.[1] Consider the following words :

- car and automobile
- long and extended
- student and pupil
- petty crime and misdemeanor
- buy and purchase
- sick and ill
- quickly and speedily
- on and upon
- died and expired

It is often said that synonyms are words with similar meanings and hence can be used interchangeably. But this is not true in all cases, e.g.,

- *pupil* as the 'aperture in the eye' is not synonymous with *'student'*.
- *died* and *expired* can't always be used interchangeably, e.g.
  - — *'he expired'* means the same as *'he died'*.
  - — But 'my *licence has expired'* can't be replaced by *'my licence has died'*.

Similarly

- long time or an extended time may become synonyms, but
  - — a *long arm* is not the same as *an extended arm.*

Thus some synonyms[2] are only synonymous in one usage and not in others. (examples above). Some authors claim that **no synonyms have exactly the same meanings** (in all contexts or social level of language) because *etymology, orthography, phonic qualities, ambiguous meaning, usage* etc. make them unique.

1. For an elaborate definition of the word 'Synonym', see wikipedia-the free encyclopedia. The list of synonyms given is not complete in any sense. It is only indicative and business related and is compiled from a host of sources mentioned in the bibliography at the end of the book.
2. According to Norman Levis "word power made easy" p. 287, ed. 2009, *onyma* is the greek prfix for name, *Syn* means with or together. Synonym is thus a word with the same name or meaning.

Synonym, as a noun means a word with the same meaning as another. When used as an adjective, it is called synonymous. Synonyms can be used interchangeably. Given below are some synonyms that may be used interchangeably in business correspondence :

Aberration : abnormality
Abeyance : discontinuance
Ability : calibre, competence
Abnormal : unusual, unnatural
Abondon : leave, forsake
Abridge : shorten, curtail
Abrogate : do away with, abolish
Abrupt : sudden
Absolute : unalterable
Absolve : exonerate, forgive, pardon
Abstain : exonerate, clear
Absurd : silly, ridiculous
Abundant : plentiful
Accumulate : collect, store
Achieve : accomplish
Acknowledgment : admission, acceptance
Acquittal : clearance, exoneration
Acting : substituted, delegated
Adept : proficient skilled
Adequate : sufficient
Admiration : praise
Affirmation : confirmation
Aggravate : intensify
Agitation : disturbance
Aid : support
Alien : foreign
Amiable : lovable
Apologise : express regret, beg pardon
Apprehend : fear
Arrangement : allocation, allotment
Assistance : help
Atonement : compensation
Attack : assault
Authentic : true, reliable
Awkward : clumsy
Beneficiary : inheritor
Bias : pre-conception, inclination
Blame : accuse

Brisk	:	bright, lively
Brutal	:	cruel, savage
Burdensome	:	onerous, oppressive
Callous	:	crude, hard
Calm	:	quiet
Candid	:	frank, sincere
Carelessness	:	negligence
Category	:	class
Certainly	:	surely
Charity	:	almsgiving, donation, dole
Cherish	:	prize, treasure
Choice	:	option, election
Circulate	:	bring out, issue
Circumstantial	:	concurrent, incidental
Cogent	:	powerful
Cold	:	indifferent
Compassion	:	sympathy, pity
Compatible	:	consistent
Concealment	:	secretion, privacy
Concise	:	short, brief
Condemn	:	blame, censure
Condense	:	compress, thicken
Conspicuous	:	noticeable
Conversant	:	familiar
Cordial	:	warm, friendly
Corrupt	:	tainted, dishonest
Courtesy	:	good manners, gentility
Criterion	:	test, standard
Custom	:	convention, usage, habit
Damage	:	loss
Debate	:	argumentation
Decision	:	conclusion, settlement
Defiance	:	opposition
Deficient	:	lacking, Inadequate
Defraud	:	cheat, swindle
Degree	:	grade, graduation, stage
Delinquent	:	defaultant
Demand	:	claim, requisition
Denounce	:	condemn
Deteriorate	:	decline
Deterioration	:	worsening

Dexterity	:	kill
Diffident	:	hesitant
Dilemma	:	quandary, impasse
Diligent	:	industrious
Disagreement	:	discord, clash
Disburse	:	pay, spend, expend
Discard	:	eliminate, reject
Disclosure	:	exposure, leak
Disgrace	:	shameful
Dismissal	:	discharge, removal
Display	:	show, presentation
Distress	:	trouble
Distribute	:	give out, handout
Distrust	:	doubt
Draft	:	sketch, outline, blueprint
Duplicate	:	copy, double, repeat
Economical	:	cheaper
Elegant	:	tasteful
Elevation	:	uplift, boost, levitation
Elimination	:	abrogation, abolition
Emancipate	:	free, liberate
Embarrassment	:	confusion, discomfort
Emphasis	:	stress
Enthusiasm	:	zeal, fervour
Equality	:	parity
Equanimity	:	composure
Eradicate	:	uproot, destroy
Exceptional	:	unusual, rare
Excess	:	too much
Exclusion	:	prevention
Expenditure	:	expense, outlay
Exquisite	:	elegant, fine
Extra ordinary	:	uncommon, exceptional
Extraneous	:	immaterial
Extravagant	:	spendthrift, wasteful
Fabricate	:	forge, construct
Fallacious	:	deceptive, false
False	:	untrue
Following	:	sequence
Foresight	:	anticipation
Fraud	:	deceit
Frequency	:	repetition

Fury	:	anger
Gaiety	:	happiness, joyous
Gigantic	:	great, colossal
Government	:	administration
Gratification	:	enjoyment, satisfaction
Gratitude	:	appreciation, thanks
Grievous	:	painful, sorrow
Hamper	:	hinder, impede
Hazardous	:	dangerous, risky
Humane	:	kind, merciful
Humility	:	politeness, modesty
Idea	:	view, conception
Immaterial	:	unimportant
Imminent	:	threatening
Importance	:	significance
Inadvertent	:	careless, negligent, unintentional
Indifference	:	disinterest, unconcern
Indignant	:	angry
Inequality	:	disparity
Influence	:	authority, effect
Information	:	news, advisory
Ingenious	:	clever, inventive
Inquiry	:	investigation, search
Irresolute	:	undecided, wavering
Jubilant	:	joyful
Judicious	:	prudent
Laborious	:	hardworking, industrious
Leadership	:	guidance, direction
Legislature	:	assembly, council
Liability	:	responsibility, blame
Liberal	:	generous
Loyal	:	faithful, devoted
Luxuriant	:	abundant
Magnificent	:	grand, splendid
Malice	:	Ill-will
Marvellous	:	wonderful
Maturity	:	full growth
Meagre	:	small
Method	:	routine, formula, way
Mistake	:	error, inaccuracy
Morbid	:	unhealthy

Motion	:	action, gesture
Negligent	:	careless
Notable	:	remarkable
Obliterated	:	destroy
Obsolete	:	old, acquainted
Obtuse	:	dull, stupid
Onerous	:	burdensome
Opportune	:	timely
Opposition	:	defiance, resistance
Ownership	:	proprietorship, possession
Pathetic	:	touching
Pensive	:	thoughtful
Persuade	:	induce, urge
Persuation	:	convincement
Plentiful	:	abundant
Portray	:	draw, sketch
Postponement	:	adjournment, stay
Precarious	:	dangerous, risky
Precedence	:	priority
Pretence	:	excuse
Prevention	:	deterrance, avoidance
Prodigal	:	extravagant
Questionable	:	doubtful, disputable
Rebellion	:	revolt, mutiny
Refined	:	elegant
Reiterate	:	repeat
Remainder	:	residue, leavings
Remorse	:	regret, repentance
Renown	:	famous, reputed
Repudiate	:	reject, discard
Resistance	:	opposition
Restoration	:	replacement
Reticent	:	silent, reserved
Rigid	:	stiff, reserved
Ruinous	:	destructive
Sane	:	sensible, sound
Scandal	:	slander
Service	:	help, aid
Shrewd	:	cunning, wily
Sordid	:	dirty, ugly
Special	:	distinctive

Specimen	:	sample
Splendid	:	grand, magnificent
Spurious	:	fake, imaginary
Sterile	:	barren, unproductive
Sterile	:	unproductive
Stiff	:	rigid, stern
Stubborn	:	rigid
Sublime	:	elevated
Submission	:	surrender, obedience
Suggestion	:	advice, proposal
Superficial	:	hollow, shallow
Surplus	:	excess
Tedious	:	monotonous, tiring
Temperate	:	moderate
Tentative	:	experimental
Thrifty	:	economical
Thrive	:	prosper, flourish
Transient	:	temporary
Uniformity	:	consistency
Unique	:	unequalled
Urbane	:	polite, courteous
Urgent	:	pressing
Value	:	worth, benefit
Various	:	several, diverse
Venerable	:	respectable
Vigilance	:	watchfulness
Vindictive	:	revengeful
Voracious	:	greedy, hungry
Wealthy	:	well-to-do, rich
Wholesome	:	healthy, sound
Wrecked	:	miserable, unfortunate
Yearn	:	desire, crave
Yield	:	surrender
Yielding	:	submissive
Zeal	:	passion
Zest	:	enthusiasm

APPENDIX IV

ENGLISH ANTONYMS[1]

Antonym as a noun means a word that means the opposite of another word. In business correspondence, antonyms may be used to give exactly opposite meaning of another word. Some of the antonyms commonly used in correspondence are given below for quick reference :

About	:	exactly
Above	:	below
Absence	:	presence
Abundance	:	shortage, dearth
Accept	:	reject, refuse
Accord	:	discord, disagreement
Acquit	:	convict
Add	:	subtract
Admire	:	dislike
Admit	:	deny
Adopt	:	reject
Advanced	:	elementary
Affirmative	:	negative
After	:	before
Against	:	for
All	:	none
Already	:	not yet
Always	:	never
Amateur	:	professional, expert
Analysis	:	synthesis
Ancient	:	modern
Antonym	:	synonym
Appreciate	:	depreciate
Approximately	:	exactly
Argue	:	Agree
Arrival	:	departure
Arrive	:	depart
Arrogant	:	humble
Artificial	:	natural
Ask	:	answer
Attract	:	repel, distract

1. This section is the compilation from a host of sources; e.g. Business Communication, Building Critical Skills : McGraw Hill by Kitty O. Locker, Stephen Kyo Kaczmarek, Business Communication by K.K. Sinha, Galgotia, Business Communication by Mary Ellen Guffy, Thomson, 3rd Ed., Business Communication by Homai Pradhan & N.S. Pradhan, Himalaya, Ed. 2009, english-hitferu.de. (learning english online) & many others.

Authentic	: spurious
Awful	: defence
Awkward	: graceful
Background	: foreground
Backward	: forward
Before	: after
Begin	: end
Behind	: in front of
Belief	: disbelief
Below	: above
Benevolent	: unkind, uncharitable
Best	: worst
Better	: worse
Big	: small
Bliss	: misery
Blunt	: sharp
Borrow	: lend
Bottomline	: topline
Break	: mend, Fix
Broad	: narrow
Build	: destroy
Buy	: sell
Callous	: tender, soft
Care	: neglect, careless
Careful	: careless
Cautious	: rash
Ceiling	: floor
Censure	: applaud, praise
Certainly	: probably
Cheap	: expensive
Cheerful	: gloomy, depressed
Clever	: stupid
Close	: open
Closed	: opened
Coarse	: fine
Compare	: contrast
Complicated	: simple
Compulsory	: voluntary
Conceal	: reveal
Condense	: expand
Confidence	: distract, doubt
Connect	: separate
Constant	: changeable

Construction	:	destruction
Correct	:	false
Coward	:	brave
Create	:	destroy
Credit	:	debit, discredit
Crude	:	refined
Damage	:	repair
Danger	:	safety
Defeat	:	victory
Defend	:	attack
Definite	:	vague, indefinite
Delay	:	haste
Deny	:	Admit
Despair	:	hope
Desperate	:	hopeful
Destruction	:	construction
Different	:	alike
Difficult	:	easy
Diffident	:	confident
Diligent	:	lazy
Discourage	:	encourage
Distant	:	near
Divide	:	unite
Early	:	late
Economy	:	extravagance
Elementary	:	advanced
Emigrate	:	immigrate
End	:	begin
Enmity	:	friendship
Entrance	:	exit
Equal	:	different
Even	:	odd
Everybody	:	nobody
Everything	:	nothing
Exactly	:	approximately
Exceptional	:	ordinary
Exclude	:	include
Explicit	:	implicit
Export	:	import
Extensive	:	intensive
Exterior	:	interior
External	:	internal
Extra ordinary	:	ordinary

Extravagant	:	economical
Extreme	:	moderate
Fact	:	fiction
Failure	:	success
False	:	true
Famous	:	notorious
Fast	:	slow
Fear	:	courage
Final	:	first
Finish	:	start
Flexible	:	rigid
Follow	:	lead
Folly	:	wisdom
Foreign	:	native
Forget	:	remember
Fortune	:	unfortunate
Forward	:	backward
Frequently	:	occasionally
Front	:	rear, back
Full	:	empty
Futility	:	utility
Future	:	past
Gaiety	:	mourning
Gain	:	loss
General	:	particular
Generosity	:	miserliness
Genuine	:	false, fake
Give	:	take
Growth	:	decline
Guilty	:	innocent
Hard	:	soft, easy
Here	:	there
High	:	low
Honour	:	shame, dishonour
Hope	:	despair
Hopeful	:	desperate
Hopeless	:	hopeful
Horizontal	:	vertical
Huge	:	tiny
Humane	:	cruel
Humility	:	arrogance
Hypocrisy	:	sincerity
Ignore	:	notice

Imperative	:	optional
Include	:	exclude
Increase	:	reduce
Industrious	:	lazy
Inside	:	outside
Interested	:	disinterested
Interesting	:	uninteresting
Interrupt	:	continue
Joint	:	separate
Junior	:	senior
Justice	:	injustice
Lack	:	enough, plenty
Land	:	take off, water
Large	:	small
Last	:	first
Learn	:	teach
Left	:	right
Legal	:	illegal
Legible	:	illegible
Liberty	:	slavery
Liquid	:	solid
Little	:	much, big
Long	:	short
Loose	:	tight
Loser	:	winner
Loud	:	quiet
Low	:	high
Loyal	:	disloyal
Major	:	minor
Malice	:	goodwill
Many	:	few, some
Material	:	spiritual
Maximum	:	minimum
Meagre	:	plenty
Merit	:	demerit
Mess	:	order
Miserly	:	generous
Moderate	:	extreme
Modern	:	ancient
Moral	:	immoral
More	:	less
Mortal	:	immortal
Much	:	little

Narrow	:	wide, board
Native	:	foreign
Natural	:	artificial
Negative	:	positive
Never	:	always
New	:	old
Noble	:	ignoble
Normal	:	abnormal
Not yet	:	already
Notice	:	ignore
Notorious	:	reputable, famous
Now	:	then
Occasionally	:	frequently
Occupied	:	vacant
Offensive	:	defensive
On	:	off
Open	:	shut, close
Opponent	:	supporter
Optional	:	compulsory, mandatory
Oral	:	written
Ordinary	:	special
Other	:	same
Out	:	in
Outside	:	inside
Outward	:	inward
Over	:	under
Part	:	whole
Partial	:	fair, impartial
Partial	:	total
Particular	:	general
Permanent	:	temporary
Permit	:	forbid
Persuade	:	dissuade
Physical	:	mental, spiritual
Please	:	displease
Plenty	:	scarce
Polite	:	impolite
Practical	:	impractical
Praise	:	condemn
Precious	:	worthless, cheap
Premium	:	discount
Presence	:	absence
Pride	:	humility

Private	:	public
Professional	:	amateur
Prospect	:	retrospect
Public	:	private
Pull	:	push
Question	:	answer
Quiet	:	loud, noisy
Raise	:	lower, demote
Rare	:	ordinary, common
Rash	:	cautious
Rear	:	front
Receive	:	give
Rectify	:	falsify
Refuse	:	accept
Regret	:	satisfied, satisfaction
Religious	:	secular
Remote	:	near
Repulsive	:	attractive
Safety	:	danger
Satisfaction	:	dissatisfaction
Savage	:	civilised
Scanty	:	plentiful
Secret	:	public, open
Seldom	:	often
Sell	:	buy
Send	:	receive
Senior	:	junior
Separate	:	joint
Simple	:	complicated
Slow	:	fast, quick
Smooth	:	rough
Sober	:	drunk, excited
Solid	:	liquid
Sometimes	:	often
Sophistical	:	naive
Special	:	general, ordinary
Spiritual	:	material
Start	:	finish, end
Stationary	:	moving
Strange	:	normal
Strict	:	gentle
Strong	:	weak
Sufficient	:	insufficient

Surplus	:	deficit
Synonym	:	antonym
Take	:	give
Tedious	:	lively, easily
Tender	:	strong, hard
Terrible	:	lovely
Theory	:	practice
Thrifty	:	extravagent
Thrive	:	decline
Tight	:	loose
Timid	:	bold
Together	:	apart
Top	:	bottom
Transparent	:	opaque
Trust	:	suspect
Under	:	over
Uniform	:	variable
Units	:	divide
Urban	:	rural
Use	:	disuse, abuse
Vacant	:	occupied
Vertical	:	horizontal
Victory	:	Defeat
Vigilent	:	careless
Violent	:	gentle
Virtue	:	vice
Voluntary	:	compulsory
Waste	:	save
Whisper	:	shout, scream
White	:	black
Whole	:	part
Wide	:	narrow
Winner	:	loser
Worse	:	better
Worst	:	best
Yes	:	no
Yesterday	:	tomorrow
Yield	:	resist
Zeal	:	indifference
Zenith	:	nadir

APPENDIX V

ENGLISH WORDS COMMONLY MIS-SPELT

The following is a tentative list of English words which are very frequently used in business correspondence, but are most commonly mis-spelt. The Business letter writer must be careful in using these words :

A

abbreviate
abridge(ment)
absurd
abundance
accede
accelerate
accentuate
accept(ance)
access(ible)
accessible
accessory
accessory
accidental
accommodate
accommodate
accompany
accountant
accrue
accumulate
accustomed
achieve
achieve(ment)
acknowledge
acquaint(ance)
acquainted
acquire
across
adhere(nce)
adjourn(ment)
adjudicator
administrator
admissible
adulterate
advantage(ous)
advertise(ment)
advisable
advisory
aerial
affectionately
affidavit
affiliate
aggrieved
agree(able)
align(ment)
all right
allege
allotment
allow(ance)
amateur
amateur
ambiguity
ambiguous
analyse
analytical
announce
annual(ly)
annually
anonymous
apologise
appearance
appendix
apprentice
appropriate
approximate
arbitrage
argument
artificial
ascertain
assessor
assistant
atrocious
attendance
audience
authorise
authoritative
automatically
auxiliary
awkward

• See also "160 Frequently misspelled words" in Business Communication by Mary Ellen Guffey: Thomson, Ed. 2005, p. 25, Business Communication by K.K. Sinha, Galgotia p. 220, Business Communication : Meenakshi Raman & Prakash Singh op. cit., etc., Essentials of Business Communication by Rajindra Pal etc. and several others.

B

bankrupt(cy)
begin(ning)
behaviour
believe
beneficent
beneficiary
benefit(ed)
biased
bouquet
broucher
bulletin
buoyant
bureaucracy
business

C

campaign
cancel(lation)
cancellation
cancelled
career
carriage
casual(ly)
catalogue
changeable
characteristic
cheque
client(ele)
clientele
collateral
collateral
colleague
colleague
collusion
column
coming
commemorate
commencement
commission
commission
commitment
committee
comparable
comparison
competent
comprehensive
compulsion
concede
condemn
conference
conscience
conscientious
conscientious
conscious
conscious
conscious
consecutive
consecutive
consensus
consideration
consign(or)
consistent
contempt
contemptuous
contradict
control
controversial
convenience
convertible
coolly
co-operation
correspondence
courteous
courtesy
criticise
curiosity
curriculam

D

debenture
deceit
deceive
decipher
deduct(ible)
defendant
defer(ence)
definite(ly)
deliberate
demonstrate
demurrage
demurrage
dependence
dependent
descend
descendant
description
desirable
despair
desparate
develop
difference
differential
disappear
disappoint
discipline
dispensable
dispensable
disputable
dissent
dissipate
dissolve
dubious

E

earnest
eccentric
economic
economical
efficiency
efficient
eightieth
elementary
eligible
eliminate
embarrass
embarrassed
encyclopaedia
endeavour

endeavour
endorse(ment)
envelope
envelope
environment
equipped
equity
escalate
exaggerate
exceed
excellent
exception
exception
excise
exclaim
exclamation
exhibition
existence
experience
expiry
explain
explanation
extraordinary

F

facsimile
failure
familiar
fascinate
fashion
favour
feasible
financial
fit(ted)
forecast
foreign
foreign
forfeit(ure)
forty
forty
fourteen
fraud(ulent)
fulfil(led)(ment)

G

gauge
gazette
generally
genuine
gilt-edged
glossary
govern(ance)
grammar
grandeur
grievance
grievous
guarantee
guardian
guidance

H

haphazard
height
hindrance
honorarium
honorary
hospitable
humorous
humour
hypothecation

I

illicit
illigible
illiterate
imaginary
immediately
immersion
imminent
inconvenience
incorrigible
incredible
indemnify
indemnity
indispensable
industrialisation
inference
inferior
influence
influential
inherit(ance)
initial
insistent
instalment
instrument
intellectual
intercede
interrupt
irrelevant
irrelevant
irreparable
irresistible
irrevocable
irritable
irritable
issuing
itinerary

J

January
jealous
jeopardise
jewel(lery)
judgement
jurisdiction
jurisprudence

K

kitchenware
knot
knowledge(able)

L

label(led)
leather
legible
leisure
Liaison
libellous
liberalise
licence
licensed

lien
lightning
liquidate
liquor
literature
loading
losing
lovely
luxurious
luxury

M

machinery
magnificent
maintenance
manage(able)
manageable
mannequin
manoeuvre
manufacture
marvellous
marvellous
mechanism
mediate
memorandum
merchant
messenger
messrs
millenium
millionaire
misappropriate
miscellaneous
mis-spelled

N

necessarily
necessary
necessitate
necessity
negligible
negotiate
neighbour
neither
nevertheless
nineteen
ninetieth
ninety
ninth
northern
notable
notice(able)
numerous

O

obedience
objection(able)
obsession
obvious
occasion(ally)
occur(rence)
occured
offence
officiate
omission
omitted
opposition
oppurtunity
overwhelming

P

pamphlet
parallel
patron(age)
peculiar
perceive
percentage
performance
perishable
permanent
permissible
permit(ted)
perpetual
perseverance
persist(ence)
persuade
persuasion
pioneer
possess
possibility
precede
predecessor
prefer(red)(ence)
prejudice
prejudice
preliminary
prevalent
privilege
probability
procedure
proceed
profession
profit(ed)
programme
promissory
pronunciation
proprietary
prospectus
provoke
psychology
pursue
pursuit

Q

quarrel(led)
question(naire)
queue
quorum

R

receipt
receive
recipient
recognise
recommend
rectify
recur(rence)
redeemable
refer(red)(ence)
register
registration
regret(table)

reliable
relieve
remembrance
remit(tance)
repeat
repetition
reputable
requiem
resolution
resource
restaurant
reveal
revenue
review
revocable
rhythm
ridiculous

S

sacrilegious
salable
sampling
satisfactory
schedule
scientific
secretary
seize
separate
separate
service(able)
several
sieve
signatory
simultaneous
sincerely
skilful
skill
specimen
speculation
statistics
statute
statutory
statutory
straight
subscribe
succeed
success
suddenness
sufficient(ly)
summary
superior
supersede
supersede
supervision
suprintendent
surprise
sympathise
synopsis
system(atic)

T

tariff
technical
technique
temperament
tenure
thoroughly
tiresome
transfer(red)
treasurer
truly
truthful
twelfth

U

unanimous
underpaid
underpriviledged
unique
unnecessarily
usable
usage
usual(ly)
utilise
utterance

V

vacation
vacuum
variable
variety
vehicle
villain
volume
voluntary
volunteer

W

waive
warranty
weekday
weird
willing
withdrawal
wholesome
writing

Y

yearn
yield

English words often confused

Here are some simple english words which are often confused for their meaning and context where they are to be used :

clothes, cloths
angle, angel
dairy, diary
loose, lose
goal, gaol
birth, berth
guard, guide
break, brake
breath, breathe
lead, led
stationery, stationary
dual, duel
artist, artisan
artistic, artificial
insure, assure, ensure
adapt, adopt
minute, minuet
sight, site
cue, queue
rest, wrest
capital, capitol
right, write, rite
accept, expect, except
latter, later, letter
trail, trial
desert, dessert
currant, current
coarse, course
ring, wring
confident, confidant
spacious, specious
affect, effect
alternate, alternative
access, assess, excess
born, borne
compliment, complement
council, counsel
country, county

disinterested, uninterested
dominate, dominant
eligible, illigible
flair, flare
honorary, honorarium
disburse, disperse
liable, libel
lapse, elapse
principal, principle
vocation, vacation
proceed, precede
resource, recourse
respectable, respectful
eminent, imminent
college, collage
staple, stable
wear, ware
illegal, illicit
tire, tier, tyre
prescribe, proscribe
uppermost, utmost
honorary, honorarium
honourable
courtesy, curtsey
formally, formerly
magnet, magnate
envelope, elope
respectively, respectfully
able, capable
adapt, adept, adopt
beside, besides
casual, causal
minor, miner
loose, lose
continuous, continual
dependent, dependant
economic, economical
equal, equitable

final, finale
exhaustive, exhausting
historic, historical
industrial, industrious
negligent, negligible
official, officious
personal, personnel
practical, practicable
rout, route
intervene, interrupt
sight, site, cite
superficial, superflous
wait, await
illicit, illegal
adverse, averse
bail, bale
abandon, abundance
momentary, momentous
all ready, already
all right, alright
altar, alter
cereal, serial
device, devise
their, there
a lot/ alot/ allot
altogether, all together
anyone, any one
a part, apart
beside, besides
bought, brought
come over, overcome
complement, compliment
decent, desent
discreet, discrete
driving test, test drive
effect, affect
e.g., i.e.
excited, exciting

expand, expend
hard, hardly
he's, his
interested, interesting
lay down, lie down
look over, overlook
lose, loose
me, my
most, mostly, the most
overtake, takeover
personnel, personal
practice, practise
precede, proceed
principal, principle
raise, rise
regard, regardless
replay, reply
stationary, stationery
there, their, they're
trainer, trainee
used to, used to do
wander, wonder
who, whom
wrong, wrongly
adopt, adept
affluent, effluent
attributed, contributed
cite, sight, site
prescribe, proscribe
discreet, discrete
elicit, illicit
imminent, eminent
forward, foreward
imply, infer
it's, its
moral, morale
objective, rationale
possible, possibly
regulate, relegate
residence, residents
respectfully, respectively
roll, role
simple, simplified, simplistic
to, too, two
unique, unusual
your, you're

* See also : Business Communication Process & Practice : Mary Ellen Guffey Thomson, Ed. 2005 p. A-24, Business Communication: K.K. Sinha op.cit. p. 217, etc., Leo Network; www.learnenglish.de/common mistakes etc.; Business Communication by Kitty O. Locker, Stephen Kyo, McGraw Hill op. ci.t, p. 311 and several others.

APPENDIX VI

NEGATIVE WORDS & WORDS WITH NEGATIVE CONNOTATIONS

The writer of a Business letter should, as far as possible, try to avoid use of *Negative words* or *Words with Negative Connotations* in letters. His attitude should always he positive even in extremely unfavourable circumstances or purely negative business situations. Given below are some examples of '*Generally Negative*' words and words conveying negative fellings, which should, preferably be avoided in business letters.

Generally Negative

afraid
anxious
avoid
bad
careless
damages
delay
delinquent
deny
difficulty
eliminate
error
except
fall
fault
fear
hesitate
ignorant
ignore
impossible
lacking
losing
neglect
never
no

Dis-words

disapprove
dishonest
dissatisfied

In-words

inadequate
inaccurate
incompetent
insincere
injury
incomplete

Mis-words

misfortune
mistake
missing

Un-words

unclear
unfair
unfortunate
unfortunately
unpleasant
unreasonable
unreliable
unsure[1]
unmanageable

Generally Negative

objection
problem
reject
sorry
worry
wrong
terrible
trivial
trouble
wait
weakness
disturbed
agitated
stupid
misinformed
horrified
senseless
punishing
destroying[2]
guess
nosy
haggle
fearful
nit-picking
obstinate
fishy-fashy
listless

1. Adapted from : Business Communication, Building Critical Skills by Kitty O. Locker & Stephen Kyo, p. 119.
2. Effective Business Communication : Harta A. Murthy, H.W. Hidlebrand, James P. Thomas, McGraw Hill, 7th ed. p. 262.

AVOIDING DOUBLE ENTRY

Many a times, writers use phrases with two words conveying the same meaning. Use of such phrases not obly gives a bad impression but also spoils the beauty of the letter. Such phrases are called 'Double entry' and can be easily simplified/avoided. Some examples of 'Double Entry Phrases' with simplified words to replace them are given below :

Double entry phrases	*Simplified words to replace them*
actual fact	fact
7 a.m. in the morning	7 a.m.
previous experience	experience
end result/ final result	result
revert back	revert
absolutely complete	complete
5 p.m. in the evening	5 p.m.
viable alternative	alternative
period of one month	
during the one month,	one month
during the year 2009	during 2009
single and only owner	sole owner
costs an amount of Rs.	costs Rs.
In my personal opinion	in my opinion
seldom ever	seldom
fullest possible extent	fully
please be kind enough	please
not too distant future	near future
leading the team as a captain	captain of the team
during the preceding year	last year
a declining bear market	bear market
a rising bull market	bull market
at the present moment	now
just sometime ago	recently
important essentials	essentials
planning in advance	plan
advance budgeting	budgeting
modern & up-to-date	modern
present work in hand	work in hand
immediately, as soon as possible	immediately
negotiating the bargain	bargaining
bad and unpleasant news	bad news
each and every individual	every individual

- See also Essentials of Business Communication: Rajendra Pal etc. op. cit., Business Communication: K.K. Sinha op. cit. p. 183. etc.

APPENDIX VII

HOW TO ORGANISE POSITIVE AND INFORMATIVE MESSAGES?

Positive messages and information may be presented in the following order[1] :

1. Give any good news and summarise the main points : Share good news immediately. Include details such as the date policies begin and the percentage of discount. If the reader has already raised an issue, make it clear that you are responding.

2. Give details, clarifications, background etc. : Information in the first paragraph should not be repeated. Answer all the questions, the reader may have, provide all the information neccessary to achieve the purposes for which the letter is written. Present details in the order of important to the reader.

3. Present any negative elements — as positively as possible : Negatives such as following should be made clear :

— There may be limits to a policy,

— The information may be premature,

— The customer may have to fulfil certain conditions to obtain a benefit

— The reader/ customer may have to satisfy requirements to get a discount[2].

However, these negatives may be presented as positively as possible.

4. Explain any Reader benefits : Most informative or positive messages suggest reader benefits.

Give enough details to make the benefits clear and convincing.

- Make it clear that the policy or information benefits the readers, not just the company.
- Explain benefits of dealing with your company as well as benefits of the product or policy.
- In a good news messages, it is often possible to combine a short reader benefit with a goodwill ending in the last paragraph.

5. Use a Goodwill ending : Positive, personal and forward looking : Shifting your message away from the message to the specific reader suggests that serving the reader is your real concern.

1. Kitty O. Locker & Stephen Kyo Kaczmarek; op. cit. p. 170 (Adapted).
2. Most Indian Sales/Sales Promotion Letters contain an asterik (*) to mean "Conditions apply" or "Terms & Conditions apply".

HOW TO CREATE POSITIVE EMPHASIS
OR
HOW TO DE-EMPHASISE NEGATIVE INFORMATION

According to Kitty O. Locker and Stephen Kyo Kaczmarek[3], the following five techniques de-emphasise negative information :

1. Avoid negative words and words with negative connotations.
2. Focus on what the reader can do rather than on limitations.
3. Justify negative information by giving a reason or linking it to a reader benefit.
4. If the negative is truly unimportant, omit it.
5. Put the negative information in the middle, and present it compactly.

3. Op. cit. page 119.

GIVING BAD NEWS TO CUSTOMERS[4] & PEOPLE OUTSIDE THE ORGANISATION

The following pattern will help writers maintain goodwill :

1. **Give the reason for the refusal before the refusal itself when you have a reason that reader will understand and accept :** A good reason mentally prepares the reader to expect the refusal.

2. **Give the negative just once, clearly :** Inconspicious refusals can be missed by a reader, making it necessary to say 'No', a second time.

3. **Present an alternative or compromise, if one is available :** An alternative not only gives readers another option to get what they want but also suggests that you care about him/her and helping them solve their problems.

4. **End with a positive note, or a forward-looking statement[5].**

GIVING BAD NEWS TO SUPERIORS

When you give a bad news to a superior[6], also recommend a way to deal with the problem. Turn the negative message into a persuasive one.

1. **Describe the Problem :** Describe what's wrong, clearly and unemotionally.

2. **Describe how it happened :** Provide the background. What underlying factors led to the specific problem ?

3. **Describe the options for dealing with it :** If one option is clearly the best, you may need to discuss one option only. But if the superior will think of other options, or if different readers will judge the options differently, describe all the options, giving their advantages and disadvantages.

4. **Recommend a solution and ask for action :** Ask for approval, so that you can go ahead to make the necessary changes to deal with the problem.

GIVING BAD NEWS TO COLLEAGUES AND SUB-ORDINATES

When you must pass on a serious bad news to colleagues and subordinates, follow a pattern different than to superiors[7].

1. **Describe the problem :** Tell what's wrong, clearly and unemotionally.

2. **Present an alternative or compromise, if one is available :** An alternative gives readers another way to get what they want and also suggest that the sender care about readers and helping them meet their needs.

---

4. Kitty O. Locker & Stephen Kyo; op. cit. p. 196 (Adapted).
5. See also "General Guidelines for saying 'No'." Jacob Neilson in useit.com
6. Kitty O. Locker & Stephen Kyo; op. cit. p. 202 (Adapted).
7. Ibid. (Adapted)

3. **If possible, ask for input or action :** People in the audience (readers) may be able to suggest solutions. And workers who help make a decision are far more likely to accept the consequences.

4. **Prepare the reader for possible negatives :** No serious negative (such as downsizing the organisation or lay off etc.) should come as a complete surprise. Managers can prepare subordinates for possible negatives by giving full information as it becomes available. Employees may sometime give suggestion that management didn't think of or rejected them as unacceptable.[8]

8. Employee suggestions enabled a San Jose Company providing Software Training, to cut the payroll by 30% without laying off any full time employees. In this slowdown, many Indian Companies like Wipro, Satyam, Air India, HCL etc. have also resorted to the same tactics.

APPENDIX VIII

BODY LANGUAGE : THE TRUTH ABOUT LIARS[1]

A growing number of contemporary "experts" on business communication are claiming to be able to detect through various body language clues when someone is lying. According to Carol Kinsey Goman, Ph. D., the following statements made in business communication are generally far from truth :

"You're next in the line of Promotion"

" Let's meet sometime"

" Let's have dinner sometime"

" I'd love to read your report."

" The Board is expected to decide favourably in your case".

We get lied to all the time. People are dishonest with us for any of the following reasons :

(i) out of politeness;

(ii) to avoid punishment;

(iii) to protect others; or

(iv) to deliberately mislead us for personal gain.

According to Carol[2], liars can "leak" nonverbal information in telltale "micro expressions" (Those genuine emotions that flash across someone's face in less than a fraction of a second) and "suppressed expressions", which slip out before realised and are than replaced with more acceptable reactions.

Behaviours Suggesting Deception :

Carol insists that there are behaviours that suggest deception.

- Incongruence between what's being said and the speaker's body language (like saying "no" while nodding "yes") and *vice versa*.
- An increased blink rate — especially over 50 blinks per minute — or eyelid flutter.
- Gazing downward after asserting innocence, or looking sideways.
- Shorter, less descriptive statements, or silence for a few moments before speaking again.
- Incomplete gestures, like a shrug that uses only one shoulder.
- A decrease in hand gestures, especially those used to illustrate speech — like drawing pictures in the air to help explain what is meant.

1. Excerpts from Carol Kinsey Goman, Ph.D., author of ***The Non-Verbal Advantage:*** *Secrets and Science of Body Langauge at Work.* see also http://www.nonverbaladvantage.com
2. Ibid. (Adapted)

- Fidgeting feet that shuffle, wind around each other, stretch and curl or kick out.
- Dilated pupils of the eyes.
- Face touching — especially around the mouth and nose, or between the eyes.
- Discrepancies in timing : when the lie is well rehearsed, deceivers start their answers more quickly than truth-tellers. If taken by surprise, however, the liar takes longer to respond.

However, lie detection is not so simple and easy. Here's why ...

(1) There is no absolute signal for deception. Most cues, including blink rates, vocal tone, pupil dilation etc. are signs of heightened anexity and stress. But there is no way of telling if the observed stress is caused by lying or by something else. Similarly, incongruence, where gestures contradict words, may be a sign of deceit or simply an indication of some inner conflict between what the person is thinking and saying.

(2) **Micro expressions** occur infrequently and are difficult for most of us to spot without video footage to review. However, **suppressed expressions** are somewhat easier to see because they appear more often and last longer.

(3) Signs of deceit may differ from person to person. Take for example ; Eye contact : some liars shift their gaze and won't meet your eyes while others give too much eye contact. One speaker may raise his vocal pitch when he lies while another speaks in a flat, unemotional tone.

(4) Nonverbal cues need to be evaluated in what is called a "gesture cluster" — movements, postures and actions that when taken together reinforce a common point. A single gesture can have several meanings or mean nothing at all. So one can't catch a liar from a single deceit behaviour.

(5) It is tough to spot deception unless one knows a person's baseline behaviour under relaxed or generally stress-free conditions. The more one understands which gestures or postures are part of someone's unique repertoire, the more one can spot significant deviation from these patterns.

(6) All non-verbal communication is influenced by cultural heritage, and the higher stress level, the more likely it is that culture-specific gestures will show up. It is extremely difficult to judge non-verbal deception cues in people from another culture.

(7) No one, not even with the help of functional MRIs to track brain activity, can identify liars who believe the lies they are telling.

APPENDIX IX

BUSINESS CORRESPONDENCE GLOSSARY

apologise : saying "sorry"

approach : method of doing something, style

attitude : outlook on life

commence : start

complimentary : free

concern : problem, issue

confidential : private

conscientious : cares about quality (of work)

contribution : individual effort or support

convenient : suitable, favourable

co-operation : the act of working together

co-ordinator : person who organises (anything)

dedication : lot of effort put into (something)

dependable : one who can be trusted

disregard : ignore, don't pay attention

dropped : fell to a lower level

effective : gives a positive response

efficient : performs well

enclosed : included inside

encouraged : inspired, persuation

enquire : inquire, looking for information

formal : set rules or requirements

grateful : thankful

guarantee : promise

impact : effect

indicate : show

invoice : purchase document (also indicates money owed)

latest	:	most modern
lay-off	:	taking a job away from an employee (without any fault)
notice	:	document indicating an event
outstanding balance	:	money still owed
pleasure	:	enjoyment
postpone	:	delay
preferred customer	:	repeat customer
professional	:	one who exhibits formal behaviours (on the job)
profound	:	deep
punctual	:	on time
records	:	files and paper that keep track of business transactions
regarding	:	being about
regret	:	feel bad, 'sorry'
reliable	:	dependable
replacement	:	in place of
representative	:	agent, who acts on other's behalf
resignation	:	the act of leaving a job
respected	:	considered good and honest
retirement	:	leaving a job due to aging
severance	:	separation compensation.
sharp	:	exact
stock	:	share (in ownership)
struggle	:	work with difficulty
sufficient	:	enough
support	:	financial help
versatile	:	with a variety of skills/abilities

APPENDIX X

BUSINESS CORRESPONDENCE VOCABULARY

attachment	:	Document or file added to an e-mail
body	:	the content of the letter; the middle portion; between opening & closing lines
bullets	:	small dark dots; that distinguish items in an un-numbered list.
coherant	:	logical; easily understandable
concise	:	to the point
confidential	:	private
diplomacy	:	showing kindness & consideration
direct mail	:	sales letter addressed to large number of recipients
enclosure	:	extra document/papers included with a letter.
formal	:	non-casual; following set rules/language/format
format	:	the organisation (set up) of a document
heading	:	a phrase or word indicating what the text below discusses.
indent	:	extra spaces at the beginning of a fresh paragraph
informal	:	casual, non-formal
inside address	:	recipient's mailing address
letter head	:	special paper with a (company) logo, name & address on the top
logo	:	symbol (image) that identifies an organisation.
margin	:	a blank space that is given at the edge of the text
memorandum (memo)	:	a document (notice) circulated within a company, internal communication
notation	:	notice to recipient that appear on an envelope. (e.g., confidential)
postage	:	cost of sending a letter (document) through post office.
proofread	:	reading a document to check for mistakes.
reader-friendly	:	easy to read
recipient	:	the addressee; one who receives the letter
salutation	:	greeting in a letter
sincerely	:	term used after closing a letter but before signing it
single spaced	:	no blank lines in between the text
spacing	:	blank area between words or lines of text.
tone	:	the feeling of the language (text)
transitions	:	words or phrases used to retain natural flow of the text.

APPENDIX XI

UNIVERSITY EXAMINATION QUESTIONS

(B.COM. (HONS.) Ist YEAR, DELHI UNIVERSITY)

Q. Design a Circular/Notice announcing a New Business English course starting in your college from the new academic session. Mention all relevant details.
(B.Com. (Hons.) Delhi Ist yr. 2005) R

Q. You work for a designer clothes store with outlets in many major cities. Your organisation wants to help people suffering from the effects of the Tsunami. Write a notice appealing to your customers for donations or old clothes that can be brought to any of your stores.
(B.Com. (Hons.) Delhi Istyr. 2005) R

Q. Draft an office circular informing employees about changes in the timings of the staff canteen. *(B.Com. (Hons.) Delhi Ist yr. 2005)* E

Q. Write a letter to your Insurance Company notifying the damage caused by a fire in your factory, asking them for an early inspeciton for the settlement of claims.
(B.Com. (Hons.) Delhi Ist yr. 2005) E

Q. Draft a memo for the Office Suprintendent asking him to keep a check on personal telephone calls from the office phones by employees. *(B.Com. (Hons.) Delhi Ist yr. 2005)* E

Q You had supplied ten steel safes that had their paint scratched due to poor handling by the Transport Company. The customer has complained asking for replacement. Though you are not responsible for the damage, you have decided to replace the entire lot. Draft a reply to the complaint mentioning all adjustments. *(B.Com. (Hons.) Delhi Ist yr. 2005)* E

Q. Draft a notification and Agenda of a meeting of the Board of Directors of a company to take up the following matters :

— confirmation of minutes
— A proposal for the modernisation of steel plant
— A proposal to open a branch in Mumbai
— Resignation of Mrs. S.C. Dabur from the Board of Directors.

(B.Com. (Hons.) Delhi Ist yr. 2005) E

Q. Draft a circular for all the employees of your company explaining the need to wear safety gear like helmets, long boots etc. at construction sites. *(B.Com. (Hons.) Delhi Ist yr. 2006)* R

Q. Draft a Notification, including Agenda, to the Heads of Departments regarding the Annual General Meetings of your company. *(B.Com.(Hons.) Delhi Ist yr. 2006)* R

Q. Write a letter to ABC Company, Mumbai, asking them to let you now if there is an agency of their goods in your area. *(B.Com. (Hons.) Delhi Ist yr. 2006)* R

Q. Draft a Memo Warning an employee, who is a habitual late comer to the Office.
(*B.Com. (Hons.) Delhi Ist yr. 2006*) R

Q. You would like to apply for the post of Telephone Executive (Marketing) at Harper and Brothers, Marine lines, Chandigarh. Write a covering letter to Mrs. Kiran Sinha, H.R. Manager of the Company to go with your CV. You donot have to write the CV.
(*B. Com. (Hons.) Delhi Ist yr. 2006*) R

Q. Write a letter to the Life Insurance Corporation of India requesting the revival of your lapsed policy. Give relevant details. (*B.Com (Hons.) Delhi Ist yr. 2006*) R

Q. Draft a circular to inform the dealers of your company about an increase in their commission on sales made, effective next month onwards. Sign it as the Marketing Officer.
(*B.com. (Hons.) Delhi Ist yr. 2006*) R

Q. The Washing Machine purchased by you is not working in a satisfactory manner. Write a letter to the company highlighting the inconvenience caused to you and seeking appropriate relief. (*B.Com. (Hons.) Delhi Ist yr. 2006*) R

Q. As the PRO of your company, draft a press release to announce the declaration of dividend and the launch of new shares by your company. (*B.Com. (Hons.) Delhi Ist yr. 2006*)

Q. Draft a notice regarding the importance of reducing the wastage of paper in the organisation and the incentives to be provided to those employees who initiate the most effective measures of saving paper. (*B.Com. (Hons.) Delhi Ist yr. 2007*) R

Q. Write a letter in response of Ms. Sunaina Sharma's enquiry about the range of office equipment your Company offers and the terms and conditions of payment and delivery.
(*B.Com (Hons.) Delhi Ist yr. 2007*) R

Q. Write a letter of complaint to Messrs. Khairatiram & Sons about the damaged condition in which the goods sent by them were received and give the redressal you are expecting.
(*B.Com. (Hons.) Delhi Ist yr. 2007*)R

Q. Write a letter to the senior manager of a Bank requesting him to order 'Stop Payment' of a cheque issued by your Company. Give all the necessary details.
(*B.Com. (Hons.) Delhi Ist yr. 2007*) R

Q. You bought a digital camera through Bazee.Com. The camera is defective. Prepare a complaint to be sent through E-mail. Use the imaginary E-mail ID.
(*B.Com. (Hons.) Delhi Ist yr. 2007*) R

Q. You have been offered a job as an Accounts officer in Punjab and Sind Bank. Write a letter declining the offer. (*B.Com. (Hons.) Delhi Ist yr. 2007*) E

Q. Write a Memo from the Vice-President, finance of a Multinational company informing employees of an increase in the Diwali Bonus. (*B.Com. (Hons.) Delhi Ist yr. 2007*) E

Q. Write a letter from Manager, Marketing to a customer offering a new range of footwear.
(*B.Com. (Hons.) Delhi Ist yr. 2007*) E

Q. You are PRO of your company. Write a Press Release presenting the Management's view of the Lock-out of the company. (*B.Com. (Hons.) Delhi Ist yr. 2007*) E

Q. Write a Memo from the Personnel officer of the firm to all heads of the department regarding scheduled meeting to discuss change in travel rules. *(B.Com. (Hons.) Delhi Ist yr. 2008)* R

Q. Write a circular announcing to the employees about the firm's Golden Jubilee Celebration in December, 2008. *(B.Com. (Hons.) Delhi Ist yr. 2008)* R

Q. Mr. Jain of Mumbai has neither settled the account nor given any reply to your reminder. Write a letter for the settlement of Rs. 7,000 owed to your company for TV sets purchased by them in September 2007. *(B.com. (Hons.) Delhi Ist yr. 2008)* R

Q. Draft the minutes of the Annual General Meeting of Shareholders of a public limited company at which the following business was conducted :

(a) Adoption of audited accounts of the company alongwith reports of Auditors and Directors.
(b) Declaration of Dividend
(c) Closing of share transfer and Register of Members.
(d) Appointment of Directors.
(e) Appointment of Auditors. *(B.Com. (Hons.) Delhi Ist yr. 2008)* R

Q. Draft a Notification, including Agenda, to the Heads of Department regarding the Annual General Meeting of the company. *(B.Com. (Hons.) Delhi Ist yr. 2009)* R

Q. Draft an office circular informing employees about changes in the timings of the Production Department. *(B.Com. (Hons.) Delhi Ist yr. 2009)* R

Q. Write a letter to the Bank Manager for the 'Stop Payment of a cheque' you have lost somewhere. *(B.A. (VS) Programme/I—2009)* R

Q. Explain the structure of a business letter. *(B.A. (VS) Programme/I—2009)* R

R = Regular, E = External

BIBLIOGRAPHY

- Kitty O. Locker, Stephen Kyo Kaz Marek : Business Communication. Building Critical Skills : McGraw Hill, Intl. 2004 Ed.
- Meenakshi Raman, Prakash Singh : Business Communication, Oxford University Press, Ed. 2006.
- Rajendra Pal, J.S. Korlahalli : Essentials of Business Communication : Sultan Chand & Sons, Ed. 2008.
- K.K. Sinha : Business Communication : Galgotia Publishing Company, Ed. 2008.
- Homai Pradhan, N.S. Pradhan : Himalaya Publishing House, Ed. 2009.
- Mary Ellen Guffey : Business Communication : Process and Product : Thomson South Western : Ed. 2005.
- Brown L. : Effective Business Report Writing.
- F.M. Rachel ; D.L. Karuth and R.E. Holmes ; Littlefield C.L., Management of office operations, Prentice Hall of India.
- Quible Z.H. : Introduction to Administrative Office Management : Cambridge Winthrop Ed. 2006.
- Dr. R.K. Chopra : Communication Management : Himalya Publishing House, Ed. 2009.
- Adair John : Training for Communication.
- Allen R.K. : Organisation Management through Communication : Harper & Row, New York.
- Alfred Gerald. J : Business Writers Hand book.
- N.H. Athreya : Effective Report Writing : Jaico Publishing House, Mumbai.
- J.L. Austin : How to do things with words. Harward University Press.
- K. Bach & R.M. Harnish : Linguistic Communication and Speech Acts, MIT Press, Cambridge.
- O.W. Baskin & C.E. Aronoff : Interpersonal Communication in organisation, Cresent Publishing Co. California.
- R.W. Bell : Write what you mean, George Ellen and Urwin, London.
- F.J. Bendev : Make your business letters, make friends, Kingswood.
- D.K. Berlo : The Process of Communication.
- K. Chandler : A Guide to sources of Information for all; McDonald and Evans, London.
- S. Chase : The Tyranny of Words; Metheron, London.
- Collins C. : English language Dictionary, Harper Collins.
- B. Cooper : The Writing of Technical Reports. Penguin, London.

- W.G. Crow & C. Riedd : How to think and write, Harper & Row, New York.
- P. Douglas : Communication through Reports; Prentice Hall, New Jersey.
- J.M.A. Fraser : Handbook of Employment Interviewing, McDonald and Evans, London.
- F. Bland : Manual of Commercial Correspondence, A.H. Wheeler & Co. Ltd. India Edition.
- Gartside : Modern Business Correspondence, McDonald & Evans, London.
- Gibbon D. : "using E-mail".
- C. Goodworth : The secret of Successful Business Letter and Reports : Hainemann, London.
- Namita Gopal : Business Communication, Oral and Writing, Galgotia, New Delhi.
- Robert D. Hey : Business Report Writing : Richard D. Irwin, Homewood, Illinois.
- G. L. Henderson and P.R. Voiles : Business English Essentials, McGraw Hill, New York.
- R. W. Jepson : A new Guide to Precis Writing : Longman, London.
- I. R. King : The Business Letter Writer : Allied Publisher, Mumbai.
- I. Lew : How to talk with People : Harper & Row, New York.
- V. Raymond & Mary R. Lyons : Report Writing for Business, Richard D. Irwin, Homewood, Illinois.
- Little Peter : Communication in Business, Longman, London — Oral and Written Communication.
- C.C. Khurst : Business Communication for Better Human Relations : Prentice Hall, New Jersey.
- Dru, Scott : The Telephone and Time Management, making it a tool and not a tyrant. Crisp Publication, California.
- R.C. Sharma and Krishna Menon : Business Correspondence and Report Writing : Tata McGraw Hill, New Delhi.
- W, Shawcross : Manual of Commercial English : Sir Issac Pitman & Sons Ltd. London.
- R.L. Shurter : Written Communication in English; McGraw Hill, New York.
- C. Sidney & M. Brown : The Skills of Interviewing, McGraw Hill, New York.
- S.Stephen : General and Business English; Sir Issac Pitman & Sons Ltd. London.
- J. Stephenson : Principles and Practice of Commercial Correspondence, Sir Issac Pitman & Sons Ltd. London.
- H.M. Taylor & A.G. Means : The Right way to conduct meetings, Conference & Discussions : Elliot Rightway Books.
- Shirley Taylor : Model Business Letters : Pearson Educating London.
- Philip R. Thilbert : Business Writing for Busy People; Penguin India, New Delhi. 2006.
- John V. Thill etc. : Excellence in Business Communication.
- C.C. Maira : Successful Business Communication; Allyn and Bacon, Boston.
- Ian Jonathan : e-mail @ work; Pearson Education Ltd. Edinburgh 2005.

- Robert Shutter etc. : Communicating in Multinational Organisation; Safe Publication.
- P.C. Wren and H. Martin : English Grammar and Composition : S. Chand & Co. New Delhi.
- W.H. Tide : Better Report Writing; Reinhold Publishing Co., New York.
- Herta A. Murphy, Herbert W. Hildebrandt, Jane P. Thomas, Effective Business Communication; McGraw Hill; 7th Ed.
- Paula Jacobs : "Strong Writing Skills Essential for Success". Infoworld 1988.
- Mark H. McCorarck : "Words you use tell a lot about you' Arizone Republic 2000.
- Kathlene Driscell : "You voice can make or break you." Democrat and Chronicle 1993.
- John R. Pierce : Communication, Scientific American 1993.
- Albert Mehrabian : "Communicating without words" Phychology Today 1998.
- Phil Bartle : Writing Better Reports, Seattle Community Net Work 2001.
- Dawn E. Waldsop : "What you wear is as important as what you say". Presentations 2000
- Joh Naisbitt : Megatrends : Ten new directions shaping our lives, Warner Books, New York.
- Dr. R.K. Chopra : Adminstrative Office Management, Himalaya Publishing House: Ed. 2009.
- Dr. R.K. Chopra & Mrs. Ankita Bhatia : Office Management; Himalaya Publishing House, 15th Ed. 2009.

http ://www.businessplansoftware.org/advice—glossary.asp

http ://www.about.com

http ://www.english.hilfen.de (learning english outline)

http ://www.office.com

http : //www.officelife.com

http : //www.useit.com

http : //www.askme.com

http : //www.infomap.com/method/html

http : //www.mhhe.com/bsc

http : //www.wisc.edu/writing/handbook/proofreading

http : //www.glasbergen.com/office

http : //www.inside.com

http : //www.planetfeed back.com/consumers/html

http : //www.office office.com

http : //www.albion.com/netiquette/html

http : //www.grammar.book. com

http : //www.io.com/writingcourse/html

http : //www.3M.com/meetingguides/html

http : //www.wildpresentations.com/articles visual/html

http : //www.sprintmail.com

http : //www.wetfeet.com/asp/article/networking

http : //www.eresumes.com

INDEX